MOON

WITHDRAWN
HO CHI MINH
CITY (SAIGON)

DANA FILEK-GIBSON

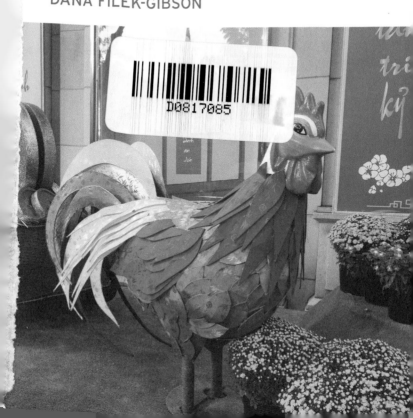

Contents

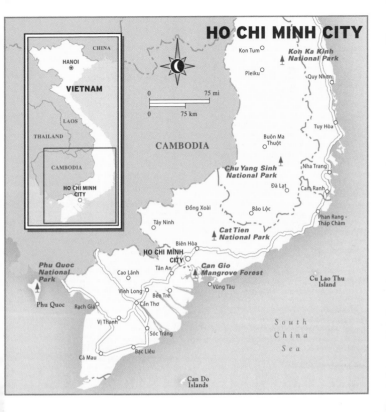

HO CHI MINH CITY

DISCOVER

Ho Chi Minh City

Get anywhere near its flashing neon lights, full-throttle traffic, sardined houses, and soaring commercial towers and it becomes clear why Ho Chi Minh City is the future of Vietnam. Indisputably the economic heart of the nation, this fast-paced, ever-expanding behemoth has charged fearlessly—and sometimes recklessly—into the 21st century, carrying along a diverse and multifaceted population, a keen business acumen, and an irrepressible spirit.

From a traveler's perspective, the city is both a blessing and a curse: HCMC provides a lively, chaotic, and occasionally dangerous atmosphere. Along with the madness of the city comes an intricate and fascinating history that announces itself time and again in the city's eclectic architecture and multifaceted cuisine. Stroll along the wide boulevards of downtown District 1, where opulent colonial-era buildings stand, or hang onto your helmet as you race down the narrow

---

Clockwise from top left: incense at Thien Hau Pagoda; Notre Dame Cathedral; coffee in Con Dao; *banh mi* vendor; the Hotel de Ville.

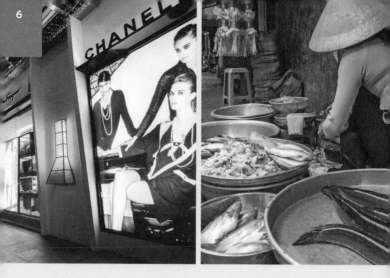

streets of Chinatown on the back of a motorbike, defying the laws of physics as you weave through traffic.

Hidden farther down the city's many alleys is another world altogether: quiet and reserved, where children play on empty sidewalks and old women sit sentinel, fanning themselves in the afternoon heat. Remnants of an earlier time remain in the aging facades of historical buildings and the one-room restaurants that continue to turn a profit, even as high-end eateries go into business next door.

HCMC is a sensory overload. Step into the chaos with optimism and you will be rewarded.

Clockwise from top left: upscale shops; vendor selling fresh fish; a water puppet performance.

Planning Your Trip

When to Go

The best months for exploring Ho Chi Minh City and its surroundings are between **November** and **March,** which also matches the region's **high season.** These months fall after rainy season has come to a close but before the sweltering heat takes over. From there, the build-up to rainy season begins, bringing high temperatures and humidity before the downpours start in mid- to late May. Things get especially busy over **Christmas** before sliding into **Tet** (Vietnamese Lunar New Year) the following month. While this is a holiday of fascinating local traditions, it makes for a poor time to visit, as the entire country shuts down for weeks before and after, particularly in Saigon, where everyone heads to the countryside to visit their relatives. Those businesses that remain open often double or triple their prices, and transportation is unreliable. While fewer foreigners travel during the summer, **July** and **August** see droves of domestic holidaymakers.

Before You Go

Passports and Visas

Visitors are required to secure a **tourist visa** prior to arrival in Vietnam. This can be arranged through any Vietnamese embassy or consulate up to six months before your trip. In 2016, the Vietnamese government debuted a one-year, **multiple-entry tourist visa** for US passport holders. The visa costs USD$135-220 and allows American citizens to stay in the country for a period of up to three months at a time.

Additionally, US citizens can apply for one- and three-month visas with both single- and multiple-entry options. Depending upon both the nature of the visa and where you apply for it—whether through your local embassy or consulate, or via an online service—the short-term visas cost USD$75-180, while the yearlong visa will set you back as much as USD$220.

Travelers entering Vietnam over land must visit an embassy or consulate to prepare their visa ahead of time. Air travelers have the additional option to apply for **pre-approval,** a significantly more cost-effective route, though this is only available to those arriving at one of Vietnam's three major airports: **Tan Son Nhat** in Ho Chi Minh City; **Noi Bai** in Hanoi; or **Danang International Airport.** Although pre-approval is not encouraged by the Vietnamese government, it is a legitimate option, provided you arrange your documents through a reliable company. International air travelers must have a passport with at least six months' validity at time of travel.

Vaccinations

While there are **no required vaccinations** for Vietnam, the Centers for

Disease Control recommend that travelers vaccinate against **Hepatitis A** and **typhoid** prior to visiting in order to prevent food-borne illness. Additional preventative measures, such as the **rabies vaccine,** are suggested for cyclists and those who may come into contact with animals. Vaccinations against **Hepatitis B** and **Japanese encephalitis** are also recommended for some travelers, depending upon your destination.

Though **malaria** does exist in Vietnam, its prevalence is low, with only rare incidences in the Mekong Delta. Most travelers opt to use insect repellent and cover up at dawn and dusk.

Transportation

Travelers to Saigon arrive at **Tan Son Nhat International Airport** and set off from there. **Public transportation** is easily accessible, from planes and trains to buses and boats. For shorter journeys, hitting the road is the cheapest option; for long-distance or over-water trips, you're better off in the air. **Budget airlines** like Jetstar and VietJet fly to a number of domestic destinations, while **overnight trains** run the spectrum from cheap hard-seat cars to air-conditioned sleeper berths.

What to Pack

Most Western amenities are available in Vietnam, though some are more affordable and accessible than others. **Sunscreen,** for instance, is available in many coastal destinations, though it can be tricky to find and is always more expensive. It's best to bring your own from home. Other items, like **contact lens solution** and **feminine products,** can be difficult to come by.

Vietnam tends to be **more formal** than the United States. In rural areas and outside of major hubs like Ho Chi Minh City and Hanoi, local women often dress more conservatively than their Western counterparts, opting for long pants and covered shoulders. Many Vietnamese women in the city have adopted a Western approach to fashion. You can get away with shorts, T-shirts, and tank tops in most tourist destinations. When visiting pagodas or sights of national importance, it's important for both men and women to opt for **conservative clothing,** wearing **long pants** and **covering shoulders,** as this is considered a sign of respect.

Tan Son Nhat International Airport

The Best of Ho Chi Minh City

Day 1

Spend your first morning in Ho Chi Minh City taking it easy with a coffee in the shadow of **Notre Dame Cathedral.** From here, both the **Central Post Office** and the **Reunification Palace** are within walking distance. Wander north toward **Turtle Lake** for lunch and then carry on to the city's **War Remnants Museum** for the afternoon.

Head to the backpacker area later in the day for a happy hour drink or dress up and spring for a cocktail at **Chill Skybar, OMG,** or the sky-high **Eon 51** to appreciate the city from a different angle.

For dinner, grab a cab to District 1's Tan Dinh neighborhood, where local favorites like **Banh Xeo 46A** and upmarket eateries like **Cuc Gach Quan** await. For live music, check out **Saigon Ranger** or **Yoko** in the evening, or hit the dance floor at **Apocalypse Now.**

Day 2

Today, visit bustling **Chinatown,** where the mammoth **Binh Tay Market** sprawls over several blocks and a tasty array of Chinese meals can be found. Back toward downtown, **Thien Hau Pagoda** is an incense-filled haze of reds and golds, lacquered woodwork, and ornate effigies, with neighboring **Chaozhou Congregation Hall** and **Cho Lon Mosque** adding an extra level of diversity to the mix.

Return to District 1 for some retail therapy at **Ben Thanh Market** and

Chaozhou Congregation Hall

Best Food

Quan Mien Cua 94 Cu specializes in soft-shell crab.

- **Street food, Northern District 1:** For a primer on the city's roadside dining, check out the famed **Lunch Lady**, who serves up a different Vietnamese noodle soup for lunch every day, or swing by **Banh Xeo 46A** for a helping of southern-style *banh xeo*, savory Vietnamese pancakes featuring shrimp, pork, and bean sprouts.

- **Pizza 4Ps:** Boasting the city's best pies, Pizza 4Ps combines fresh ingredients—including homemade artisanal cheeses from its farm in Dalat—with a menu of both traditional and innovative Neapolitan-style pizzas, in a trendy, modern setting.

- **Quan Mien Cua 94 Cu:** Amid the bustle of District 1, this long-standing eatery focuses on one main ingredient: soft-shell crab. Whether accompanied by a mountain of glass noodles or steamed in a savory tamarind sauce, these small, easy-to-eat crustaceans make for a hearty meal.

- **Chinese noodles from Quan Thien Thien:** For the more adventurous crowd, an evening trip to Chinatown is in order. The *mi sui cao* (dumplings with egg noodle soup) at Quan Thien Thien are the cream of the crop. Don't forget to spring for a sweet tea to accompany your meal.

the ornate Opera House

along posh **Le Loi**, passing by the colonial-era **Hotel de Ville** and local **Opera House.** Pop into one of the many watering holes along the **Nguyen Hue pedestrian street** for a sunset drink or return to the backpacker district for a laid-back evening.

Excursion to Phu Quoc Island

A large, palm-fringed island west of Vietnam's border with Cambodia, Phu Quoc has become one of the country's most visited tourist destinations almost overnight. The island now boasts over a million annual visitors thanks to its close proximity to Saigon and a host of daily flights from the country's budget carriers. This itinerary outlines the best way to spend one day on the island—but many people allot longer than this to lounge on the beautiful beaches.

Flights to the island are cheap and plentiful. VietJet Air, Jetstar, and

Bai Sao, one of Phu Quoc's most popular beaches

Best Hotels

- **Saigon River Boutique Hotel:** The staff at this charming boutique hotel goes above and beyond to make guests feel welcome.

- **Hong Han Hotel:** This hotel is an oasis of relative calm amid the chaos of the city's backpacker district. The clean, comfortable beds are a good find on their own, but add to these a charming communal balcony and a friendly staff, and Hong Han makes for a great budget option in a central location.

- **NN99 Hotel:** For younger budget travelers, NN99 is a great choice. It's in a prime location not far from Pham Ngu Lao's best nightlife and outfitted with cozy, affordable rooms. It's hard to get any closer to the action than this place, and NN99's easygoing staff are a helpful bunch who can point you in the right direction.

- **Town House 50:** While most budget venues are not known for their decor, the charming Town House 50 manages to be both stylish and cost effective. Though it's in an unorthodox location north of the backpacker district, this delightful little spot has won over many a traveler with its well-appointed dorm rooms and bright, colorful design.

- **Cinnamon Hotel Saigon:** The swanky, red-and-black Cinnamon Hotel stands apart in many ways, from its elegant and inviting reception area to the beautiful, spacious rooms and its attentive staff. The cinnamon-scented rooms, too, are a nice touch, making you feel welcome from the moment you set foot inside.

Vietnam Airlines all offer daily service between Saigon and Phu Quoc for incredibly low prices. The hour-long flight lands at Phu Quoc's new international airport in the center of the island.

Start off by heading for Phu Quoc's **Coconut Tree Prison,** a large, sunscorched complex which housed prisoners of war during the French and American conflicts. When you've finished, unwind on the shores of **Bai Sao,** Phu Quoc's most popular beach on the eastern coast, or head down to the small fishing village of **An Thoi** for a glimpse of local life.

In the afternoon, continue your beach crawl by heading back past Duong Dong, the island's main town, and north toward Phu Quoc's more secluded stretches of sand. Both **Bai Dai** and **Ganh Dau** are sights to behold with their white sand and crystal blue waters.

As dusk approaches, move closer to **Duong Dong** for a quick exploration of the town, including its pungent **fish sauce factories,** as well as a sunset near **Dinh Cau,** a small temple wedged between Phu Quoc's main beach and the local harbor. Round out the end of the day with a seafood dinner at the local **night market,** where the catch of the day goes from a tank to a grill to your plate.

Ho Chi Minh City

Look for ★ to find recommended sights, activities, dining, and lodging.

Highlights

© AVALON TRAVEL

★ **Reunification Palace:** This opulent palace was once home to the presidents of the short-lived Republic of Vietnam (page 22).

★ **Ben Thanh Market:** Frenetic and fast-paced, the city's most iconic market hosts dozens of multilingual vendors and over 3,000 stalls packed to the ceilings with everything you could imagine (page 28).

★ **War Remnants Museum:** Thoughtful and at times harrowing, Saigon's best museum provides insight into life during and after the American War (page 34).

★ **Thien Hau Pagoda:** A centuries-old Chinese pagoda in the heart of bustling District 5 was built by Chinese refugees as a thank-you to the goddess of the sea after their treacherous emigration (page 38).

★ **Street Food in Northern District 1:** The best of Vietnamese cuisine finds its way to the dented metal carts and bamboo poles of Saigon's street vendors (page 67).

★ **Northern Beaches of Phu Quoc Island:** Secluded beaches like **Bai Dai** and the stunning **Ganh Dau Beach** offer an unparalleled piece of paradise (page 119).

Shackled by heavy-handed governmental policies after the Vietnam War, Ho Chi Minh City (HCMC) hit the ground running in the mid-1980s, as the nation's *doi moi* economic reforms flung open the door to international business and trade.

A decade of pent-up energy was unleashed, sending the city on a frantic, determined mission to become Vietnam's cosmopolitan leader. HCMC—still known to locals as Saigon—packs all of southern Vietnam's best food, art, culture, and diversity into the jumbled houses and narrow alleyways of the country's most ambitious metropolis.

Settled on the sticky, humid, pancake-flat marshland just east of the Mekong Delta, the city began only a few centuries ago but has exploded in population over the past two decades. Even today, immigrants travel from near and far, hoping to make a home and a living amid the bustle of Vietnam's largest city. Government statistics put the urban population at around 8.1 million residents and counting, but this number hardly seems enough when you sit bumper-to-bumper in midday traffic or squeeze onto a tiny patch of sidewalk for a nighttime *ca phe bet* (streetside coffee). Others estimate the actual population is as high as 10 million people. Whatever the number, HCMC shows no signs of stopping. Already, outlying districts are swallowing up nearby towns like Di An and Bien Hoa, and the population of the greater metropolitan area is expected to grow to as many as 14 million in 2025.

Opener: busy street traffic; large Buddha in Vung Tau. **Opposite:** a tank at the War Remnants Museum. **Above:** view of the Bitexco Financial Tower, home to the Saigon Skydeck.

The outlines of modern-day Saigon began to take shape in 1674, as communities settled along the Ben Nghe River. To the east, Vietnamese farmers raised buffalo in what is now District 1, while a large, business-minded community of Chinese refugees, who had fled the persecution of the Ming dynasty, appeared in present-day District 5. Over the next 200 years, these two settlements grew closer to one another, forming the boundaries of Vietnam's largest metropolis.

After the French arrived in 1859, the city underwent major changes. Few were quick to welcome the French to Vietnam, but colonialism provided Saigon with several important and lasting things. At the center of town, the French erected churches, theaters, government buildings, and a post office, many of which remain in use today. To the west, much of the Chinese neighborhood was left as a separate entity, and so its residents carried on living as they had prior to colonization.

While Saigon's Chinese residents were able to live undisturbed, the Vietnamese resented European authority. Tensions rose steadily between foreign and local residents. By the 1940s, a healthy opposition force had grown. Their efforts briefly stalled during WWII, when Japanese forces wrested power from the French for a short time in 1944, but Vietnam ultimately prevailed.

When the French finally left in 1954, south Vietnam set up its own government, with Saigon as the capital. Aided by the United States, the Republic of South Vietnam began in the spirit of democracy but quickly grew unpopular thanks to the policies of its leader, Ngo Dinh Diem. Once again, dissent turned the city into a staging ground for protests and other acts of political opposition. Rallies were held, Buddhist monks self-immolated in protest, and, across the city, plots to overthrow the government were plentiful. Finally, in 1963, Diem and his brother, Ngo Dinh Nhu, met their end after hiding out in a church in District 5, and the country quickly rolled into armed conflict.

For the better part of the American War, Saigon proper remained safe, and foreign journalists flocked to the city to cover the conflict, making Saigon something of an international hub. That is, until Communist forces crashed through the Independence Palace gates on April 30, 1975, officially ending the war. From then on, the southern hub became Ho Chi Minh City in honor of the man who crusaded for Vietnam's independence.

Closed to the world and still reeling from decades of battle—against the French, Americans, Cambodians, and Chinese—Vietnam began to rebuild. Economic reforms in the mid-1980s allowed HCMC to begin realizing its full potential, with brightly colored billboards and trendy foreign shops opening across town. By the 1990s, an ever-growing number of foreign tourists began to visit HCMC and since then the city has taken off.

Though the jumble of traffic and mismatched buildings can seem infinite, the city's downtown area is small. Most of the city's major sights and activities can be covered within four or five days, as attractions tend to be concentrated around Districts 1 and 5.

Do your sightseeing in the morning to avoid the heat, especially if you're visiting pagodas and other non-air-conditioned places. Afternoons are great for activities, eating, and taking in the buzz of the city. Though businesses stay open at lunchtime, many Vietnamese take siesta around noon, particularly those working at museums and government-run buildings, so avoid these places at midday. Once the sun goes down, street vendors set up along sidewalks, restaurants open, and tiny roadside stalls sling beer and *do nhau* (drinking food). The heat also lets up, making the evening a perfect time to wander through a night market, grab a bite to eat, or delve into the city's nightlife.

Set aside a day or two to escape the downtown area and pay a visit to the Cu Chi Tunnels and Tay Ninh's mammoth Cao Dai temple. Budget at least 2-3 days to visit Phu Quoc because it requires either more money (for the plane ticket) or more time to get there (by way of a speedboat), so it's worth sticking around for an extra day or two.

You should have no trouble finding English speakers downtown, though you may occasionally have to rely on the pick-and-point method. When heading out for the day, grab a business card from your hotel or jot down the address of wherever you're headed: While most taxi and *xe om* (motorbike taxi) drivers know the city's major landmarks, it pays to have the address and district on hand for lesser-known locations.

The biggest holiday of the year is Tet (Lunar New Year, late Jan.-mid-Feb.), a day when everyone in Vietnam returns to their hometown to celebrate. During this time, HCMC is virtually a ghost town. Most streets are empty and businesses deserted. Many services are not available or if they are prices go up considerably to compensate.

ORIENTATION

Ho Chi Minh City is divided into 19 districts and five communes. The majority of visitors only make it to a few of the more centrally located neighborhoods.

District 1

At the heart of the city is District 1 (considered the city's downtown), perched on the banks of the Saigon River, where the best shopping, nightlife, hotels, restaurants, and trendy cafés can be found. **Ben Thanh Market**, one of HCMC's most famous landmarks, and **Pham Ngu Lao street** (the **backpacker district,** where most travelers stay) are located in the southwestern part of

Ho Chi Minh City

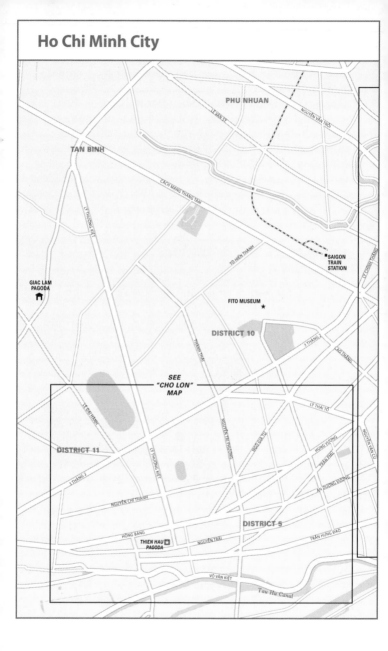

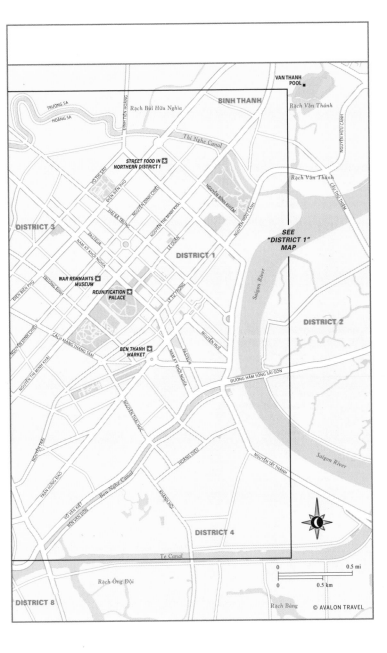

District 1

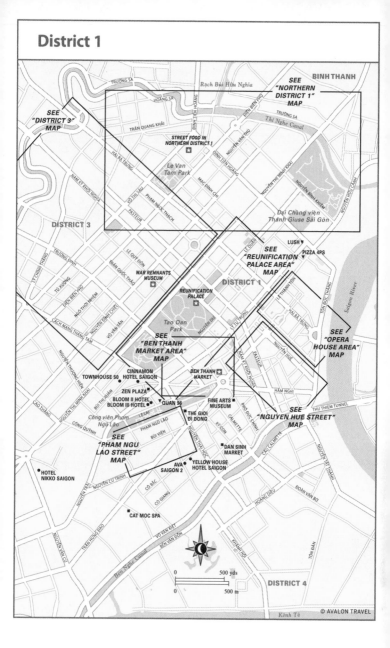

this district. Several of the city's other famous sights, such as the **Reunification**
Palace and **Notre Dame Cathedral,** are slightly farther north. The **Opera House** is a destination for high-end shopping and numerous nightlife spots. Also within District 1 is **Nguyen Hue street,** a large, open pedestrian-only square featuring high-end shops, cafés, and snack vendors and street performers.

Comprising the **northern** part of the district are a quieter web of streets packed with plenty of mouthwatering Vietnamese cuisine, and a handful of sights, including the Jade Emperor Pagoda.

District 3

Also in the middle of the action, District 3, to the northwest of District 1, is quieter. District 3 contains the **War Remnants Museum,** Vinh Nghiem Pagoda, Turtle Lake, and the historic Xa Loi Pagoda. (Some of these sights sit right on District 3's border with District 1.) This area is home to excellent restaurants, particularly vegetarian eateries, at more affordable prices than its downtown counterpart.

Cho Lon

The city's famous Chinatown, also known as Cho Lon, is a haze of noise, light, and traffic. Here you'll find the vast majority of HCMC's vibrant Chinese-Vietnamese community, along with scores of pagodas, temples, and assembly halls. Cho Lon literally means "big market," named after the enormous Binh Tay Market. This neighborhood lies across Districts 5 and 6. This area became a safe haven in the 16th and 17th centuries for Chinese refugees fleeing the persecution of the Ming dynasty and, later, the Tay Son rebellion.

lion dance celebrating Tet, the Lunar New Year, in Cho Lon

Sights

Ho Chi Minh City has seen a lot in its short history. Its sights are a testament to its diverse and intricate past. The streets are brimming with churches, temples, markets, museums, and everything from French-inspired halls to Chinese-style pagodas, offering proof of its many cultural intersections.

HCMC is not the place for grand photo ops or immense, awe-inspiring structures. Though there are some stunning sights within the city limits, it is the stories of these places and the ways in which they continue to function today that make them worth appreciating. Hop on a motorbike and jet out to Cho Lon, the city's Chinatown and one of the most hectic districts. Write a friend—or yourself—a postcard in the Central Post Office, a lasting relic of an earlier time, or grab a coffee outside the striking Notre Dame Cathedral and see how people live in the country's biggest metropolis.

REUNIFICATION PALACE AREA
★ Reunification Palace

The **Reunification Palace** (135 Nam Ky Khoi Nghia, D1, tel. 08/3822-3652, www.dinhdoclap.gov.vn, 7:30am-11am and 1pm-4pm daily, VND30,000) is a colossal white building that punctuates the end of Le Duan Boulevard. Set on 12 hectares of shaded, well-manicured lawns, the palace once served as the seat of government for both the French colonial regime and the short-lived Republic of Vietnam. Its interior remains almost exactly the same as it was 40 years ago, from the pale pink rotary phones in the situation room to the art-deco ambience of the upper floors.

Christened Norodom Palace in 1868, the palace was an official colonial dwelling until WWII when Emperor Bao Dai, Vietnam's last king, abdicated the throne. Once the war ended, the French reclaimed the palace until 1954, when power was officially transferred to politician Ngo Dinh Diem, who became south Vietnam's first president the following year. Diem renamed

the Reunification Palace

it the Independence Palace and installed his family in the house, which included a rooftop dance floor, several sitting rooms, dining areas, offices, a kitchen, and a series of underground bunkers. Following an assassination attempt in 1962, Diem commissioned Vietnamese architect Ngo Viet Thu to build a new structure in its place. This served as the headquarters of the south Vietnamese government until Communist forces crashed through the palace gates on April 30, 1975, officially putting an end to the American War.

Enter the palace to the left of the main gates and head toward the left side of the building, where free guided tours are offered every 15 minutes (7:45am-11am and 1:15pm-4pm daily). Signage is virtually nonexistent, so it's a good idea to hop on one of these tours. It takes about an hour to see the palace's four floors as well as its eerie bomb-shelter basement. There is also an educational video offered at the end of the tour but you can skip it. The palace gardens make for a pleasant stroll back to the entrance. To the right of the building are two tanks parked at the edge of the lawn. These vehicles were among the group that broke through the palace gates in 1975.

Notre Dame Cathedral

Set amid the hustle and bustle of downtown is the imposing figure of **Notre Dame Cathedral** (1 Cong Xa Paris, D1, tel. 08/3822-0477, 8am-11am and 3pm-4pm daily). Completed in 1880, this iconic Roman Catholic church is known for its soaring Gothic arches and bright red brick.

Every item that went into Notre Dame's construction was imported from France. The famous red-brick exterior is a product of Marseille. The pair of 190-foot bell towers were added in 1895, and still house functioning bells, though they are rarely used.

In front of the church is the **Our Lady of Peace statue,** completed in

A Long Weekend in Ho Chi Minh City

As one of Vietnam's younger cities, Ho Chi Minh City has infectious energy. When experienced like a local, this massive, fast-paced behemoth is a wonderful place. Plan for three action-packed days around town, whizzing past the city's sights and enjoying all the sounds, smells, and vibrancy of life in Vietnam's largest metropolis.

Day 1

Start your adventure at the **Reunification Palace** with a free guided tour. When you've finished, stroll through **30-4 Park,** stopping for a *ca phe bet* (sidewalk coffee) if you need a caffeine fix, or popping into one of the posh air-conditioned cafés nearby. The opposite end of the park opens onto **Notre Dame Cathedral** and the **Central Post Office.** From here, walk up toward **Turtle Lake** for lunch. There are plenty of options overlooking the roundabout and on the side streets surrounding 30-4 Park. You can also head west to **Khoai** or **...hum** before spending the afternoon at the **War Remnants Museum.**

Head back toward the backpacker district as the day winds down, passing through **Tao Dan Park** en route. Stop by **Chill Skybar** or **OMG** for cocktails and bird's-eye views of the city, or simply rest up before heading off for dinner. District 1's Tan Dinh neighborhood is a good choice. For street food, **Banh Xeo 46A** offers a great introduction into local cuisine, while **Cuc Gach Quan** adds an upscale environment to its delicious Vietnamese menu. Not far from this area, seafood lovers will also appreciate **Quan Mien Cua 94 Cu.**

After dinner, return to the backpacker neighborhood for cheap **street beers** or a laid-back drink at **The View.** Dance floors are abundant throughout this area, with live bands playing nightly at **Universal Bar** and **Thi Cafe.**

Day 2

Jet out to **Cho Lon** first thing in the morning to explore Chinatown's enormous wholesale market. You can grab breakfast from one of the many market vendors before hitching a *xe om* ride over to **Thien Hau**

1959 by an Italian sculptor and shipped from Rome. This is the second sculpture to stand in its place. The first was a statue of the Bishop Pigneau de Behaine, who helped Emperor Gia Long rise to power. The bishop's statue was removed in the 1940s. The red marble base upon which Our Lady of Peace now stands is a leftover from this original work.

Our Lady of Peace is one of Saigon's biggest celebrities. Early in the morning, you can see local Catholics before the statue, hands folded in prayer. By the afternoon, she is the subject of countless tourist photos.

Notre Dame is most impressive when viewed from outside. Inside, a set of arched door frames give way to high ceilings crisscrossed with a wooden detail. Visitors are forbidden beyond the back area of the church, but it is still possible to see a few stained glass panels as well as a figure of Jesus above the altar. The alcoves on either side of the entrance house statues of

Pagoda, stopping in at the nearby Chaozhou Congregation Hall and Cho Lon Mosque while you're there. When you've had your fill of District 5, head back downtown to bustling Ben Thanh Market for shopping and lunch. Wander down Le Loi street, passing by the city's charming colonial Hotel de Ville building and the Opera House as you reach a more upscale part of town.

statue at the Jade Emperor Pagoda

Enjoy a sunset drink from the rooftop of Broma or grab a cocktail at the swanky Racha Room. Dinner in this neighborhood is an international affair, with Ciao Bella, The Refinery, and Pizza 4Ps within walking distance, as well as a few local eateries, such as Bo Tung Xeo and the Temple Club.

For a night on the town, Last Call, a classy cocktail lounge, is nearby, as is Phatty's, an expat sports bar, and the dance floor of Apocalypse Now. The city's best live music venues are Yoko and Saigon Ranger.

Day 3

Spend your last day in the city with a local. Art enthusiasts can sign up for Sophie's Art Tour to learn more about Vietnam's history through the eyes of its artists. Foodies will appreciate Back of the Bike Tours, which go around town, savoring all the best local fare. If you prefer an activity, you can spend the morning honing your culinary skills with a cooking class or treat yourself at one of the city's spas.

When you're ready for lunch, pay a visit to the famous Lunch Lady for one of her tasty soups before walking to the Jade Emperor Pagoda nearby. From here, spend the rest of the afternoon unwinding at a café or wandering around the city.

the Virgin Mary and St. Anthony. Around each statue, stone tiles express reverence and thanks in French, English, and Vietnamese. To see the building in its entirety, attend the English version of Sunday mass at 9:30am, during which time you can gain full access to the main hall.

Central Post Office

On the eastern side of the Cong Xa Paris square is another vestige of French colonialism, the Central Post Office (2 Cong Xa Paris, D1, tel. 08/3924-7247, 7am-7pm Mon.-Fri., 7am-6pm Sat., 8am-6pm Sun.). More reminiscent of a train station, this large building was designed by Gustave Eiffel. The massive clock and grand entrance are a favorite photo op among tourists. High yellow-and-green arches line either side of the vast hall. The two maps near the main entrance depict the Vietnam of an earlier time. No

the Central Post Office

matter where you stand, you're sure to catch a glimpse of modern Vietnam's founding father, Ho Chi Minh, affectionately known as Uncle Ho, who watches over the building from a portrait mounted on the back wall.

The Central Post Office functions as the city's main postal hub. A number of other services are also available here, including international phone calls, which can be made from a tiny, antique wooden phone booth. There are also postcards available for purchase and a set of writing desks farther back if you want to send your postcard on the spot. You might also catch Duong Van Ngo, Saigon's last professional letter writer, hard at work. A post office employee since 1946, Ngo is fluent in English, French, and Vietnamese and specializes in both translating and writing letters.

OPERA HOUSE AREA

A block away from bustling Nguyen Hue, dapper security guards and lavish store displays signal a more upscale part of town.

Opera House

At the end of Le Loi Street, Saigon's **Opera House** (7 Cong Truong Lam Son, D1, tel. 08/3823-7419, www.hbso.org.vn), also known as the Municipal Theater, is a well-preserved historical gem and one of the city's oldest supporters of the arts. When the opera house opened in 1900, it became Saigon's premier center for the arts, hosting scores of ballets and musical acts, as well as other performances.

Following the end of the French colonial government, the building was transformed from a cultural center into the Lower Assembly of the Republic of Vietnam as part of the south's new administration. It remained a government office until the end of the war in 1975.

Opera House Area

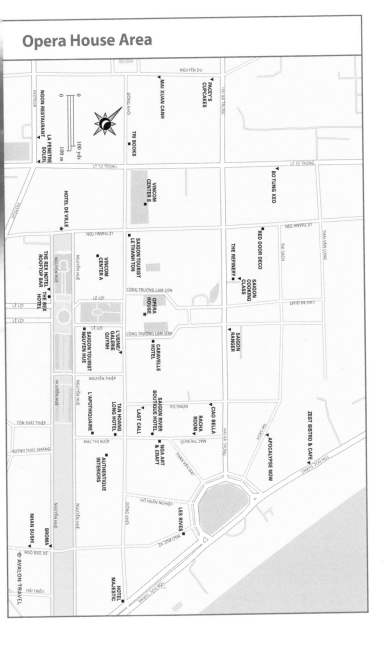

After reunification, the Opera House was restored to its original function as a performance space. Renovations later brought back its former architectural glory as well, and today it continues to hold cultural events, showcasing both domestic and international performers. Outside of performances, the Opera House is normally closed to the public. Its exterior is the most impressive aspect, with a wide set of front steps and a massive arched facade.

Rex Hotel

On the northwest corner of the block is the **Rex Hotel** (141 Nguyen Hue, D1, tel. 08/3829-2185, www.rexhotelvietnam.com), yet another downtown building that has evolved according to Saigon's history. The Rex has survived many incarnations, from an early 20th-century French garage to an energetic trading center to a property of the American Cultural Center. Its greatest claim to fame is as the site of the American Information Service's daily press briefings during the war, better known as the "five o'clock follies," when foreign journalists would gather to hear news from the front lines. The five-star Rex boasts over 100 luxury rooms and a popular rooftop bar. There's not much to do here unless you're a guest, but it's worth passing by.

Hotel de Ville

Positioned at the end of Nguyen Hue's long, open pedestrian street is the **Hotel de Ville** (86 Le Thanh Ton, D1), a stunning colonial building from the turn of the 20th century. Set amid the old-world grandeur of the nearby buildings, the Hotel de Ville remains a piece of colonial Indochina in the modern age. The Vietnamese flag flies high above the French-made building. Now the home of the local People's Committee and the center of city government, the building is not open to the public.

BEN THANH MARKET AREA
★ Ben Thanh Market

Easily the most recognizable structure in Saigon, **Ben Thanh Market** (Le Loi and Tran Hung Dao, D1, tel. 08/3829-2096, 6am-6pm daily) is the original commercial heart of the city and a prime spot for souvenir shopping, with over 3,000 small businesses and an army of multilingual vendors. Using the city's waterways to transport goods, Ben Thanh became the Vietnamese answer to Chinatown's Binh Tay Market, with each attracting traders from both their local communities and neighboring states. When the French arrived and began to incorporate their architecture into Saigon's landscape, the market was formalized as a large, thatched-roof building near the river. Ben Thanh's present-day site is at the north edge of Quach Thi Trang roundabout. The building was completed in 1914 and dubbed the "New Ben Thanh Market."

Since its inception, Ben Thanh has been a major commercial hub and the site of many historical events. During the tumultuous 1950s and '60s, several significant protests occurred outside its massive gates. The most

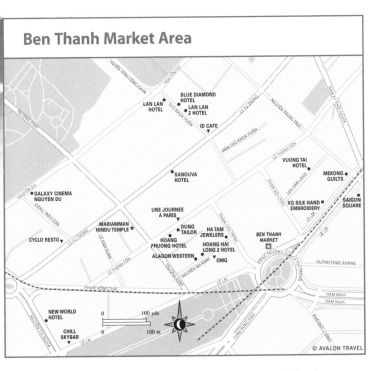

Ben Thanh Market Area

notable of these occurred on August 25, 1963, when thousands of students and Buddhist monks gathered at the roundabout in front of the market to protest American forces and the presidency of Ngo Dinh Diem. As the protest grew in size and strength, shots were fired to subdue the crowd and one young protester, 15-year-old student Quach Thi Trang, was killed. Since then, the roundabout has been referred to as Quach Thi Trang roundabout.

Ben Thanh Market

Vendors begin setting up as early as 4am each day. The outer shops open their doors first, followed by the market's main gates. Once the day market has closed its doors to the public, an equally popular night market sets up shop around the building on Phan Chu Trinh and Phan Boi Chau streets from 6pm until about midnight.

Mariamman Hindu Temple

The **Mariamman Hindu Temple** (45 Truong Dinh, D1, 7am-7pm daily), northwest of Ben Thanh Market, comes as a surprise with its colorful towers rising high out of the downtown traffic. The largest of three Hindu temples in the city, this shrine is dedicated to Mariamman, the fickle south Indian goddess of rain and disease.

This temple was built in the late 19th century by Tamil immigrants and is today visited by the small remaining Hindu community and many local Vietnamese. Mariamman is housed inside a large central sanctuary and flanked by her two guardians: Maduraiveeran on the left and Pechiamman on the right. A walk around the back of these shrines reveals a series of brightly hued statues carved into the far wall.

Beside the entrance is a lion statue, which was once used for Hindu processions around the city. An impressive and beautifully decorated *rajagopuram* (tower) stands nearly 40 feet high, the tallest Hindu structure in Saigon, and features images of the temple's guardian as well as other Hindu deities.

Dress modestly when visiting and remove your shoes on the raised platform. Silence is observed indoors, and it is forbidden to enter the gated area surrounding the central sanctuary.

NGUYEN HUE STREET
Saigon Skydeck

Saigon Skydeck (2 Hai Trieu, D1, tel. 08/3915-6156, www.saigonskydeck. com, 9:30am-9:30pm daily, VND200,000), 49 stories above the city, is the official viewing platform of the lotus-shaped Bitexco Financial Tower. Standing at 262 meters (860 ft.), this is the tallest building to grace the city skyline. The tower boasts 68 floors, a shopping mall, several restaurants, and a helipad topped with a Vietnamese flag so large that it is visible from the street below.

The Bitexco opened its doors for the first time in 2010. A year later came the inauguration of the Skydeck, providing locals and tourists with a unique opportunity to see the city from above.

Since most of Saigon's buildings are low-lying structures, finding a bird's-eye view like this is no easy feat. On the 360-degree viewing deck, a series of displays help to orient visitors, offering snippets of historical information about the landscape and the buildings below. You can catch a close-up look at the city's more famous sights through the binoculars situated around the platform.

If you're looking for nice views and some peace and quiet, head a few

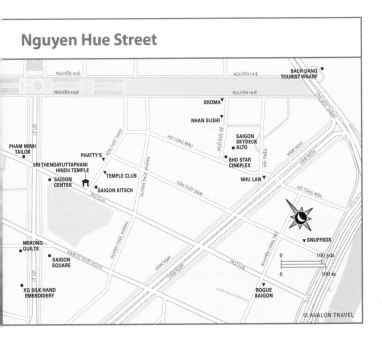

Nguyen Hue Street

floors up to **Eon 51** (tel. 08/6291-8752, www.eon51.com, 8am-11pm daily, VND100,000-500,000), which spans the 50th to 52nd floors and includes a bar, café, and restaurant. Prices are more expensive than other bars, but instead of shelling out cash to stand on the 49th floor, you get the added benefit of a seat and a drink, slightly higher up. Hours of operation vary depending upon the venue. The café is open longest, from 8am to 11pm, while the restaurant has more limited lunch and dinner hours, so be sure to check the website before dropping by.

Sri Thendayuttaphani Hindu Temple

The **Sri Thendayuttaphani Hindu Temple** (66 Ton That Thiep, D1, 6am-7pm daily) is an interesting fusion of Hindu and Buddhist traditions. Built over 100 years ago, this structure is the work of a once-thriving south Indian community. In its heyday, the temple was regularly used and Hindu processions took place in the streets of Saigon. After 1975, racial and religious persecution escalated and many south Indians fled the country.

The Sri Thendayuttaphani Temple worships both Hindu and Buddhist deities. In the main sanctuary, a statue of Thendayuttaphani, also known as Lord Muruga, sits at the center of the temple. Images of Hindu deities line the surrounding walls alongside famous Indian faces. Most notable is the photograph featuring former Indian Prime Minister Jawaharlal Nehru in a meeting with Ho Chi Minh. A statue of Quan Am, a popular Buddhist bodhisattva, sits on the right side of the courtyard. Hidden at the back of the temple is a statue of the Buddha.

Wear appropriate clothing and, when stepping onto the raised platform, remove your shoes. Before you leave, take the narrow staircase on the right up to the roof, where a single blue-and-white incense pot sits before the temple's colorful tower, covered with depictions of Hindu gods and goddesses.

NORTHERN DISTRICT 1
Saigon Zoo and Botanical Garden

Rounding out the eastern end of Le Duan Boulevard is the **Saigon Zoo and Botanical Garden** (2B Nguyen Binh Khiem, D1, tel. 08/3829-1425, www.saigonzoo.net, 7am-6:30pm daily, VND50,000), one of the oldest zoos in the world. Part menagerie, part beautiful park, and part children's carnival, this is a nice place to trade the urban chaos for a rare glimpse of nature in the bustling city. Once one of Saigon's nicest features, the zoo was first developed in 1864. Louis Adolph Germain, a military veterinarian with the French Expedition Army, was tasked with developing the 12-hectare park's roads, animal cages, and nurseries.

The zoo section of the park has not retained its former glory. While the various plants, trees, and flowers packed onto the grounds provide a gorgeous backdrop for an afternoon stroll, the zoo would likely not be considered humane by Western standards due to small and crowded enclosures. Anyone sensitive to animal rights should avoid this part of the park.

Instead, stick to the shaded walkways and stone benches of the botanical garden or the butterfly garden, an enclosure often brimming with dozens of the brightly colored creatures. There is also a children's petting zoo (9am-11am and 2pm-4pm weekends) stocked with billy goats and sheep. If you prefer a quiet stroll around the gardens, it's best to go during the week.

orchids on display at the Saigon Zoo and Botanical Garden

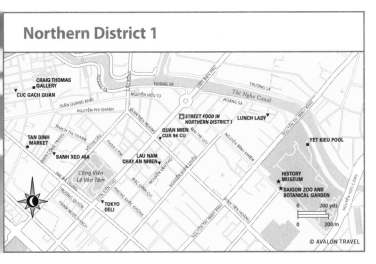

© AVALON TRAVEL

HISTORY MUSEUM

Within the gates of the Saigon Zoo and Botanical Garden, the city's **History Museum** (2 Nguyen Binh Khiem, D1, tel. 08/3829-8146, www.baotanglich-suvn.com, 8am-11:30am and 1:30pm-5pm Tues.-Sun., VND15,000) has seen several iterations, from ancient Asian art museum to the country's national museum. It's been the History Museum since 1979. The beautiful grounds surrounding the building add to its already-stunning colonial architecture, which bears the telltale yellow paint and sloping roof of many early 20th century structures in the city.

The museum's exhibits are divided into two parts: Vietnam's cultural history, from 5,000 years ago until the mid-20th century; and the ancient art of some of Vietnam's southern minorities, including the Champa and the Oc Eo. Though many of the more modern exhibits feature beautiful, functional pieces—lacquer trays, ceramic vases, ivory trinkets—there is little signage or additional information. The most educational exhibits are the Champa and Oc Eo sections, in which a few simple placards guide you through the Hindu and Buddhist influences that helped create these works of art.

There are no photographs allowed without a photo ticket (VND40,000), though most visitors won't feel the need. There are also traditional water puppet shows here (six shows per day Tues.-Sun., VND50,000).

Directly across from the museum is the **Hung Kings Temple,** which is guarded by a famous Ho Chi Minh quotation carved onto a large stone slab: "The Hung Kings built this country; we must uphold it." This building once served as a memorial honoring the Vietnamese soldiers who died during WWI. After 1954, locals began coming here to worship the historic Hung Kings. The temple is an impressive structure, particularly inside, where its walls and ceiling are full of ornate red-and-gold carvings. Taking photos is allowed within the temple, but ask permission first.

Jade Emperor Pagoda

Just off busy Dien Bien Phu street sits the **Jade Emperor Pagoda (Chua Phuoc Hai)** (73 Mai Thi Luu, D1, 7am-6pm daily), one of Saigon's more prominent places of worship. Cantonese immigrants completed the building in the late 19th and early 20th centuries, though it was never meant to be a pagoda. Phuoc Hai originally belonged to followers of Minh Su, one of the five syncretic religions brought to Vietnam by the Chinese, and was only later handed over to the Buddhist Association to ensure its preservation.

Inside, massive wooden warriors loom just beyond the main doorway, guarding the entrance to the pagoda. Locals usually pay respects to these imposing figures before heading into the main hall, where the King of Heaven and his court sit, waiting to decide who is admitted into paradise. On the left side of the hall, a series of wood carvings depict the 10 levels of hell in gruesome detail.

Turn right out of this room, follow the signs reading "Dien Quan Am," and take the wooden staircase up to where the goddess of fertility resides. Less fearsome than her counterparts downstairs, she is often visited by pregnant women and those hoping to conceive. A small balcony at the top of the staircase offers up-close views of the pagoda's elaborate roof.

Outside of the narrow corridor beside the main hall is a small pond brimming with turtles of varying size; this is why the pagoda is also called the Tortoise Pagoda. Out front, vendors sell fish and baby turtles, which can be released into their respective ponds. With Phuoc Hai's already-over-crowded waters, it's better to leave these creatures where they are.

DISTRICT 3
Turtle Lake

Turtle Lake (Cong Truong Quoc Te, D3, daily 24 hours), an enormous circle surrounded by several cafés, used to be known as Soldier's Park, where bronze statues honored the fallen French soldiers of WWI. Not long before his assassination in 1963, then-president Ngo Dinh Diem did away with the French park, and his successor, General Nguyen Van Thieu, used the land to erect the monument you see today: a large, somewhat murky pond sitting beneath a series of concrete walkways and a statue of a towering lotus, the national flower of Vietnam. The park originally included a statue of a turtle, but it was destroyed shortly after Saigon fell in 1975. The statue was never replaced, but the name stuck.

During the day, vendors gather around the park, selling snacks and refreshments to office workers and students. The higher floors of the surrounding cafés make a good spot to take a break and people-watch over a *ca phe sua da* (Vietnamese iced coffee with milk). This is a good stop en route to the War Remnants Museum and the rest of District 3's sights.

★ War Remnants Museum

The **War Remnants Museum** (28 Vo Van Tan, D3, tel. 08/3930-6664, www.baotangchungtichchientranh.vn, 7:30am-noon and 1:30pm-5pm

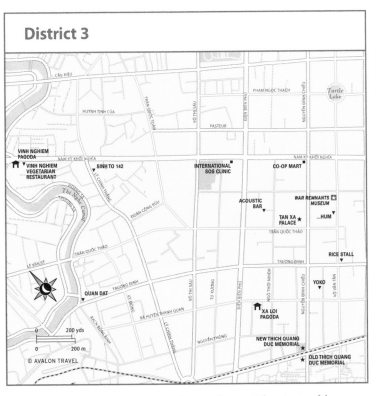

District 3

daily, VND15,000), located behind the Reunification Palace, is one of the city's most-visited sights. This museum serves as an important reminder of Vietnam's recent past and a conflict that many locals remember firsthand.

During the years between the end of the American War and the country's normalization of relations with the United States in 1995, this building housed the Museum of Chinese and American War Crimes. Though the name has changed, the sentiment remains largely the same: each floor of the building touches upon a different topic, from the global community's fierce opposition toward U.S. involvement in Vietnam to the atrocities committed by American soldiers against Vietnamese civilians. Though several of these exhibits are laden with propaganda, they paint an accurate picture of the struggles that many Vietnamese endured during the war and continue to face today.

Outside the main building, military vehicles line the border of the property, including a helicopter and different types of tanks, all of which were used during the conflict. There is also a smaller exhibit dedicated to tiger cages, the brutal form of punishment once used at the infamous Con Dao and Phu Quoc prisons, where thousands of Vietnamese were tortured and often died at the hands of their captors.

Allow yourself plenty of time, as the building shuts down promptly at midday so that employees can break for lunch and all guests are ushered

military helicopter outside the War Remnants Museum

off the premises until 1:30pm. Most people spend about two hours here, so plan your visit either in the early morning or the early afternoon. While this is a valuable and eye-opening experience for locals and foreigners, it is not an easy place to visit. Families with children should steer clear, as some of the exhibits are graphic.

Tan Xa Palace

The oldest private residence in the city is **Tan Xa Palace** (180 Nguyen Dinh Chieu, D3, tel. 08/3930-3828, 8am-5pm daily), a small, one-room building hidden in the shadow of the lavish Archbishop's residence. Now a chapel, this modest structure is credited to the man who would later become Emperor Gia Long. Before ascending the throne, Nguyen Phuc Anh arranged its construction in 1790 as a thank-you gift to then-Bishop Pigneau de Behaine for his help in reclaiming the Nguyen dynasty's power after the Tay Son rebellion. The place later became a home for missionaries and bishops before being converted into a chapel.

It is possible to see the palace up close, but you can also get a good feel for it from the street, where you can look through the fence to see the decaying wood of the structure. To get on the property, check with the security guard at the side gate, located on Tran Quoc Thao street, before entering. The chapel itself is no longer in use and no one is permitted inside, but the neighboring buildings are functioning offices for the local Catholic church.

Vinh Nghiem Pagoda

Before you can even see the building, the 40-meter, seven-tiered tower of **Vinh Nghiem Pagoda** (339 Nam Ky Khoi Nghia, D3, tel. 08/3896-6798, www.vinhnghiemvn.com, 6:30am-11:30am and 1pm-6pm daily) alerts you to the largest Buddhist structure in Saigon. Built in 1971, this fairly modern complex is comprised of not only a pagoda but also a library and classrooms for Buddhist study. Three staircases lead up to the main hall, an open space that becomes jam-packed during holidays and special occasions. Inside, the front half of the pagoda is used for Buddhist ceremonies and worship, with religious paintings and other artwork lining the walls. A walk around the main altar reveals hundreds of tiles commemorating the dead, which are kept behind glass at the back.

Outside, the corners of the pagoda's impressive roof curl skyward in the northern style, and its stark, gray tower rises high above the surrounding structures. Though it is not possible to enter the tower itself, visitors can look out over bustling Nam Ky Khoi Nghia street from the balcony and admire the maze of Buddhist flags zigzagging across the complex.

Xa Loi Pagoda

Xa Loi Pagoda (89B Ba Huyen Thanh Quan, D3, tel. 08/3930-0114, www.chuaxaloi.vn, 7am-11am and 2pm-5pm daily) has seen a lot in its short history. Originally built to house sacred relics of the Shakyamuni Buddha, this pagoda is known as a major center of Buddhist study. Today the sacred relics can be seen in a red compartment above the enormous Buddha residing in the main hall.

Xa Loi is also known for its outspoken opposition to the government of south Vietnam in the early 1960s. Most notably, on the morning of June 11, 1963, the Venerable Thich Quang Duc, a senior monk at Xa Loi, sat in the middle of a busy downtown intersection and, surrounded by supporters, lit himself on fire in response to President Ngo Dinh Diem's religious persecution. He was the first of several monks who completed this act of protest against Diem's government.

Today, Xa Loi is a quiet place, equipped with a library and study center. Two massive staircases curve up to the main hall of the pagoda, an airy room that houses one large floor-to-ceiling Buddha as well as several smaller statues. Both outside and in, Buddhist flags sway in the breeze, and a smaller statue honors Quan Am, the most well-known female bodhisattva in Mahayana Buddhism. A short walk down the road leads to the **Thich Quang Duc Memorial** (Cach Mang Thang Tam and Nguyen Dinh Chieu, D3), honoring the fallen monk.

CHO LON

If you think District 1 is busy, meet its noisy neighbor to the west. The farther you travel along the Saigon River, the faster the motorbikes begin to move, speeding down wide and hectic Vo Van Kiet street. Buses blare their siren-like horns into the fray, followed by cars, transport trucks, and the occasional motorized tractor, chugging along with its cargo.

Binh Tay Market

One look at the massive entrance of **Binh Tay Market** (57A Thap Muoi, D6,

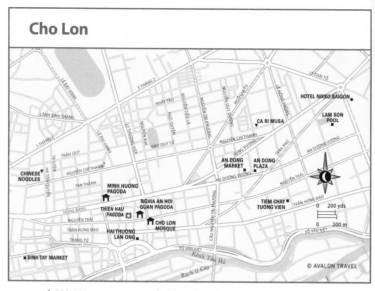

Cho Lon

tel. 08/3857-1512, 6am-7pm daily) is all it takes to understand how the trading center got its name. Still known by locals as Cho Lon—"big market" in Vietnamese—this mammoth building was constructed in the late 1800s. Cho Lon drew traders and businessmen from across the city as well as from neighboring countries, such as Cambodia, Malaysia, and India. Cho Lon fast grew into the wholesale market of the south. After the original location grew too large, the new Cho Lon was constructed, using a combination of Chinese-style architecture and French building techniques. A small bust of Quach Dam, the market's founder, stands in the center of the market.

Binh Tay is a major commercial center in the city, housing over 2,300 separate stalls and serving not only the large Chinese-Vietnamese community nearby—roughly a quarter of the vendors within the market are ethnic Chinese—but also the rest of the city. The bustle inside the market embodies much of the pace at which this part of Saigon moves, buzzing with activity from morning until night. At the time of writing, Binh Tay is closed for renovations; it's unclear how long these upgrades will take, so it's wise to ask around about the market's status before you visit.

★ Thien Hau Pagoda

The teetering, haphazard, multi-story houses of Chinatown mix with the shops and offices of a modern city. But stuck firmly in a bygone era is **Thien Hau Pagoda** (710 Nguyen Trai, D5, 6am-5:30pm daily), a beautiful building constructed in 1760. Southern Chinese refugees arrived in south Vietnam and began to settle around the Cho Lon area, then known as Tai Ngon. The Chinese expressed their thanks to Thien Hau, goddess of the sea, by crafting the ornate wood carvings and terra-cotta scenes depicted around this pagoda. This single-story structure shows its age gracefully in the worn exterior and intricate designs on the roof.

Before you step inside you'll be accosted by a wave of incense, which burns ceaselessly from the massive pots indoors, not to mention a collection of incense coils that hang from the ceiling. Flanking the walls on either side of the pagoda are stone engravings that list the building's benefactors over the years. The final third of the main hall is easily the most impressive. Vivid red and gold adorns the building's columns, while up above countless incense coils twist and flutter in the breeze. Dozens of locals and foreigners pay their respects with incense sticks, candles, and other offerings, which are available for purchase. A statue of Thien Hau sits at the back, ornate and heavily decorated. The pagoda is one of the more unique buildings in Saigon. Despite the click of cameras and the curious tourists, locals are friendly and seemingly unaffected by the many foreign visitors.

SIGHTS

Chaozhou Congregation Hall

A short walk down the road from Thien Hau Pagoda is the newer and bigger **Chaozhou Congregation Hall (Nghia An Hoi Quan)** (678 Nguyen Trai, D5, 6am-6pm daily), obscured by a high stone wall. Honoring the great Chinese general Quan Cong, this structure is the work of the local Chaozhou Chinese Congregation. The gilded woodwork of the exterior forms a splash of color that runs along the thick cylindrical beams of the building and up to the detailing on the roof.

Inside, a statue of a red-faced Quan Cong sits, beard in hand, at the center of the pagoda, with his horse tucked on the left of the entrance. Farther into the pagoda, bright neon hues contrast against a pair of stone walls. Remove your shoes as you step onto the raised platform at the back, where a larger statue of the general sits, flanked by towers of golden figurines and other ornamentation. Look up: Much of this building's stunning decor and architecture is tucked inside the rafters of the high-ceilinged structure.

Thien Hau Pagoda

Cho Lon Mosque

A marked contrast from the colorful ornamentation of nearby pagodas, the pastel blue **Cho Lon Mosque** (641 Nguyen Trai, D5, no phone, 4:30am–6:30pm daily) is easy to miss amid the hectic market outside its front door. This no-frills building became a house of worship for Tamil immigrants in 1935. After 1975, much of the Tamil community left Vietnam. Today, the mosque serves mostly Malaysian and Indonesian Muslims living in the city, though there are also a few Vietnamese believers. To the left of the entrance is an ablutions pool, where the religious wash before praying, and opposite the entrance of the mosque is a Halal restaurant serving mostly Malaysian dishes.

Minh Huong Pagoda

Near the corner of Thuan Kieu street just a block north of the string of pagodas lining Nguyen Trai is the **Minh Huong Pagoda** (184 Hong Bang, D5, 6am–5pm daily), also known as the Phuoc An Assembly Hall. Originally completed in the late 19th century by immigrants from the Guangdong, Fujian, and Zhejiang provinces of China, this vibrant building once stood beside the Cho Lon Railway Station. In the small courtyard out front, statues of the Buddha and Quan Am, a popular Buddhist bodhisattva, flank the main entrance. The pagoda's front door features a beautiful, iridescent red lacquer, but its most unique element is the collection of mosaic incense pots throughout the pagoda. Carefully tiled with colorful patterned pieces of broken china, these massive standing pots catch your eye amid a main hall full of vivid embellishment. At the back of the hall, famous Chinese general Quan Cong sits in the middle, accompanied by Ong Bon, a Fujianese god, on the left and the Ngu Hanh goddesses of the five elements on the right. Above the red, yellow, and green decor, enormous incense coils burn slowly, taking as long as a full month to burn down.

incense coils at the Minh Huong Pagoda

Slightly off the beaten path, the **Fito Museum of Traditional Medicine** (41 Hoang Du Khuong, D10, tel. 08/864-2430, www.fitomuseum.com.vn, 8:30am-5pm daily, VND120,000) is an unusual and worthy attraction that is slowly gaining popularity among tourists. It's owned and operated by the Fito Pharmaceutical Company, which produces and sells traditional Vietnamese remedies within Vietnam and abroad. The energetic museum staff are eager to educate visitors on the nation's long history of traditional medicine. Designed to reflect Vietnamese architecture in various parts of the country, from the northern structures of Hanoi down to Mekong Delta-style houses, the museum is filled with dozens of artifacts dating as far back as a few thousand years. Free guided tours cover the origins of Vietnamese medicine, the many plant and animal ingredients involved in traditional remedies, and the practices of traditional Vietnamese pharmacists. The tour ends downstairs with a cup of tea and a chance to peruse the museum's small shop of traditional medicine, including teas and oils.

Though it's never busy, the museum sees a steady stream of visitors; there is almost always someone available to lead a tour. Informational pamphlets are available at the front desk for guests who arrive after a tour has begun. Photos are also allowed here and even encouraged on the third floor, where visitors can try on traditional Vietnamese garb and snap a picture with the museum's collection of grinding apparatuses, once used by pharmacists.

If there's time, swing by Hai Thuong Lan Ong street near Binh Tay Market, better known as the traditional medicine street, where dozens of traditional pharmacists sell their remedies.

GIAC LAM PAGODA

About four miles outside of downtown, **Giac Lam Pagoda** (565 Lac Long Quan, D Tan Binh, , no phone, 6am-noon and 2pm-8pm daily) is the city's oldest pagoda. A large, open complex made up of several buildings, the

Giac Lam Pagoda

grounds of Giac Lam boast over 100 statues of the Buddha as well as a staggering collection of shrines honoring the relatives of local residents.

In the seven-tiered tower just inside the gates, each floor houses a different statue of the Buddha or a popular bodhisattva. This is one of the only Buddhist towers in the city that you can ascend. Though the very top is off-limits to visitors, a narrow balcony on each floor offers a nice view of the surrounding area.

Beyond the tower is a small garden decorated with dozens of miniature idols as well as a large statue of Quan Am, one of Buddhism's most famous bodhisattva. A second set of gates leads into the main building, where dozens more Buddhas are on display, as well as headstones and nameplates with ages and birth dates scrawled across lacquer plaques and stone carvings.

The largest statue of all, a towering white Buddha, sits cross-legged to the right of the main walkway. Another small garden precedes the main pagoda, while the far end of the complex is home to a series of ornate tombs belonging to the pagoda's founders.

TOURS

There are scores of travel agencies in the city that offer half- and full-day tours. Larger companies like **Sinh Tourist** (246-248 De Tham, D1, tel. 08/3838-9593, www.thesinhtourist.vn, 6:30am-10:30pm daily) and **TNK Travel** (220 De Tham, D1, tel. 08/3920-4766, www.tnktravelvietnam.com, 7am-10pm daily) provide inexpensive, cookie-cutter tours to most of the city's major sights and cost VND150,000-500,000. Though by far the most inexpensive option, these tour buses often shepherd groups of 20-30 people around town. Being on such a large tour diminishes the experience, as it can be difficult to hear the tour guide or get much of the benefit that paying for a tour is meant to provide.

Motorbike Tours

Hands down, the ultimate way to experience the city is as most locals do—on a motorbike. **XO Tours** (tel. 09/3308-3727, www.xotours.vn, 9am-10pm daily, VND1,100,000-1,700,000) does just that, ferrying visitors around town on the back of a scooter. In addition to visiting the city's major sights, XO provides tours tailored to food, nightlife, and shopping, all with experienced, traditionally clad local guides who double as motorbike drivers. The same goes for **Vietnam Vespa Adventures** (169A De Tham, D1, tel. 09/0836-7997, www.vietnamvespaadventures.com, 7am-2am daily, VND1,600,000-2,100,000), which runs food and nightlife city tours as well as one-day trips to the Mekong Delta.

Foodies should book a trip with **Back of the Bike Tours** (tel. 09/3504-6910, www.backofthebiketours.com, 9am-10pm daily, VND1,200,000-3,600,000), the brainchild of husband-and-wife team Chad and Thuy Kubanoff, a pair with a serious passion for the city and its delectable street food. Tours leave from District 1 and take guests outside of Saigon's central area to dine in some of the less-visited neighborhoods, offering a more unique, authentic take on Vietnam's southern hub.

Cultural Tours

For a unique perspective on Vietnamese history and art, sign up for **Sophie's Art Tour** (tel. 09/3375-2402, www.sophiesarttour.com, 9am-1pm Tues.-Sat., VND1,500,000). A longtime Saigon resident and the former curator of local Galerie Quynh, Sophie Hughes spent over a year researching and compiling this living project, which tells the tumultuous history of 20th-century Vietnam through its greatest artists. Divided into four chapters, the tour whisks visitors to a series of private galleries as well as the Fine Arts Museum, focusing on different aspects of local history before and after colonialism and the American War. Sophie's interactive approach and continuing research keep the story fresh, adding new anecdotes and information all the time and encouraging visitors to get involved. The tour leaves from a small café in District 3 and its fee includes transportation as well as admission to museums, cold drinks, and, of course, the expertise of a local resident.

Entertainment and Events

NIGHTLIFE

As the sun sets over Saigon, street barbecues and curbside watering holes pop up all over town, serving a variety of *do nhau* (drinking food) and slinging bottles of Saigon Red and Tiger beer.

Though there are hundreds of bars across town, the best of the city's nightlife is in District 1. For backpacker bars and nonstop activity, head to Bui Vien, where there is always a party. Drinks are dirt-cheap and most places have nightly specials. More spacious and slightly more expensive environments can be found down the narrow streets surrounding Nguyen Hue and the Opera House, where laid-back lounge options abound, not to mention larger expat bars and a handful of trendy nightclubs. Saigon is big on rooftop venues, which are a nice place to take in the city at night, removed from the bustle down below.

Petty theft is common during daylight hours; this problem only increases at night. When heading out on the town, take only the essentials, travel in groups, and opt for taxis over motorbikes where possible. There have been instances in which passengers have been accosted on a *xe om* and robbed, sometimes by a thief in cahoots with the motorbike driver. Though it's just as likely that you won't have trouble in the evening, it's best to keep your wits about you and an eye on your belongings at all times.

Bars

OPERA HOUSE AREA

Saigon Ranger (5/7 Nguyen Sieu, D1, tel. 09/4192-4388, 6pm-1am daily, VND40,000-180,000) is one of a handful of venues in the city to regularly feature live music. From hard rock and hip-hop to a host of local DJs, Saigon Ranger maintains a steady calendar of events. There is an occasional cover fee, but usually you're free to just pop in, grab a drink, and enjoy the music. Unlike most of Saigon's clubs, the dance floor is not obstructed by tables and chairs.

Open well past most other venues in the city, **Last Call** (59 Dong Du, D1, tel. 09/3314-6711, www.lastcallbarsaigon.com, 6pm-late daily, VND150,000-600,000) is a chic and cozy spot to end the evening. Decked out in animal print cushions and smoked glass, the dimly lit bar houses an extensive collection of wine, beer, and liquor and prides itself on its hand-crafted cocktails. The bar is located across from the Saigon Sheraton and often has regular drink specials, like its buy-one-get-one happy hour from 6pm to 9pm, as well as weekend promotions and events.

NGUYEN HUE STREET

On the corner of Ngo Duc Ke and Nguyen Hue, **Broma** (41 Nguyen Hue, D1, tel. 09/0278-8848, bromasaigonbar@gmail.com, 5pm-2am daily, VND80,000-180,000) has made a name for itself among the younger Vietnamese and expat crowds, mostly for its laid-back rooftop seating. Take the narrow staircase up to the roof and you'll find a small-but-steady flow of people enjoying the cozy open-air terrace, which is decked out in tea lights and greenery. The bar is usually open late; closing time depends on the number of customers, so don't be surprised if you arrive in the wee hours to find that they've already closed for the evening.

Saigon's original craft brewery, **Pasteur Street Brewing Company** (144 Pasteur, D1, tel. 08/3823-9562, www.pasteurstreet.com, 11am-11pm daily, VND70,000-150,000) combines American-style brewing techniques with Vietnamese ingredients to create some of the city's tastiest and most innovative beers. Whether it's the signature jasmine IPA, featuring dried jasmine flower, or more adventurous seasonal refreshments like the jackfruit wheat ale or a surprisingly pleasant durian beer, Pasteur Street always has an array of brews on tap, and its cozy second-floor bar makes for a nice spot to enjoy a drink.

For more of a sports bar atmosphere, **Phatty's** (46-48 Ton That Thiep, D1, tel. 08/3821-0796, 8am-midnight daily, VND40,000-320,000) is a popular expat haunt just off Nguyen Hue. Serving beer, cocktails, and hearty pub food, the bar keeps a schedule of major sporting events, which it plays on the multiple televisions around the bar, and exudes a bit more class than its Pham Ngu Lao counterparts.

A new addition to the city's nightlife scene, **Rogue Saigon** (13 Pasteur, 2nd fl., D1, tel. 09/0236-5780, www.saigonoutcast.com, 4pm-midnight Sun.-Thurs., 4pm-2am Fri.-Sat., VND40,000-VND150,000) is a modest downtown watering hole that serves several of Saigon's ever-growing array of craft beers. The spot is bare bones, but there's a nice little balcony overlooking the street as well as outdoor seating upstairs. Rogue's owners keep things interesting with regular DJs and the occasional live music night.

BEN THANH MARKET AREA

Starting around late afternoon, dozens of plastic stools begin to appear on Bui Vien. This is a good place to start, as beers are inexpensive and the setup makes it easy to meet other travelers. As the evening goes on, the crowd of backpackers creeps out onto the street, making it hard to tell that this real estate actually belongs to several different businesses. Each small shop slings a variety of cheap local beers. To get an idea of the chaotic ambience and shoulder-to-shoulder seating, head to **Bia Sai Gon** (73 Bui Vien, D1, no phone, 5pm-1am daily, VND12,000-25,000) for an ice-cold brew and a street-side view of the action.

For more space and a proper chair, nearby **Universal Bar** (90 Bui Vien, D1, tel. 012/0887-2248, 24 hours daily, VND25,000-120,000) is right in the mix of the busy backpacker scene and boasts beer, liquor, a dart board, several international sports channels, and live music nightly from 9:30pm. The bartenders are chatty, and the place tends to get busy as soon as the music begins.

Just off Bui Vien near the looming neon sign of Crazy Buffalo, **Thi Bar** (224 De Tham, D1, tel. 08/2210-2929, 5pm-1am daily, VND60,000-150,000) has the best of both worlds with a lively bar area downstairs and relaxed, comfortable seating up top. The house band starts to play around 10pm every night, turning the narrow area around the bar into a dance floor and sending the noise level through the roof. For a livelier scene, stay downstairs, where it gets busy around 11pm, or if you prefer to sit and chat, head upstairs and grab one of the cushioned seats along the wall.

For a rooftop view without the sky-high prices, Duc Vuong Hotel's **The View** (Duc Vuong Hotel, 195 Bui Vien, D1, tel. 08/3920-6992, 8am-1am daily, VND30,000-180,000) offers cheap beer and cocktails to the budget traveler set. Its heavily decorated rooftop area, which overlooks the backpacker neighborhood, is a pleasant escape from the hustle and bustle at street level and the friendly atmosphere makes this an easy place to make friends.

While it's not quite as high up as other rooftop watering holes, **OMG** (15-19 Nguyen An Ninh, D1, tel. 09/3720-0222, 5pm-1am daily, VND80,000-250,000) has an incredible view of both Ben Thanh Market and Quach Thi Trang roundabout. Located on the top floor of Tan Hai Long Hotel, the bar offers both indoor and outdoor seating, but no matter where you sit you'll be able to take in the view, thanks to the floor-to-ceiling glass windows facing the traffic circle.

Twenty-six stories above the city, **Chill Skybar** (76A Le Lai, AB Tower, 26th and 27th fl., D1, tel. 08/6253-8888, www.chillsaigon.com,

5:30pm-1:30am Sun.-Thurs., 5:30pm-4am Fri.-Sat., VND150,000-350,000) is worth a visit for its view. Though drink prices are steep, the outdoor bar boasts a 180-degree panorama of the downtown area that becomes all the more impressive at night, when Saigon is lit up and motorbike headlights race along the darkened streets. To save a little cash, time your visit between 5:30pm and 9pm, when happy hour specials make cocktail prices reasonable. Be aware that the bar enforces a strict dress code, which Chill describes as "smart casual": no flip-flops, shorts, athletic clothing, or men in sleeveless tank tops. There is an indoor lounge and restaurant area if you prefer to admire the view from inside, though these are equally overpriced. For a quieter but equally upscale atmosphere, grab a drink just downstairs at **Sorae** (24th Fl., AB Tower, 76A Le Lai, D1, tel. 08/3827-2372, www.sorae-sushi.com, 11:30am-2pm and 5:30pm-1am daily).

Lounges
OPERA HOUSE AREA
Tucked away above a shop on the corner of Ly Tu Trong and Pasteur, **La Fenetre Soleil** (44 Ly Tu Trong, D1, tel. 08/3824-5994, www.lafenetresoleil. com, 10am-midnight Mon., 10am-1am Tues.-Wed., 10am-2am Thurs.-Sun., VND70,000-150,000) oozes cool. This trendy night spot is home to a cozy interior room surrounded by low couches and tables lining the outer wall. Regular live music and DJ events take place, though it's definitely a more laid-back vibe than you'll find in downtown nightclubs. While the lounge doesn't have a website, La Fenetre Soleil updates its Facebook page regularly to reflect upcoming events, and it also doubles as a café and restaurant during the day, when the countless windows around the exterior make it a bright and pleasant place to spend an afternoon.

A short jaunt away from Nguyen Hue's walking street, **Racha Room** (12-14 Mac Thi Buoi, D1, tel. 09/0879-1412, http://theracharoom.com, 11:30am-midnight Mon.-Fri., 4pm-midnight Sat.-Sun., VND80,000-300,000) is the perfect place for a happy hour refreshment. Its exposed brick interior, dim lighting, and dark red upholstery add a bit of class, as do its array of expertly crafted signature cocktails. While the upscale vibe attracts an equally sophisticated clientele, the place lacks pretense, making this an excellent spot to while away an evening. You're best to visit during happy hour (5pm-8pm Mon.-Sat.), when cocktails are half-price.

NGUYEN HUE STREET
Hidden in an old French colonial apartment building, **Snuffbox** (14 Ton That Dam, D1, tel. 012/6387-2603, 5pm-late daily, VND80,000-200,000) is Saigon's only speakeasy. The door to the laid-back lounge is unassuming, but indoors the venue gives off a vintage vibe that feels straight out of the Roaring '20s, complete with Art Deco accents and plush furniture. At the bar, you'll find a healthy mix of beer, wine, and hand-crafted cocktails, while the seating arrangement allows for large gatherings downstairs and

more intimate conversations in the tiny upstairs loft. Though Snuffbox doesn't have set closing hours, it typically stays open late, until around 2am or 3am.

Nightclubs
OPERA HOUSE AREA

Thumping music and spacious dance floors have turned **Apocalypse Now** (2B Thi Sach, D1, tel. 08/3825-6124, www.apocalypsesaigon.com, 8pm-2am daily, VND80,000-200,000) into a local institution. The self-proclaimed "first nightclub in Saigon" is slightly removed from Pham Ngu Lao, but is still frequented by the backpacker set, blasting bass-filled hits well into the night. Its smaller outdoor area makes for a good spot to relax, but most of the action happens indoors, where several rooms play different genres of music.

A massive compound on the corner of Dinh Tien Hoang, **Lush** (2 Ly Tu Trong, D1, tel. 08/3824-2496, 8pm-3am Tues.-Sun., VND90,000-200,000) is one of the city's best-known clubs due to its ladies' nights (9pm-midnight Tues.), during which time women drink for free. When it gets busy around 10:30pm, it brings together the local population, from a handful of tourists to expats and locals. The DJ sets up just beyond the large circular bar at the center of the room. There are quieter areas to sit at the back of the club and just beside the main entrance. Ladies' night here is a fun, cheap night on the town, but it's not worth visiting on other days, as it gets less crowded and drinks are overpriced. The dress code requires semi-formal attire.

If you're up for a night on the town, **Qui Lounge** (22 Le Thanh Ton, D1, tel. 08/3828-8828, www.quilounge.com, 5:30pm-2am daily, VND130,000-400,000) gets busy on weekends, when the city's social butterflies come out to drink and dance. The layout of the place makes busting a move a little tricky—in Vietnam, clubgoers often prefer lounging to dancing—but the DJ spins plenty of dance-able tunes until late. Drinks are expensive here, as they are in most local clubs, and a more formal dress code is enforced.

Live Music

One of Saigon's pioneer music venues, **Yoko** (22A Nguyen Thi Dieu, D3, tel. 08/3933-0577, 8am-midnight daily, VND80,000-180,000) was once an intimate one-room venue packed with couches and a precarious wooden balcony. Nowadays, the venue boasts a bigger stage and more comfortable seating, not to mention both original local acts and the odd international performer. The atmosphere is very laid-back and the venue remains cozy enough that you can enjoy the show no matter where you sit. Talented musicians appear nightly from 9pm, performing rock-infused covers of old and new hits as well as original music.

Easily the only venue of its kind in the city, **Sax N Art Jazz Club** (28 Le Loi, D1, tel. 08/3822-8472, 9pm-midnight daily, VND100,000) is the pet project of master saxophonist Tran Manh Tuan, one of Vietnam's renowned jazz musicians. With eight solo albums to his credit, Tuan operates and often performs at the club. The long, narrow building makes for a great performance space, and a rotating group of Vietnamese and foreign musicians joins the mix. Live music begins at 9pm, at which time a cover charge is enforced.

A popular, if a little cramped, live music venue is **Acoustic Bar** (6E1 Ngo Thoi Nhiem, D3, tel. 012/7677-7773, 7pm-midnight daily, VND70,000-150,000), set at the back of an alley packed with cafés and karaoke lounges. While Acoustic often features sugary, pop-fueled performances, the bar feels intimate, with a lively audience lined up shoulder-to-shoulder in front of the stage. Live music starts at 8pm every day, and you'll catch a crowd of young Vietnamese hanging out here.

THE ARTS

A burgeoning community of painters, filmmakers, visual artists, and enthusiastic supporters of the arts have begun to appear in the city. While more traditional performances and cultural showcases have long been a mainstay at the Opera House, smaller venues like cafés and independent galleries also exhibit artwork and hold regular film nights as well as artist workshops. Keep an eye out for these smaller events through the calendars on **Saigoneer** (www.saigoneer.com) or **Any Arena** (www.anyarena.com). Several regularly scheduled film screenings like **Future Shorts** (www.futureshorts.com), a quarterly international short film festival, also take place.

Performing Arts

Most of the city's English-language theatrical performances take place at the historic **Opera House** (7 Cong Truong Lam Son, D1, tel. 08/3823-7419, www.hbso.org.vn). A regularly changing schedule of shows passes through the theater, from plays, ballets, and circus acts to cultural shows and musical performances. Box office hours vary along with the show; however, you can book your tickets through the opera house itself or through **Saigon Tourist** (102 Nguyen Hue, D1, tel. 08/3521-8760; 45 Le Thanh Ton, D1, tel. 08/3827-9279, www.saigon-tourist.com, 8am-7pm daily).

The labor of a group of talented Vietnamese-European musicians and circus performers, **AO Show** (tel. 012/4518-1188, www.luneproduction.com, box office: 9:30am-6pm daily, VND630,000-1,470,000) is Vietnam's answer to Cirque du Soleil. Inspired by the rapidly changing pace of Vietnam, from the quiet, laid-back life of the countryside to the mayhem of its cities, this hour-long show, performed at the Opera House, has received rave reviews from local media and visiting travelers for the acrobatics and agility of its performers, as well as the cultural element it brings to a circus-based show. AO Show takes place in the evenings several times a week. When the main show is traveling, a pair of similar shows—The Mist and Teh Dar—both created by the production company behind AO, also play at the city's opera house.

A long-standing northern tradition, the colorful wooden puppets of *roi nuoc* (Vietnamese water puppet theater) have been around since the 11th century. This unique form of theater is one of the more popular cultural performances in town. The **Golden Dragon Water Puppet Theater** (55B Nguyen Thi Minh Khai, D1, tel. 08/3930-2196, box office 8:30am-11:30am and 1:30pm-7:30pm daily, VND200,000), located within the grounds of the Labor Cultural House, holds two daily performances in the early evening at 5pm and 6:30pm. Musicians play traditional Vietnamese instruments such as the *dan nhi*, a sort of two-stringed violin, and lend their voices to a lively cast of characters, who splash around in the miniature pool that serves as a stage. Hidden behind a bamboo screen are the show's masterful puppeteers. The entire show runs 50 minutes, and each scene is accompanied by music and vocals. Though the performance is entirely in Vietnamese, no translation is required. Reserve your ticket at least one day in advance, as seats fill up quickly. Request a seat behind the front row if you prefer to stay dry during the performance—the puppets can get rowdy. Call the theater's hotline or visit their box office in order to get the best price.

Galleries and Museums

The **Fine Arts Museum** (97A Pho Duc Chinh, D1, tel. 08/3829-4441, www.baotangmythuattphcm.com, 9am-5pm Tues.-Sun., VND10,000) is housed in the former residence of a wealthy Chinese family. This three-story, colonial-style building was constructed in 1929. It was the first building in the city to feature an elevator, which is on display on the ground floor. Since its opening to the public in 1992, the museum has housed permanent exhibits in the main house as well as a rotating collection of special exhibits, which are on display in a smaller building nearby. The exhibits are organized chronologically, beginning with ancient Champa and Oc Eo sculpture from the 7th to 17th centuries and continuing through modern-day Vietnamese art. There is also a display of what's called "combat art." During the American War, artists followed rebel forces to the front lines and drew the people and battles before them. These works are displayed in the second-floor corridors. Allot a few hours here, as the collection is deceptively large. There are information desks located at the front of the main building.

For a constantly changing lineup of both local and international artists, **Galerie Quynh** (151/3 Dong Khoi, level 2, D1, tel. 08/3824-8284, www.galeriequynh.com, 10am-7pm Tues.-Sat.) regularly curates new exhibits from around the world. The joint effort of Vietnamese-American art critic Quynh Pham and Englishman Robert Cianchi, Galerie Quynh has been working to promote contemporary art in Vietnam and the larger region since 2000, when it first came on the scene as an online entity showcasing the talents of local artists. The gallery boasts a modern space that is at the forefront of contemporary art in southern Vietnam.

A major player in the local art scene is the **Craig Thomas Gallery** (27I Tran Nhat Duat, D1, tel. 09/0388-8431, www.cthomasgallery.com,

11am-6pm Mon.-Sat., noon-5pm Sun.), tucked at the back of a wide alley in northern District 1 not far from Tan Dinh Market. Inside the gallery gates, golden bicycles scale the front wall of the building, up and over its awning. Indoors, two high-ceilinged rooms showcase the work of talented contemporary Vietnamese artists. Gallery founder Craig Thomas has been an active member of the Vietnamese art scene since 2002, mentoring young Saigon artists working in all mediums, and fostering the nascent artistic community of southern Vietnam. The gallery regularly changes its exhibits and is willing to open for private showings (call to arrange).

FESTIVALS AND EVENTS

Roughly a month after the Western world ushers in a new year, the entire nation of Vietnam takes a long holiday in honor of Tet, the Lunar New Year. During this time, Saigon is an empty city, deserted by many of its year-round residents who return home to enjoy the holiday with their extended families. Despite the mass exodus, HCMC still holds a well-known annual **Flower Street Festival** (Jan.-Feb.), at which time the length of Nguyen Hue Boulevard is shut down in order to accommodate an impressive floral display, usually featuring the Vietnamese zodiac animal of that particular year. Gardeners will twist and shape these colorful plants into a dragon, a cat, or a slithering snake. The flower festival is the one thing that draws people out of their homes at Tet to admire the vivid decorations along Nguyen Hue.

Though the **Mid-Autumn Festival** (mid-late Sept.) is a holiday celebrated throughout the country, Saigon's festivities are particularly lively. Beginning about a month before the holiday, the tiny street of Luong Nhu Hoc in District 5 becomes a *pho long den* (lantern village). Vendors sell colorful paper lanterns and decorations in honor of the coming day of festivity. Go in the evening, after the sun has set, to get the full effect of the lanterns. The closer the holiday is the more likely it is to be packed shoulder-to-shoulder with people.

lanterns for the Mid-Autumn Festival

From droves of street peddlers on Pham Ngu Lao to the high-end boutiques and colossal shopping centers of District 1, Saigon is the commercial heart of Vietnam. The city's shopping obsession runs deep, extending out into the frenzied markets of Chinatown and down narrow streets that specialize in everything from guitar-making to used bicycles to high-quality fabrics. Designer clothes line Nguyen Hue and Dong Khoi streets. Closer to the backpacker area, shopping hubs like Ben Thanh Market and Saigon Square are packed with inexpensive souvenirs and colorful clothing. Bargaining is a common practice, giving you the opportunity to hone your haggling skills while picking up a new wardrobe.

SHOPPING

MARKETS

Market culture is alive and well in Saigon. It is in the mayhem of these open-air buildings that many locals do their shopping. Vendors sit outside their stalls and call to passing shoppers, advertising T-shirts and fabric, souvenirs, shoes, and every food under the sun.

Ben Thanh Market

A Saigon institution, **Ben Thanh Market** (Le Loi and Tran Hung Dao, D1, tel. 08/3829-2096, 6am-6pm daily) is a symbol of the city. The current market, built in 1914, houses every item imaginable, from souvenirs and clothing to accessories, electronics, packaged food, and foreign items that can't be found elsewhere in the city. Squeeze your way through the aisles of fabric stalls or peruse the coffee selection along the main corridors. The majority of the market's outer shops, which line the perimeter of the building, try to maintain a fixed-price policy. Still, you do have some room to bargain, particularly if you are buying multiple items at a time. Inside, vendors beckon from all sides. The food area is concentrated close to the

Saigon Square, off Le Loi

middle, and there are a handful of luggage and backpack shops on the very exterior of the building near the northern entrance.

At 6pm, Ben Thanh closes its doors, but a busy outdoor night market begins, going until about midnight. The night market is considerably smaller, though it does have a good number of outdoor dining options and some shopping.

Located near the northern entrance to Ben Thanh Market, **Dung Tailor** (221 Le Thanh Ton, D1, tel. 08/3829-6778, dungtailor@hcm.vnn.vn, 8am-7:30pm daily) designs suits, button-up shirts, and other dress clothes specifically for men. The shop is clean and comfortable with a range of ready-made items to choose from as well as plenty of fabric options. Prices are expensive, with a men's button-up shirt going for about VND600,000, but the quality of the work is undeniable and it's worth the investment.

Even with its close proximity to Ben Thanh, it would be easy to miss **The House of Saigon** (258 Le Thanh Ton, D1, tel. 08/3520-8178, www.thehouseofsaigon.com, 8:30am-9pm daily), as it's not directly surrounding the market. The housewares, jewelry, clothing, and knick-knacks sold here make it worth a visit. Though prices are steeper than in the market, items are of high quality and beautifully made, from wicker-and-porcelain serving dishes to buffalo horn chopsticks. The shop also features clothing and souvenirs.

Binh Tay Market

The large and imposing **Binh Tay Market** (57A Thap Muoi, D6, tel. 08/3857-1512, 6am-7pm daily) boasts an ornate Chinese-style roof visible from a mile away. This is the heart of Cho Lon, home to Saigon's large ethnic Chinese population. The mammoth market houses dry goods, clothing, fabrics, food, cosmetics, and household items. It's more of a local market than the foreign-influenced Ben Thanh. Inside is a small courtyard devoted to Quach Dam, a wealthy Chinese immigrant and the benefactor of modern-day Binh Tay. Beyond and around that, the market is a flurry of activity that features Chinese products as well as local offerings. Binh Tay closes in the evening but the area remains busy well into the night. For practical items or specific Vietnamese goods, Binh Tay is a better place to go than Ben Thanh, as its prices are often cheaper. At the time of writing, Binh Tay is undergoing renovations and is closed to the public. It's unclear how long these upgrades will take. Ask around about the market's status before you make the trek.

Tan Dinh Market

Considerably smaller than other downtown markets, **Tan Dinh Market** (Hai Ba Trung and Nguyen Huu Cau, D1, tel. 08/3829-9280, 6am-6pm daily) houses the usual smorgasbord of household goods, clothes, and food items but is best known for the fabric vendors in the market and across the street on Hai Ba Trung and Nguyen Huu Cau. Stalls are packed to the ceiling with silk, cotton, and other materials, from plain colors to intricate,

What a Bargain!

t-shirt vendor at a Saigon market

Bargaining in Ho Chi Minh City's markets is almost always acceptable. In bigger, more central markets, prices are higher and room for negotiation is greater. In Ben Thanh Market, for instance, you may be able to drive the price down as much as 40-50 percent. Vendors in these heavily touristed areas tend to sell the same products, which gives you more bargaining power. If you attempt to haggle with a local vendor and are unsuccessful, you can move next door and find the same things on offer.

Many travelers find their first trip to the local market overwhelming. Stalls are small and cluttered, cramming innumerable items into one space, and, particularly in tourist areas, vendors can be pushy. Remain patient and only bargain seriously for something you really want. The most important thing to remember when bargaining is that as long as both you and the vendor are pleased with the transaction, then the price is acceptable. You may pay slightly more than a local might, but there's a good chance it's still cheaper than what you would pay at home.

sequined patterns. Around the market's exterior along Hai Ba Trung, fruit vendors set up a nice display to attract passing customers.

An Dong Market

If you're on the lookout for wooden or lacquer handicrafts, visit **An Dong Market** (34-36 An Duong Vuong, D5, no phone, 6am-6pm daily). This ancient building doesn't see nearly as much traffic as An Dong Plaza, its newer, fancier counterpart down the block, but it boasts a wider selection of statues, dishes, and other handicraft items. The first floor of the market is mostly food stalls; upstairs is an array of fabric, shoes, purses, clothing, and handicrafts. This is a quieter, more relaxed bargaining environment than Ben Thanh Market, and vendors tend to be friendlier.

Dan Sinh Market

Dan Sinh Market (104 Yersin, D1, tel. 08/3825-1130, 6am-6pm daily), sometimes known as Yersin Market, sells an eclectic combination of construction materials and war memorabilia. Tucked in the heart of this dank makeshift building are a plethora of stalls carrying army gear and personal effects of soldiers from both sides of the American War. In addition to combat helmets, compasses, bullets, canteens, and all manner of camouflage, you'll find rusted antique lighters and cameras as well as piles of photographs once carried by Vietnamese soldiers. The market offers authentic antiques as well as cheaper reproductions of most items.

SHOPPING DISTRICTS
Nguyen Hue and Le Loi Streets

On the eastern side of Ben Thanh Market is **Le Loi,** a street devoted almost exclusively to shopping and geared toward the tourist crowd. Many of the same souvenirs sold inside Ben Thanh are featured here, but alongside more expensive local shops as well as international brands. Intermixed with these smaller boutiques are one or two shopping malls, namely the brand-new **Saigon Center** (65 Le Loi, D1, tel. 08/3829-4888, www.saigoncenter. com.vn, 9:30am-9:30pm daily), a seven-level shopping complex adjoined to Japanese department store Takashimaya. Farther down the street, take a right onto Nguyen Hue and you'll find more retail shops squeezed in among the nicer hotels and Western restaurants.

For cheap local fashions, visit the gargantuan **Saigon Square** (77-89 Nam Ky Khoi Nghia, D1, tel., 9am-9pm daily), which is something of a cross between a local market and a Western-style shopping mall. Here you'll find boatloads of inexpensive souvenirs, bags, coffee, clothes, and various electronic odds and ends. Haggling is acceptable and, though the place is usually a madhouse, it is slightly more organized than nearby Ben Thanh Market. There is also a second location, known as **Saigon Square 3** (179-183 Hai Ba Trung, D1, 9am-9pm daily), which is equally hectic.

The folks at **Saigon Kitsch** (43 Ton That Thiep, D1, tel. 08/3821-8019, saigonkitsch@gmail.com, 8am-9pm daily) take old propaganda images and spruce up T-shirts, notebooks, drinking glasses, magnets, and other odds and ends, including propaganda-style renditions of famous movie posters.

Bambou (26 Luu Van Lang, D1, tel. 09/1564-2688, www.bamboucompany.com, 8am-10:30pm daily) produces items from locally grown bamboo and milk fiber, selling super-soft T-shirts and dresses as well as funky leather shoes.

Pham Minh Tailor (132 Pasteur, D1, tel. 09/0378-2220, phamminhtailor@yahoo.com.vn, 8am-7:30pm daily) is a reputable tailor for men and women. This store boasts fabrics from all over the world, including Vietnam, India, Italy, and China. The experienced seamstresses can complete a job on a tight deadline. You may be able to pay a visit to Ben Thanh Market with the tailor to choose your fabric.

Even if the embroidered portraits and landscapes at **XQ Silk Hand Embroidery** (106 Le Loi, D1, tel. 08/3822-7724, www.xqvietnam.com, 8am-9:30pm daily) are beyond your budget, visiting this store is educational and fascinating. Artisan Hoang Le Xuan and her husband, Vo Van

Quan, opened a training center in Dalat, teaching women how to hand-stitch intricate landscapes and portraits. The enormous, framed works of art are nearly six feet wide and four feet tall. Visitors are able to watch the embroidering process at the back of the store, where women in *ao dai* (the traditional garment of Vietnam) work on new pieces. A small image can take one person several months to complete; larger images are often the product of a whole team of women.

Mekong Quilts (68 Le Loi, tel. 08/2210-3110, www.mekong-creations. org, 9am-7pm daily) carries plush, colorful quilts as well as bamboo and papier-mâché products, handmade by women in southern Vietnam and Cambodia. This nonprofit enterprise employs over 300 people. Designs come from the women themselves as well as professional designers, and 50 cents of each dollar spent at the shop goes directly back to the villages, providing each employee with a sustainable income.

Pham Ngu Lao Street

Also known as the backpacker area, **Pham Ngu Lao** is home to a wide variety of reasonably priced souvenir and clothing shops, as well as street vendors carrying everything from knock-off Ray Bans to photocopied books, fans, and other goods. This neighborhood provides the same products as Ben Thanh Market with a slightly lower degree of chaos and fewer bargaining opportunities.

Nearly every shop in this neighborhood has a section devoted to travel necessities like outlet adapters, headphones, backpacks, sleeping bags, and camera gear. It's also a good spot for buying bootleg DVDs and boxed sets, as well as English-language books. Shops are open from early morning to late at night. If you see a price tag on an item, it is not up for negotiation. If the product does not have a listed price, there is a chance you can bargain.

The **Ginkgo Concept Store** (254 De Tham, D1, tel. 08/6270-5928, www. ginkgo-vietnam.com, 8am-10pm daily) sells well-made, locally produced

Pham Ngu Lao

Pham Ngu Lao Street

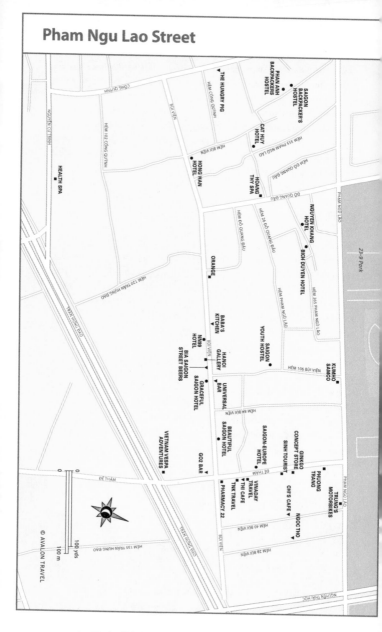

souvenirs like buffalo horn jewelry and lacquer dishware, in addition to its signature T-shirt line. The company is a fair-trade enterprise, so the higher prices for T-shirts go to providing workers with a sustainable living. There is a second location (54-56 Bui Vien, D1, tel. 08/3837-3077, www.

ginkgo-vietnam.com, 8am-10pm daily) in the Pham Ngu Lao area as well as a larger location on Le Loi (92-96 Le Loi, D1, tel. 08/3823-4099, www. ginkgo-vietnam.com, 8:30am-10pm daily).

On Bui Vien is a massive sign advertising "Old Propaganda Posters." This is the **Hanoi Gallery** (79 Bui Vien, D1, no phone, 9am-9pm daily), where high-quality reproductions of Communist propaganda are sold at bargain prices. Prices aren't listed on the items, so it's possible to bargain, especially if you purchase more than one. Take a peek upstairs, where there are more prints available for sale. Beware of "original" posters: There are very few remaining originals left in Vietnam. Chances are it's just a good reproduction for several times the normal cost.

Dong Khoi Street

Beginning at Notre Dame Cathedral and running south toward the Saigon River, **Dong Khoi** and the maze of narrow streets that surround it are full of interesting and unique local handicrafts, antiques, and artwork, as well as some designer clothing. A handful of local designers specializing in silk and other fine fabrics are featured here.

A prominent part of the city's current skyline, the **Vincom Center B** (72 Le Thanh Ton, tel. 08/3936-9999, www.vincom.com.vn, 9:30am-10pm daily) houses several notable Western brands like Zara, Marks & Spencer, and Yves Rocher beside homegrown retailers. Though you wouldn't guess it from the outside, Vincom's shopping facilities are surprisingly large, with several underground floors that offer shopping, a food court, and a supermarket.

Not far from Dong Khoi, **Diamond Plaza** (34 Le Duan, D1, tel. 08/3822-5500, www.diamondplaza.com.vn, 9:30am-10pm daily) is one of the city's better-known department stores, and also includes a bowling alley and movie theater on its upper floors. While prices are more expensive than in the market or at certain shopping centers, Diamond Plaza offers a wider range of sizes, which can be helpful to Western travelers, as what may pass for a small garment in North America may be considered medium to extra large in Vietnam.

Crisp white walls, exposed lightbulbs, and an industrial decor make **L'Usine** (151/1 Dong Khoi, D1, tel. 08/6674-3565, www.lusinespace.com, 7:30am-10:30pm daily) the city's center of cool. This café-restaurant-boutique sells a variety of men's and women's clothing as well as Lomography cameras, shoes, and jewelry. Housed in a French colonial building, L'Usine pulls its look into the 21st century with an eclectic clothing selection, drawing upon contemporary designers from Vietnam, Europe, and beyond. Prices are quite high for Vietnam, but the items are worth every penny. L'Usine also has a second location (70 Le Loi, D1, tel. 08/3521-0702, 7:30am-10:30pm daily) closer to Ben Thanh Market.

Nga Art & Craft (91 Le Thanh Ton, D1, tel. 08/3823-8356, www.huongngafinearts.vn, 8am-9pm daily) provides home furnishings in unique designs and colors, adding contemporary flair to the age-old lacquer-ware tradition. After harvesting, pieces undergo a lengthy lacquering process—even something as small as a tray requires at least 75 days to create. The resulting products are unique and durable. Larger items like dressers and coffee tables can be purchased and shipped, but there are plenty of smaller creations like dishware, paintings, and frames.

For beautifully made ceramic dishware, **Authentique Interiors** (71/1 Mac Thi Buoi, D1, tel. 08/3823-8811, www.authentiquehome.com, 9am-9pm daily) produces and sells plates, bowls, and teapots, from simple monochromatic sets to intricately patterned pieces. Downstairs is kitchenware, including utensils, while upstairs holds a small selection of bedding and table runners. Items are affordable and high in quality. The shop also has a second location (113 Le Thanh Ton, D1, tel. 08/3822-8052, 9am-9pm daily).

Nguyen Trai Street

From morning to night you'll see the flashing lights of **Nguyen Trai** advertising brand-name clothes as well as knock-off handbags and other bargain items. Companies like The Gap, Banana Republic, and Nike have factories in Vietnam, so there are lots of discounted clothes here that are either the real deal or a good imitation of it. Brand names from other Asian countries also make an appearance on this stretch, particularly closer to the backpacker area. In addition to air-conditioned stores and shopping malls, vendors set up along the sidewalk, hawking helmets, shoes, purses, and other goods. This is a decidedly more local shopping area, with lower prices but also Vietnamese-only sizes; if you're taller than the average local, you might need to stick to the tourist trail.

Roughly a block away from the massive roundabout that houses Vietnam's original Starbucks location, **Zen Plaza** (54-56 Nguyen Trai, D1, tel. 08/3925-0339, www.zenplaza.com.vn, 9:30am-10pm daily) is an eclectic combination of Asian brands packed into a tall and narrow building. With loads of women's and men's clothing, some from major brands like Nike and others from small designer labels, this shopping mall is compact, unique, and close to Pham Ngu Lao and the shopping street of Nguyen Trai, making it worth a quick visit.

Hai Ba Trung Street

Busy **Hai Ba Trung** offers a more local collection of shops. Here, you'll find a large selection of fabrics in and around Tan Dinh Market, whose southern side faces a row of tailors capable of stitching together anything from men's suits and ladies' dresses to *ao dai* (the traditional garment of Vietnam). This area is particularly well known for its fabrics, but there are also shops dedicated to skincare and ready-made clothes. Farther down the road, **Saigon Square 3** (179-183 Hai Ba Trung, D1, 9am-9pm daily) is bustling day and night with local shoppers.

Though it's not an especially sporty place and the great outdoors are hard to come by amid the traffic and droves of people, Saigon maintains its fair share of parks, swimming pools, and day spas, all of which offer a great way to unwind and experience local culture at the same time.

PARKS

Saigon's parks are oases amid a chaotic urban landscape. It's worth paying a visit to these well-manicured green spaces in the morning, when locals flock to the park for their daily exercise. Men stretch and practice tai chi while groups of women gather around a massive speaker on wheels, bouncing to the beat of techno music during their daily aerobics class. Still more groups hone other skills, from martial arts to ballroom dancing, or play a rousing game of badminton.

Tao Dan Park

One of the larger parks in District 1, **Tao Dan Park** (Truong Dinh and Nguyen Thi Minh Khai, D1), is bisected by the fast-paced traffic of Truong Dinh. The park stays busy from dawn to dusk, but the early hours are particularly hectic, with locals tracing the paths that loop around the park. On the western side, foliage helps to shelter the grounds from traffic.

Manicured topiaries line the walkway up to the Hung Kings Temple at the center of the grounds. Flanked by two dragons sculpted out of the greenery, this temple is an homage to the first kings of Vietnam, who ruled during the Hong Bang dynasty (2879-258 BC). The temple is small but popular. Visitors come to burn incense or offer fruit.

To the east, the sidewalk winds through a series of angular stone statues. It's a quiet, pleasant change from the mayhem of traffic that buzzes outside its grounds.

23-9 Park

Sandwiched between Pham Ngu Lao and Ben Thanh Market, **23-9 Park** (Pham Ngu Lao and Nguyen Thi Nghia, D1), also known as Lover's Park, holds regular events, from food festivals and cultural performances to dance recitals and concerts. This is a green space in two parts, with its grounds interrupted by Nguyen Thi Nghia. While locals use it for their morning exercise routines, this park sees the most activity at night, when young Vietnamese gather here. The long, narrow grounds are sometimes occupied by local students hoping to practice their English with a foreigner; you are sure to attract at least one conversation partner if you decide to sit beside the lotus pond.

Le Van Tam Park

Farther north and east in District 1 is **Le Van Tam Park** (Hai Ba Trung and Dien Bien Phu, D1), one of the nicer fresh-air spots downtown. Le Van

23-9 Park

Tam maintains beautiful, well-kept grounds that can be a peaceful escape from the din of the surrounding streets. A long, flowered walkway leads up to the park's main gathering area, at the center of which stands a large Communist-era statue. At the back of the park are a handful of coffee stalls and a playground. At time of writing, half the park was cordoned off for metro construction, which is expected to take several years.

This park is named after national hero Le Van Tam, who, as a teenager, dressed in gasoline-soaked garments and lit himself on fire before running into a gasoline depot owned by the French, destroying the structure in protest of colonial rule. It has since been revealed that the story was propaganda invented to boost public support of the anti-colonial revolutionary cause.

30-4 Park

Bordered on one side by the sweeping grounds of the Reunification Palace and on the other side by the imposing structure of Notre Dame Cathedral, **30-4 Park** (Nam Ky Khoi Nghia and Le Duan, D1) is a lush, green area zigzagged with walkways and park benches where young people gather to enjoy a coffee or mid-afternoon snack in the shade.

AMUSEMENT PARKS

To cool off and get away from the noise and chaos of city traffic, pay a visit to **Dam Sen Water Park** (3 Hoa Binh, D11, tel. 08/3858-8418, 9am-6pm Mon. and Wed.-Sat., 8:30am-6pm Sun., VND130,000). The huge venue, located northwest of the city center, boasts a well-manicured wooded area as well as a water park, where local and foreign visitors flock on hot days to enjoy the slides, rides, and cool water of the wave pool. All rides are supervised by park staff, and changing rooms are available. The cost of

entry goes down after 4pm (VND110,000), though it's better to make an
afternoon of the trip, as Dam Sen is far from downtown. There is also an
on-site restaurant.

SWIMMING

The pool at **Van Thanh Tourist Area** (48/10 Dien Bien Phu, D Binh Thanh,
tel. 08/3512-3026, 6am-8pm daily, VND60,000-70,000 adults, VND30,000-
40,000 children) is the perfect way to escape the city without actually having to leave the city. Hidden down an alley off Dien Bien Phu street in Binh
Thanh District, Van Thanh is a pleasant surprise, with lush green lawns
and tree-lined walkways that create the illusion that you've left Saigon
behind. The pool is clean and big, with a separate, smaller swimming
pool for young children, and there are plenty of lounge chairs nearby. Van
Thanh has a restaurant and several activities for young kids. The place gets
crowded on weekends and holidays.

MASSAGES AND SPAS

Massages are all the rage in Saigon, with dozens of spas located in the
District 1 area alone, ranging in price from dirt-cheap to exorbitant. Many
hotels and guesthouses also offer spa services, but these are often overpriced and, in truth, you're usually better off visiting a spa on your own.
While tipping is not common in restaurants or cafés, it is expected that you
offer a 15-20 percent tip to a masseuse or masseur. In some places, masseuses will have a tip form for you to fill out, noting the amount you are
giving. While this can be uncomfortable for some—having to write down
your tip amount and give it to the masseuse before you pay—it is the norm
in many places here.

For the lower end of the budget, without sacrificing quality, **Hoang
Thy Spa** (35 Do Quang Dau, D1, tel. 08/3836-4404, 8am-9pm daily,
VND50,000-300,000) is a great spot for a massage or manicure. The facility
itself is pretty bare bones, but the staff are incredibly friendly and the spa's
services, from hair and nails to massages, waxing, foot care, masks, and
facials, are inexpensive. A manicure or pedicure will set you back around
VND50,000, while body massages cost VND120,000-300,000.

If you don't mind venturing a few more blocks outside the backpacker
area, **Health Spa** (36-38 Nguyen Cu Trinh, D1, tel. 08/2220-2132, 9:30am-
10:30pm daily, VND50,000-860,000), formerly known as Ngoc Anh Spa,
has a range of affordable massage services beginning at VND200,000, tips
excluded. This massive building has separate floors for men and women,
as well as a sauna and steam room, and the masseuses are well trained and
speak some English.

The mid-range **Cat Moc Spa** (61-63 Tran Dinh Xu, D1, tel. 08/6295-8926,
www.catmocspa.com, 9am-10pm daily, VND120,000-820,000) is an excellent value. The modest storefront belies the spa's impeccable service. Guests
are greeted with a glass of iced tea in the cozy seating area before choosing
from massages, body scrubs, facials, hair care, and waxing. The friendly

and experienced staff speak English. Afterward, you'll be offered a glass of *chanh muoi* (lemon juice and salt), a refreshing local treat. Spa packages (VND548,000-1,628,000) are available for those looking to make a day of it.

The cheerful, purple-clad staff at **L'Apothiquaire** (100 Mac Thi Buoi, D1, tel. 08/3822-2158, www.lapothiquaire.com, 10am-6pm daily, VND320,000-1,200,000) carry their own line of skincare products, as well as offering massages, wraps, facials, manicures, pedicures, and waxing services. Packages can be purchased to combine several services for a full day at the spa. Walk-ins are welcome, but book ahead in order to receive the best service possible. L'Apothiquaire's larger flagship location (64A Truong Dinh, D3, tel. 08/3932-5181, 10am-6pm daily) also provides the same treatments in a more peaceful setting with touches of French colonial decor.

COOKING CLASSES

There are a handful of excellent culinary courses offered in Saigon. Class prices are higher here than other places, so you may be better off waiting, particularly if you are also traveling to central coast cities like Hue and Hoi An.

The most well-known culinary course is **Saigon Cooking Class** (74/7 Hai Ba Trung, D1, tel. 08/3825-8485, www.saigoncookingclass.com, 8am-5pm Tues.-Sun., VND870,000-990,000 adults, VND550,000-616,000 kids under 12), which operates out of Hoa Tuc, an upscale Vietnamese restaurant. The three-hour hands-on course teaches students how to prepare a three-course Vietnamese meal, with the dishes changing daily. An English-speaking Vietnamese chef gives instruction. For an extra fee, you can accompany the chef to the market, where he shows students how to select and purchase the necessary ingredients. Classes are capped at 12 people, and children seven years and up are welcome.

For a slightly more affordable option, the **Cyclo Resto Cooking Class** (6/28 Cach Mang Thang 8, D1, tel. 08/6680-4235, www.cycloresto.com.vn, 9am-6pm daily, VND700,000) combines a market visit and cooking class with sightseeing. Ride to the local market in a cyclo, taking in the city as you go, before exploring the stalls of fresh produce and meat. A taxi ferries you back to the cooking center, where you'll learn several dishes from a professional and knowledgeable English-speaking staff. Cyclo Resto has smaller class sizes and more one-on-one interaction.

Saigon is obsessed with food. Everywhere you turn, people are crouched over bowls of noodle soup or picking at fruit and *banh trang tron* (a salad-like mix of rice paper, dried meat, green mango, and seasonings eaten from a plastic bag with chopsticks) in the park. Women hustle across intersections, bamboo poles bouncing beside them, as they carry mobile kitchens from one location to the next; empty stretches of sidewalk become a maze of tiny tables at lunchtime.

While the southern city doesn't have many specialties to call its own, HCMC has managed to appropriate the best of Vietnam and the world so that you can find just about anything to please your palate. Dine in the quiet garden courtyard of an upscale eatery or share tables with a stranger amid the chaotic buzz of a street food stall—wherever you are, there's a solid chance you'll find yourself going back for seconds.

REUNIFICATION PALACE AREA
Cafés and Bakeries

Quiet, charming, and in possession of some of the best sweets in town, **Pacey Cupcakes** (53G Nguyen Du, D1, tel. 08/3823-3223, www.paceycupcakes.com, 9am-10pm daily, VND30,000-60,000) is opposite the south side of the Central Post Office. The café sells a variety of cupcakes, including green tea, double chocolate, passion fruit, red velvet, and banana chocolate. Upstairs, the bar-style seating (made from a sheet of glass atop cupcake tins) and wide-open bay window look directly onto busy Nguyen Du. There is a line of booths that hug the far wall, making for a cozy atmosphere.

Vietnamese

Ngon Restaurant (160 Pasteur, D1, tel. 08/3827-7131, 7:30am-10:30pm daily, VND40,000-120,000) is a tourist favorite and the perfect spot for a

street vendor

Street Food

No trip to Saigon is complete without experiencing street food. From morning to night, locals crowd around cracked plastic tables and miniature stools on every sidewalk in town. Some of the best food in the city comes from a cart. A visit to these mobile businesses brings you the best of Hue, Nha Trang, Can Tho, or Hanoi, all with a southern twist. People from all walks of life flock to these makeshift eateries for a quick *banh mi* (Vietnamese sandwich) or a bowl of pho.

Eating street food can be safer than dining in a local restaurant. Because the kitchen is visible and the meal you're about to enjoy is already on display, you can tell whether or not the cart in question is clean, safe, and worth a visit. There are several good streets, where the food masters congregate. **Huynh Man Dat** in District 5, not far from Nguyen Trai, does a fair turn in Chinese-style street food, while **Nguyen Thuong Hien** in District 3, north of Nguyen Thi Minh Khai, is a popular spot for delicious rice and noodle dishes.

crash course on local food, offering every meal under the sun at reasonable prices. This large, colonial-style building boasts spacious seating and gives the restaurant a marketplace feel, with cooks set up along the outer edges of its open-air courtyard so that guests can peruse their options before ordering.

Mediterranean

Exactly as the name suggests, **Au Parc** (23 Han Thuyen, D1, tel. 08/3829-2772, www.auparcsaigon.com, 7:30am-11pm daily, VND115,000-295,000) boasts a beautiful location overlooking 30-4 Park. This chic café serves up Mediterranean dishes like hummus, baba ganoush, and shish kebabs. This is also a great place to enjoy a morning coffee or tuck in to either of the Turkish or New York brunches, which are served every weekend. For more local fare, you can also pop in next door at Au Parc's sister restaurant, **Propaganda** (21 Han Thuyen, D1, tel. 08/3822-9048, www.propaganda-saigon.com, 7:30am-10:30pm, VND50,000-175,000), for fresh spring rolls and modern Vietnamese cuisine.

OPERA HOUSE AREA
Vietnamese

Guests become chefs at **Bo Tung Xeo** (31 Ly Tu Trong, D1, tel. 08/3825-1330, 10am-10pm daily, VND120,000-430,000), a spacious open-air spot, where an extensive menu of do-it-yourself barbecue dishes are on offer. Sturdy clay pot fires are brought to your table, along with a grill and a plate of raw meat. Barbecue your own meat as you like it and choose the accompanying side dishes. Stick to tried-and-true beef, fish, and chicken or try crocodile, ostrich, deer tendon, or goat breast. Meals are reasonably priced and the waiters keep a steady flow of Saigon Red coming.

Formerly the Saigon Opium Manufacture, **The Refinery** (74 Hai Ba Trung, D1, tel. 08/3823-0509, www.therefinerysaigon.com, 11am-late daily, VND130,000-420,000) has come a long way from its past involvement in the drug trade. The restaurant offers French cuisine and is outfitted in the style of a Parisian bistro. Meals are top-notch, featuring barbecued swordfish, steak frites, gourmet cheeseburgers, and homemade pasta dishes. Come for the weekend brunch (11am-4pm Sat.-Sun.), when a complimentary chocolate fountain occupies the front dining room.

FOOD

Italian

An affordable, white-tablecloth affair, the atmosphere at **Ciao Bella** (11 Dong Du, D1, tel. 08/3822-3329, www.ciaobellavietnam.com, 8am-11pm daily, VND125,000-575,000) is cozy and communal. With New York-style Italian dishes and an intimate dining space, this restaurant prides itself on its diverse menu and constantly changing list of specials, featuring old favorites such as spaghetti al pomodoro and chicken parmesan as well as more unique dishes. Entrées are generous, and servers are attentive. A nice wine selection is also on offer.

Pizza

With hip European decor and an excellent handle on Italian food, ★ **Pizza 4Ps** (8/15 Le Thanh Ton, D1, tel. 012/0789-4444, www.pizza4ps.com, 10am-11pm daily, VND90,000-420,000) is, surprisingly, a Japanese creation. Only when you flip past the margherita and quattro formaggi to toppings like calamari seaweed and salmon miso cream do the restaurant's roots become apparent. Meals at 4Ps are more expensive than other local Italian places, but the extra money spent is well worth it if you're craving a good pie. Book a table before you go, as this is one of the only places in town that usually requires a reservation. You can also grab a pie at their **Ben Thanh location** (8 Thu Khoa Huan, D1, tel. 012/0885-4444, 10am-2am Mon.-Sat., 10am-11pm Sun., VND90,000-420,000).

Western

Inside the gates of the Ton Duc Thang Museum, **Zest Bistro & Cafe** (5 Ton Duc Thang, D1, tel. 08/3911-5599, 7am-10pm daily, VND77,000-255,000) follows a simple mantra: "Good drinks, good food, good company." The back wall of this Western café and eatery is covered with a propaganda-inspired mural paying homage to these very things, while the front windows open onto the museum's peaceful courtyard. Zest's menu features hearty meat-and-potato meals, as well as a selection of vegetarian options and interesting coffees and teas.

NGUYEN HUE STREET
Vietnamese

The narrow corridor leading up to the **Temple Club** (29-31 Ton That Thiep,

D1, tel. 08/3829-9244, www.templeclub.com.vn, noon-midnight daily, VND140,000-285,000) is a step back in time. Lined with white elephant statues and Chinese wood carvings, the red-tiled entryway leads to an opulent dining room, where dark wooden furniture and deep red curtains create an old-world feel. The menu features expertly prepared Vietnamese, Chinese, Khmer, and French cuisine. Though prices are slightly higher than other local restaurants, the upscale atmosphere and food are worth it. Book a table before going, as dinnertime can be very busy.

Japanese

Expensive, but worth every penny, **Nhan Sushi** (62 Ngo Duc Ke, D1, tel. 08/3915-2280, nhansushibito@gmail.com, 10am-2:30pm and 5pm-11:30pm daily, VND75,000-350,000) is a tiny restaurant opposite the Bitexco Tower. Its menu features an impressive list of authentic Japanese fare, including a handful of excellent lunch sets. Reservations are a good idea in the evenings, as the place fills up once the work day ends.

Thai

Squeezed down a narrow alley off Mac Thi Buoi, **Lac Thai** (71/2-71/3 Mac Thi Buoi, D1, tel. 08/3823-7506, www.lacthairestaurant.com, 10am-2pm and 5pm-10pm daily, VND130,000-280,000) offers some of the most authentic Thai food in the city. From noodles and tom yum soup to Thai curries, the menu runs from conventional to unexpected, and the intimate dining area is decked out in plush sofas and low tables. Both upstairs and downstairs seating are available. Its hidden location gives the place a serene, laid-back vibe.

BEN THANH MARKET AREA
Cafés and Bakeries

Calm, cool, and centrally located, **ID Cafe** (34D Thu Khoa Huan, D1, tel. 08/3822-2910, www.idcafe.net, 7am-11:30pm daily, VND35,000-125,000) is a trendy café not far from Ben Thanh Market that is popular among locals and foreigners. Customers gather around its solid wood tables for coffee, smoothies, and decent Vietnamese food. Vintage records decorate the walls and mood music plays in the background, adding to the laid-back vibe. There is also a larger **second location** (61B Tu Xuong, D3, tel. 08/3932-0021, 7am-11:30pm daily) in District 3.

French

Just behind Ben Thanh Market is the French-owned and -operated **Une Journee A Paris** (234 Le Thanh Ton, D1, tel. 08/3827-7723, 7am-7:30pm Mon.-Sat., VND80,000-200,000), a Parisian-style bakery and sandwich shop decked out in pink and purple. Its glass display case features pain au chocolat and croissants as well as several other cakes, all of which are made fresh. Sandwiches are also served on European-style baguettes.

Street Food

A stone's throw from the backpacker area, **Quan 96** (96 Le Lai, D1, tel. 08/3839-9317, 5pm-10:30pm daily, VND75,000-180,000) is one of the few street-side restaurants that has an actual menu. With a few plastic tables and chairs and a barbecue, this place serves up standard pork and chicken dishes, frog, eel, and Vietnamese hotpot. The tastiest dish is the *ga chien nuoc mam* (fried chicken wings in fish sauce), which pairs perfectly with an ice-cold beer.

FOOD

Western

A narrow, barely there shop on the far side of Pham Ngu Lao, the **Hungry Pig** (144 Cong Quynh, D1, tel. 08/3836-4533, 7am-9pm daily, VND70,000-110,000) shows great potential with its varied lineup of bacon sandwiches. Beyond the fat pink pig emblazoned across the shop's awning, a large menu on the back wall lists sandwich combinations as well as a build-your-own menu with different types of bacon, cheese, veggies, and sauces. Solid iron-and-wood picnic-style furniture takes up most of the space indoors and out. The walls feature antique, black-and-white portraits of—you guessed it—pigs.

Southeast Asian

The masterful chefs at **Baba's Kitchen** (164 Bui Vien, D1, tel. 08/3838-6661, www.babaskitchen.in, 11am-11pm daily, VND60,000-110,000) supply Saigon with cheap, authentic Indian food smack-dab in the heart of the backpacker district. The menu lists standard Indian fare, including masalas, curries, daals, and vindaloos, and everything is made in-house, including the paneer. Though there are a couple of more upscale Indian ventures in town, this is the best.

Vegetarian

The An Lac Pagoda, located in Pham Ngu Lao, has drawn a handful of vegetarian restaurants into the area, including **Ngoc Tho** (175/9 Pham Ngu Lao, D1, tel. 08/3836-0162, 10:30am-10:30pm daily, VND30,000-300,000). This no-frills eatery churns out delicious meat-free Vietnamese food, and has recently expanded its menu to include Western dishes and some carnivorous fare.

NORTHERN DISTRICT 1
★ Street Food

Ever since Anthony Bourdain visited HCMC in 2009, Nguyen Thi Thanh, better known as ★ **The Lunch Lady** (23 Hoang Sa, D1, from 11am daily, VND40,000), has become a local celebrity. Her cart, at the edge of a clearing not far from the Saigon Zoo, serves up a different soup every day, from spicy *bun bo Hue* (soup with beef and rice noodles) to pho or Cambodian-style *hu tieu* (rice noodle soup). Around noon the sidewalk becomes a mess of diners hoping to get a bowl. The Lunch Lady has no set closing time and sells her soup until it's sold out. Get there no later than mid-afternoon or you may find that she's done for the day.

Just north of the massive Tan Dinh Church is **Tan Dinh Market** (Hai Ba Trung and Nguyen Huu Cau, D1, 6am-6pm daily, VND20,000-75,000), which houses several food stalls along Nguyen Huu Cau. A variety of local dishes are available, including vegetarian fare, as well as juices and smoothies. One of its best offerings is *banh canh cua* (crab soup with thick, rope-like rice noodles).

The namesake specialty at ★ **Banh Xeo 46A** (46A Dinh Cong Trang, D1, tel. 08/3824-1110, 10am-2pm and 4pm-9pm daily, VND60,000-150,000) is the star here. Cooks crouch over piping hot pans, dishing up large *banh xeo* (southern-style Vietnamese pancakes). A deft waiter will rush over with a pile of fresh greens, fish sauce, and pickled vegetables, and from there it's up to you. Roll your pancakes up in the accompanying lettuce leaves, throw in a few herbs for flavor, dip in fish sauce, and enjoy. The pancakes come in regular and large sizes and can be easily split between two people. The restaurant offers a handful of other items, like fresh and fried spring rolls and barbecued meat.

Vietnamese

★ **Quan Mien Cua 94 Cu** (84 Dinh Tien Hoang, D1, tel. 08/3910-1062, 10am-10pm daily, VND80,000-500,000) is a well-known local spot that specializes in soft-shell crab. A row of live crabs sits outside the storefront, waiting to be turned into soup or spring rolls, fried or steamed. The *mien xao cua* (crab with glass noodles) and tamarind soft-shell crab are particularly noteworthy. There are a few impostors located nearby: Quan Mien Cua 94 Cu is the shop just before the corner, not directly on it.

Cuc Gach Quan (9-10 Dang Tat, D1, tel. 08/3848-0144, www.cuc-gachquan.com.vn, 9am-11pm daily, VND80,000-220,000) is a return to the basics. Inspired by his grandmother's street food stall, owner and architect Tran Binh transformed this French colonial house into an intimate restaurant serving traditional countryside fare. Each meal is arranged on antique earthenware dishes, and chopsticks are kept in recycled milk tins. The menu may overwhelm, but knowledgeable servers will recommend dishes like pork stewed in a claypot, morning glory sautéed in garlic, or homemade fried tofu with chili and lemongrass. Binh's pledge to "eat green, live healthy," means that ingredients are all natural, down to the drinking straws, which are hollow vegetables. All meals are served family-style.

Vegetarian

With an emphasis on Buddhist tenets and healthy living, the folks at **Lau Nam Chay An Nhien** (94 Nguyen Van Thu, D1, tel. 08/3910-1129, www.lau-namchayannhien.com, 9:30am-9:30pm daily, VND30,000-250,000) create delicious vegetarian dishes without mock-meat or any artificial products,

Know One, Teach One

When Vietnamese-Australian Jimmy Pham first opened the KOTO hospitality training center in Hanoi over a decade ago, it was his goal to provide a small number of Vietnam's disadvantaged youth with a better future. Years on, **KOTO** (39 Le Duan, Kumho Link Plaza, 3rd fl., D1, tel. 08/3822-9357, www.koto.com.au, 11am-10pm daily, VND65,000-350,000) has not only given young people without resources a steady income and hope for the future but also the necessary skills and training to succeed in the hospitality industry at an international level. KOTO, which stands for Know One, Teach One, has two training centers in Hanoi and Ho Chi Minh City and recruits roughly 30 young people between the ages of 16 and 22 to the program every six months. The Saigon branch is located on the top floor of Le Duan's Kumho Link Plaza with nice views of the boulevard from its rooftop.

FOOD

instead using mushrooms and other all-natural ingredients. The menu runs the gamut from spring rolls and southern specialties like *hu tieu My Tho* (rice noodle soup) to a meatless hotpot and an excellent, aromatic rendition of pho. The dining area is clean, spacious, quiet, and comfortable. Best of all, prices are affordable, with most one-person dishes setting you back no more than VND50,000.

DISTRICT 3
Cafés and Bakeries
An extension of the Fly Cupcakes chain, **Fly Garden** (25A Tu Xuong, D3, tel. 08/3932-2299, www.flycupcake.vn, 7am-11pm daily, VND40,000-100,000) is a cross between a Western coffee shop and a Vietnamese *san vuon* (garden) café. The bakery, lined with fairy lights in cupcake wrappers, offers sweets like cream puffs, tarts, and cupcakes. The wall of vines outside brings a hint of green to the city, while inside the whimsical decor and mellow music make this a pleasant place to unwind. There is an eclectic food menu featuring Vietnamese, Western, and Japanese items.

A local institution, the perpetually busy **Sinh To 142** (142 Ly Chinh Thang, D3, tel. 08/3848-3574, 8am-11pm daily, VND20,000-40,000) is exactly like a local café but without the coffee. From sunup to sundown, this open-front shop slings an assortment of fresh smoothies and juices, ranging from conventional single-fruit drinks to more unusual combinations, like avocado-mung bean, tomato-mango, or the deceptively delicious carrot-coconut.

Japanese
For cheap Japanese cuisine, visit **Tokyo Deli** (187 Dien Bien Phu, D1, tel. 08/3826-5888, www.tokyodeli.com.vn, 11am-9:30pm daily, VND40,000-150,000), a popular sushi chain with multiple locations around Districts 1 and 3. These large restaurants have prix fixe lunches (about VND100,000) and also offer an à la carte menu throughout the day. The service isn't

stellar, but the space is nice and the price makes it worth a visit if you're in the mood for something different.

Street Food

Popular with local office workers, the **rice stall** (Truong Dinh between Nguyen Thi Minh Khai and Vo Van Tan, D3, 11am-2pm Mon.-Fri., VND20,000-50,000) on Truong Dinh street just north of Tao Dan Park cooks up at least a dozen different dishes for lunch every day, including pork, eggs, tofu, beef, and a variety of vegetables to go along with rice, not to mention soup and iced tea. Low tables are set up along the sidewalk and the place gets busy around noon. While everything on the cart is delicious, the *ga muoi* is particularly noteworthy.

Vegetarian

Located inside the grounds of the Vinh Nghiem temple, **Vinh Nghiem Vegetarian Restaurant** (339 Nam Ky Khoi Nghia, D3, tel. 08/3848-1829, www.vinhnghiemchay.vn, 7am-9pm daily, VND40,000-100,000) is one of the city's most well-known vegetarian restaurants and, due to its location, also one of the more peaceful places to sit and have a quiet meal. The restaurant serves up a range of Vietnamese dishes without the meat, including soups, tofu, and fried rice options.

With its placid courtyard and back-to-basics philosophy, **...hum** (32 Vo Van Tan, D3, tel. 08/3930-3819, www.humvietnam.vn, 10am-10pm daily, VND65,000-150,000) is a pleasant escape from the roar of the city. Concealed by a high wall, a floating walkway leads over a mossy pond and into the courtyard. The decor is simple, with wooden furniture and chopsticks wrapped in pandan leaves. The menu lists tofu and vegetable dishes, and explains the specific health benefits of each meal. The spring rolls and spicy tofu are especially good. In addition to the flagship location, a slightly trendier lounge downtown (2 Thi Sach, D1, tel. 08/3823-8920, 10am-10pm daily, VND65,000-150,000) also serves the same delicious dishes in a hip setting.

Vietnamese

Behind the Reunification Palace is **Khoai** (3A Le Quy Don, D3, tel. 08/3930-0013, www.khoairestaurant.com, 7am-10pm daily, VND55,000-155,000), a cozy restaurant specializing in southern coastal cuisine from Nha Trang. The majority of its dishes feature seafood, the most famous being *bun cha ca*, a rice noodle soup with grilled pressed fish. The restaurant itself is nothing special, but the food is tasty and the location convenient for hungry sightseers.

Slightly removed from downtown, **Quan Dat** (16 Truong Dinh, D3, tel. 08/3843-7390, 10am-10pm daily, VND70,000-200,000) serves incredible, affordable meals to a local crowd. Mastering the art of Phan Rang cuisine, seafood-infused southern food featuring a savory peanut sauce, Quan Dat's most popular dishes are *banh can* (small egg-and-rice-flour cakes topped with meat or seafood) and a smaller, seafood version of *banh xeo* (savory Vietnamese pancakes). Sit downstairs near the window overlooking the street or in the spacious second-floor dining area, where wooden tables and chairs line the room.

CHO LON
Street Food

Well off the beaten path and a challenge to find, **Ca Ri De Musa** (001 Bldg. B, Su Van Hanh Apts., D5, tel. 08/3886-6679, 10am-11pm daily, VND50,000-150,000) is a small, bustling eatery that does an excellent rendition of *ca ri de* (goat curry). Take a seat at one of the many metal tables indoors or out and tuck into a hearty helping of the dish, accompanied by a baguette. Foreigners are few here, so you might draw attention during your visit. To find the restaurant, look for the flashing red-and-blue sign reading "Ca Ri An Do" beside 202A Su Van Hanh.

On a street packed with dumpling shops and touts waving at passersby, the ★ **Chinese noodles** (193 Ha Ton Quyen, D11, 11am-midnight daily, VND15,000-50,000) at **Quan Thien Thien** are the best of the best. Order a piping hot bowl of *mi sui cao* (dumplings with egg noodle soup) with Chinese-style dumplings and take in the bustling chaos of this eating street. The shop is out of the way, but the reward is an authentic, mouthwatering bowl of noodles. Don't forget to grab a *tra hong* (sweet tea) to go with your meal.

Vegetarian

Off the beaten path, **Tiem Chay Tuong Vien** (58-62 Huynh Man Dat, D5, tel. 08/6275-8938, 6am-9pm daily, VND25,000-50,000) is like any local restaurant but for its lack of pork, beef, or chicken. This humble shop serves everything from mock-meat barbecue to vegetarian pho and Chinese-style stir-fried noodles. Prices are easy on the wallet, and at lunchtime you'll find impressive mock-meat renditions of many Vietnamese dishes, including vegetarian claypot catfish and barbecued pork. Their menu does not have an English version, but it's fine to point at what you want to order.

Accommodations

From the bare-bones hostels hidden down the alleys off Pham Ngu Lao to the high-end hotels overlooking the Saigon River, accommodations in HCMC run the spectrum. Dorm beds cost as little as VND100,000 a night, while the peak of luxury will set you back several hundred dollars.

Base yourself in District 1, where the majority of the city's sights, shopping, restaurants, and English-speaking services are located. Due to the many hotels in this area, making a reservation is usually unnecessary, though you may want to check availability ahead of time if you're in town during a holiday.

Most budget travelers base themselves in Pham Ngu Lao, the backpacker neighborhood. Just outside of the backpacker area, Nguyen Trai is an excellent choice if you're looking to get away from the nonstop noise of Pham Ngu Lao but still remain close to the heart of downtown. Mid-range accommodations are packed onto the streets around Ben Thanh Market. Several historic five-star hotels are close to the Opera House.

Light sleepers should be extra selective, as Saigon's noise pollution is second to none. Hotels located in alleys tend to be quieter than those on the street. (Conversely, hotels on busy streets are safer at night, where front doors are more visible and well lit.)

If rates are listed higher than VND500,000 per night, check if the hotel gives a discount for booking ahead of time. Budget accommodations often discount their rates for someone walking in off the street in order to fill rooms.

Don't bother requesting an airport pickup from your hotel: Taking a cab from the airport to District 1 costs at least half the going rate offered by hotels.

OPERA HOUSE AREA
VND525,000-1,050,000

Clean and spacious, rooms at the **Tan Hoang Long Hotel** (84 Mac Thi Buoi, D1, tel. 08/3827-0006, www.tanhoanglong-hotel.com, VND905,000-1,200,000, breakfast included) are a good value, with plenty of natural light and a private working desk as well as daily coffee, tea, and bottled water. In some of the larger rooms, sofas and street views are available. The staff is courteous and the hotel's location is close to the downtown shopping area, Dong Khoi, and the market.

VND1,050,000-2,100,000

Boasting colorful decor and large rooms, the ★ **Saigon River Boutique Hotel** (58 Mac Thi Buoi, D1, tel. 08/3822-8558, www.saigonriverhotel.com, VND630,000-1,890,000) provides more upscale lodgings with an exceptional level of service and cleanliness. This boutique hotel boasts modern facilities as well as an amiable staff. Each room includes a safety deposit box, cable TV, free Wi-Fi, toiletries, and air-conditioning. For a bit more, you can get a room with a balcony at the front of the hotel, where there are nice views of the street below. The hotel has a restaurant serving Asian and Western dishes as well as a rooftop bar and café.

Over VND2,100,000

The five-star **Hotel Majestic** (1 Dong Khoi, D1, tel. 08/3829-5517, www.majesticsaigon.com, VND5,500,000-17,000,000) has been in business since 1925, located at the intersection of Ton Duc Thang and Dong Khoi, formerly the famous Rue Catinat. The stunning arches and ornate detail of the building's exterior are a fitting welcome. The interior boasts equally impressive decor, with rich wooden surfaces and opulent antique furniture.

the five-star Hotel Majestic

River-view rooms include a balcony, and each room comes equipped with a safety deposit box and spacious marble bathrooms. The hotel has fitness facilities, a serene outdoor swimming pool, and the grandiose Catinat Lounge.

The Rex Hotel (141 Nguyen Hue, D1, tel. 08/3829-2185, www.rexhotelvietnam.com, VND2,700,000-4,800,000) is a Saigon institution. Topped with its iconic crown and featuring high-end designer shops on the ground floor, the Rex is best known as the site of daily press briefings from the American Information Service during the Vietnam War. The deluxe hotel boasts 159 individually designed rooms as well as a top-notch spa and fitness center, a rooftop pool and bar, and several restaurants. Each room comes with plush queen- or king-size beds, complimentary breakfast, shower and bathtub, and daily newspaper service.

On the far side of the Central Post Office, the beautifully furnished **InterContinental Saigon** (Corner Hai Ba Trung and Le Duan, tel. 08/3520-9999, www.intercontinental.com/saigon, VND5,000,000-8,500,000) features modern facilities with an Asian-inspired decor. Its sleek guestrooms boast plush beds and spacious bathrooms. The hotel features on-site fitness facilities, a concierge, room service, and a rooftop swimming pool. Next door, the Kumho Asiana Plaza offers a variety of restaurants and high-end shopping.

Beside the Opera House, the **Caravelle Saigon** (19-23 Lam Son Square, D1, tel. 08/3823-4999, www.caravellehotel.com, VND3,800,000-10,700,000) is one of the city's largest and best-known five-star hotels. In the heart of downtown, this enormous building served as a meeting place for foreign journalists during the war. The original 10-story structure has been joined with a larger, 24-floor tower. The well-known Saigon Saigon Bar is found on the rooftop of the smaller building. The Caravelle boasts 335 guest rooms, as well as six different eating and drinking venues, a spa, pool, and fitness center. Deluxe rooms are plush and comfortable and include standard amenities. Higher-end rooms on the Signature Floor include complimentary breakfast and evening cocktails, and spacious suites have sweeping views of the city and a comfortable living room.

BEN THANH MARKET AREA
VND525,000-1,050,000

Down a side street is **Vuong Tai Hotel** (20 Luu Van Lang, D1, tel. 08/3521-8597, vuongtaihotel@gmail.com, VND840,000-1,050,000, breakfast included), which offers service well above its two-star label. Rooms range from deluxe to VIP and include complimentary bottled water, cable TV, and a safety deposit box. Higher-end rooms feature bathtubs and a desk. All guest rooms have windows.

A high-quality, three-star facility, the **Alagon Western** (28-30 Nguyen An Ninh, D1, tel. 08/3823-2999, www.alagonhotels.com, VND945,000-2,200,000, breakfast included) boasts well-appointed rooms with contemporary decor and modern facilities. Larger rooms include a small sitting area as well as city views and standard amenities, like air-conditioning and toiletries. This hotel is part of a larger group of three-star hotels, with the more expensive original Hoang Hai Long just a stone's-throw away on Pham Hong Thai.

VND1,050,000-2,100,000

The bright and spacious **Sanouva Hotel** (177 Ly Tu Trong, D1, tel. 08/3827-5275, www.sanouvahotel.com, VND1,130,000-2,500,000, breakfast included) is close enough to Ben Thanh to be convenient without the added noise that comes with staying directly beside the market. Each room has natural light, as well as chic, contemporary decor, large bathrooms, and the usual amenities, including toiletries and cable TV. Larger rooms feature a small sitting area. The staff is exceptionally helpful.

Rooms at the **Blue Diamond Hotel** (48-50 Thu Khoa Huan, D1, tel. 08/3823-6167, www.bluediamondhotel.com.vn, VND1,150,000-3,220,000, breakfast included), just north of the market, are spacious with plush, cozy beds and plenty of natural light. All rooms include a large bathroom with bathtub, daily newspaper, free Wi-Fi, air-conditioning, and complimentary bottled water, tea, and coffee. A small fitness center is available, as are professional foot massages. The on-site restaurant serves Vietnamese and Western cuisine.

The **Lan Lan 2 Hotel** (46-46bis Thu Khoa Huan, D1, tel. 08/3822-7926, www.lanlanhotel.com.vn, VND885,000-1,535,000, breakfast included) boasts five different types of guest rooms, from small but adequate standard rooms to large suites. The hotel is decorated in dark wood and rich colors. Each of its 100-plus rooms includes cable TV and air-conditioning. The hotel also has a small fitness center, a restaurant, room service, and laundry. The original **Lan Lan Hotel** (73-75 Thu Khoa Huan, D1, tel. 08/3823-6789, www.lanlanhotel.com.vn, VND1,500,000-2,535,000) is up the road and is equally suitable.

PHAM NGU LAO STREET

Pham Ngu Lao is the most inexpensive area to stay, though it is also party central. The main streets in the backpacker area—De Tham, Bui Vien, and Pham Ngu Lao, along with their respective alleys—are brimming with budget hotels that do most of their business in walk-in customers.

Pham Ngu Lao is a loud and happening place morning, noon, and night. Don't shell out more than VND1,000,000 per night for hotels in this area. For more upscale rooms, head to the Ben Thanh Market area or downtown, where there is a little more flash and a little less debauchery.

Under VND210,000

The **Saigon Backpacker's Hostel** (373/20 Pham Ngu Lao, D1, tel. 08/3837-0230, sgbackpackershostel@gmail.com, VND157,000-180,000) is one of the nicer dorms in the area. Each dorm room has thick mattresses, clean bedding, a locker for each guest (bring your own lock), air-conditioning, and an en suite bathroom with hot water. Eight-bed mixed dorms and four-bed female-only dorms are available in addition to double rooms (VND495,000 d). Don't confuse this place with the Saigon Backpacker's Hostel on Cong Quynh; they are not affiliated.

Hidden in one of Pham Ngu Lao's alleys, the **Saigon Youth Hostel** (241/32 Pham Ngu Lao, D1, tel. 08/3920-3665, www.saigonyouthhostel.com, VND115,000-400,000) has mixed and all-female dorms, as well as private single and double rooms. Clean and comfy beds are available, with breakfast included for a small fee. The hostel provides lockers for dorm guests and each private room features an en suite bathroom with hot water. Two computers are available for guest use, and the common room is well stocked with DVDs, reading material, and a Foosball table.

The entrance to alley 373 of Pham Ngu Lao is down the road from the heart of the backpacker area. The beds and staff at **Phan Anh Hostel** (373/6 Pham Ngu Lao, D1, tel. 08/3920-9235, www.phananhbackpackershostel.com, VND180,000 dorm, VND520,000-680,000 d, breakfast included) make it worth the walk. Clean, comfortable, and reasonably priced, each room features basic amenities, including air-conditioning and free Wi-Fi. The six-bed dormitories have en suite bathrooms and lockers, and there is a common room with a flat-screen TV. Unlike other hostels, Phan Anh has an elevator.

VND210,000-525,000

★ **Hong Han Hotel** (238 Bui Vien, D1, tel. 08/3836-1927, www.hochiminhguesthouse.com, VND480,000-710,000, breakfast included) offers clean and spacious rooms as well as a nice communal balcony. The guesthouse has a variety of room options, from double and twin beds to triple rooms, all of which have air-conditioning, hot water, cable TV, and free Wi-Fi. The staff goes out of their way to be hospitable and are happy to offer advice and local recommendations.

Owned by the same people that operate the Hong Han Hotel, **Bich Duyen Hotel** (283/4 Pham Ngu Lao, D1, tel. 08/3837-4588, www.hochiminhguesthouse.com, VND380,000-680,000) is an equally relaxing option. Situated down an alley off the main road, the rooms at Bich Duyen are quiet and comfortable and include breakfast, free Wi-Fi, air-conditioning, cable TV, hot water, and a fridge. The friendly staff help with travel services in the city and throughout Vietnam. Bich Duyen does not have an elevator.

Though the rooms are not as modern or well-appointed as others in town, the staff and value at **Ava Saigon 2** (126 De Tham, D1, tel. 08/3920-8647, www.avasaigon.com, VND390,000-860,000, breakfast included) make it a nice place. The hotel offers complimentary laundry services, international phone calls, and Wi-Fi. Ava 2 is located just across Tran Hung Dao, close to the backpacker area without being directly at the center of the noise. Though there are cheaper standard rooms available, spring for a room with a window, as it's a better deal.

Away from the heart of the backpacker area, the **Yellow House Saigon Hotel** (114/32 De Tham, D1, tel. 08/3920-6503, yellowhousehotel@gmail.com, VND450,000-945,000) boasts a plethora of options, from standard rooms (with or without a window) to spacious superior and deluxe offerings. Standard rooms are smaller than average, but the bathrooms are larger. Upgrade to a superior for more space and light.

VND525,000-1,050,000

The **Graceful Saigon Hotel** (63 Bui Vien, D1, tel. 08/3838-6291, www.gracefulsaigonhotel.com, VND565,000-900,000, breakfast included) is worth every penny. Tidy, well-decorated rooms come with in-room computers, safety deposit boxes, toiletries, hot water, cable TV, and small bathrooms. Each of the hotel's 11 rooms has a window. Graceful Saigon is right in the middle of the party area. Particularly on weekends, the street noise can be loud. Friendly staff assist in renting scooters or motorbikes as well as providing travel and visa services.

Rooms at the ★ **NN99 Hotel** (99 Bui Vien, D1, tel. 08/3836-9723, www.nn99hotel.com, VND550,000-750,000) are a steal. Though small, NN99 features clean, comfortable, large beds, cable TV, air-conditioning, and modern decor. The staff is helpful and attentive. In addition to free Wi-Fi throughout the building, there is a computer in the lobby for guest use. Don't bother spending the extra money for a room with a balcony, as it's small.

The **Beautiful Saigon Hotel** (62 Bui Vien, D1, tel. 08/3836-4852, www.beautifulsaigonhotel.com, VND680,000-1,600,000) is a good value with modern, if small, rooms. Each room comes equipped with cable TV and air-conditioning, and has a window. The hotel is on the main drag, so opt for a higher floor for quiet. The superior and deluxe rooms have in-room computers, bathtubs, and complimentary fruit baskets.

Though there are clean, comfortable rooms and a nice reception area, it is the staff that makes the experience at **Nguyen Khang Hotel** (283/25 Pham Ngu Lao, D1, tel. 08/3837-3566, www.nguyenkhanghotel.com, VND545,000-815,000, breakfast included). Down an alley, removed from the city noise, Nguyen Khang has rooms with and without windows as well as free Wi-Fi, cable TV, and air-conditioning. The friendly receptionists can recommend restaurants and activities. Book in advance, as the hotel's 13 rooms fill up quickly.

With the assurance that it's "not an ordinary one-star hotel," the **Cat Huy Hotel** (353/28 Pham Ngu Lao, D1, tel. 08/3920-8716, www.cathuyhotel.com, VND685,000-820,000, breakfast included) does not disappoint. Featuring large, well-decorated rooms and impeccable service, this family-owned mini-hotel is an excellent spot, near enough to the backpacker area but tucked down an alley. All rooms have air-conditioning, free Wi-Fi, and cable TV. The hotel also offers services such as laundry and travel arrangements.

While rooms at the **Saigon-Europe** (207 De Tham, D1, tel. 08/3837-3879, www.beautifulsaigonhotel.com, VND700,000-1,500,000, breakfast included) are on the small side, modern decor and impeccable cleanliness more than compensate, not to mention the flat-screen TVs and computers in each room. Rooms (with or without windows) come with in-room safety deposit boxes, toiletries, minibar, and complimentary fruit basket. The friendly staff assist with additional services such as laundry and motorbike rentals.

Over VND2,100,000

On the edge of one of Saigon's busiest roundabouts, the **New World Hotel** (76 Le Lai, D1, tel. 08/3822-8888, www.saigon.newworldhotels.com, VND4,300,000-7,000,000) boasts over 500 of the nicest rooms in town. Its tower offers sweeping views of the city from the perfect vantage point, not far from Ben Thanh Market. Each plush guestroom features a marble bathroom, a large bed, and satellite television. The hotel has two restaurants serving Western and Asian cuisine, as well as a spa, outdoor swimming pool, fitness center, and tennis courts.

NGUYEN TRAI STREET
VND525,000-1,050,000

Bloom Hotel III (120/4 Le Lai, D1, tel. 08/3839-5780, www.bloomhotel.com.vn, VND680,000-1,200,000) provides clean beds and quality service at reasonable prices. It's located in a quiet alley. The amiable staff is always around to help and each spacious room is equipped with air-conditioning and hot water. This is a stairs-only place. If you prefer an elevator, **Bloom**

Hotel II (5 Nguyen Van Trang, D1, tel. 08/3925-0253, www.bloomhotel. com.vn, VND680,000-1,200,000) is around the corner. It's equally good, with some more expensive room options.

Down an alley, **Ono Saigon Hotel** (7/8 Nguyen Trai, D1, tel. 08/3925-2345, onosaigon@gmail.com, VND450,000-1,100,000, breakfast included) is spare in its decor but clean, comfy, and spacious. Basic amenities such as air-conditioning and television are available, as well as hot showers and free Wi-Fi. Ms. Rose, the general manager, is always willing to recommend restaurants and other activities.

The bright and cheery ★ **Town House 50** (50E Bui Thi Xuan, D1, tel. 09/0374-0924, VND240,000-1,050,000, breakfast included) is a pleasant surprise. Set back from the street, this beautiful mini-hotel is decorated in vibrant colors. Though dorm lodging is more expensive than in Pham Ngu Lao, beds are comfy and spotless. This is one of only a few places to offer all-female dorms. The massive common area has a homey feel. The staff are knowledgeable and can offer recommendations for eating, sightseeing, and other activities. Private rooms are more expensive but equally clean and spacious, with large en suite bathrooms, air-conditioning, hot showers, cable TV, and free Wi-Fi.

VND1,050,000-2,100,000

Despite its modest sign and inconspicuous location, ★ **Cinnamon Hotel Saigon** (74 Le Thi Rieng, D1, tel. 08/3926-0130, www.cinnamonhotel.net, VND1,500,000-2,000,000) exceeds expectations. Dressed in red-and-black *ao dai* (traditional Vietnamese garments), employees are outgoing and personable. Each of the hotel's beautifully furnished rooms features large beds and great attention to detail, with even the air-conditioning units masked by crafty embellishments. The hotel does not have an elevator. From the sumptuous breakfast to the occasional complimentary foot massage and the service-minded staff, this spot is worth the extra cash. Service charges and tax are not included in the price.

Over VND2,100,000

Towering above its surroundings, the chic five-star **Hotel Nikko Saigon** (235 Nguyen Van Cu, D1, tel. 08/3925-7777, www.hotelnikkosaigon.com. vn, VND2,600,000-5,200,000) offers a different vantage point to experience the city. Hotel Nikko's Japanese-inspired minimalist design is evident in its muted, earth-toned rooms. Rooms feature king-size beds, large flat-screen televisions, and in-room safety boxes. In addition to its outdoor swimming pool, Hotel Nikko has a fitness center, on-site spa, and a handful of luxury restaurants.

TOURIST INFORMATION

Saigon Tourist (23 Le Loi, D1, tel. 08/3829-2291, www.saigon-tourist.com, 8am-6:30pm daily) is able to provide helpful information to travelers, as well as free city maps. It is a for-profit entity, so your questions may be answered with a pamphlet or a travel brochure. There is also a second office near the corner of Dong Khoi (45 Le Thanh Ton, tel. 08/3827-9279, 7:30am-6:30pm daily).

Most hotels in the backpacker area have travel agencies attached to them, and even if you don't purchase a trip through their business, chances are the receptionist can give you practical information.

If you're looking for information about transportation or day trips outside the city, a better spot to visit is **Sinh Tourist** (246-248 De Tham, D1, tel. 08/3838-9593, www.thesinhtourist.vn, 6:30am-10:30pm daily) near Pham Ngu Lao. This massive company provides travel services within Saigon, throughout the country, and into Cambodia. Employees speak English well and are helpful in presenting options, though this is a for-profit company so you will likely be encouraged to book a tour. **Vinaday goREISE** (228 De Tham, D1, tel. 08/3838-8382, www.goreise.com, 10am-10pm Mon.-Fri., noon-8pm Sat.) is another reliable and friendly source in the backpacker area that provides helpful information to travelers, even if you forgo their tours and venture out on your own. The company also handles hotel reservations and other logistical services.

BANKS AND CURRENCY EXCHANGE

ATMs are plentiful in the city. Drawing money directly from your account is often a better deal and less hassle than trying to exchange dollars or traveler's checks at a local bank.

There are countless currency exchange kiosks advertised around District 1, particularly in the Pham Ngu Lao area and around Nguyen Hue. You can also visit one of the gold shops near Ben Thanh Market to exchange currency. **Ha Tam Jewelers** (2 Nguyen An Ninh, D1, tel. 08/237-243, 8am-9pm daily) is a reliable place to buy and sell foreign bills.

International banks like **ANZ, HSBC,** and **Citibank** follow the typical business day, opening 8am-5pm Monday-Friday; the majority of local banks in Saigon keep odd hours, breaking for lunch in the middle of the day and opening again for only a few hours in the afternoon. A trip to a local bank can often be a tedious affair. But, if you need a local bank, visit **Vietcombank** or **Techcombank.** Several of these institutions provide Western Union wire services. For the most part, you're better off visiting an institution with some foreign affiliation.

While a growing number of high-end boutiques, restaurants, and hotels in Saigon have begun to accept credit cards, Vietnam remains, for the most part, a cash-only country, so check before trying to use your credit card.

INTERNET AND POSTAL SERVICES

A handful of shops in District 1 sell postage stamps, but there are no mailboxes in Vietnam. To send mail, you'll need to go to a post office. Pay a visit to the **Central Post Office** (2 Cong Xa Paris, D1, tel. 08/3924-7247, 7am-7pm Mon.-Fri., 7am-6pm Sat., 8am-6pm Sun.) near Notre Dame Cathedral. In addition to being a worthy sightseeing spot, it is the city's main post office.

There is a **DHL** (3bis Nguyen Van Binh, D1, tel. 08/3844-6203, www. dhl.com.vn, 8am-6pm Mon.-Sat.) around the western side of the Central Post Office building as well as a **UPS** (1 Nguyen Van Binh, D1, tel. 08/3811-2888, www.ups.com, 8am-noon and 1pm-6pm Mon.-Fri., 8am-noon Sat.). Sending large or expensive items from Vietnam is not advised. Even reputable international companies have been known to tack on additional fees and prices change inexplicably.

Wireless Internet is available throughout the city at most hotels, cafés, and restaurants; all you need to do is ask for the password. Many hotels keep a desktop computer in their lobby for guests to use.

PHONE SERVICE

For anyone planning to stay in Vietnam beyond a couple weeks, a mobile phone is a good idea. Cheap but reliable Nokia phones can be purchased new or secondhand at **The Gioi Di Dong** (136 Nguyen Thai Hoc, D1, tel. 1/800-1060, www.thegioididong.com, 8am-10pm daily) starting from VND350,000. Tourist SIM cards are available in the Pham Ngu Lao area and at the post office for around VND90,000. These are less expensive than a regular SIM, but only make domestic calls. Vietnamese mobile service runs on a pay-as-you-go basis, and phone credit is sold throughout the city. There are several carriers, most notably Viettel, Vinaphone, and Mobifone; look for these names posted outside *tap hoa* (convenience stores). Credit can be purchased in VND20,000, VND50,000, VND100,000, and VND200,000 increments.

EMERGENCY AND MEDICAL SERVICES

Vietnam has no single phone number for general emergency services. Dial 113 for the police, 114 for the fire department, and 115 for a local ambulance. Don't expect any of these operators to speak English or for help to come quickly. Emergency services in Vietnam are not often helpful and can be more hassle than they're worth.

In the event of a medical emergency, go directly to a foreign medical center. Local hospitals have aging and overcrowded facilities, and it is doubtful that you'll find an English-speaking doctor. All of the best-equipped facilities in town have 24-hour emergency services. **Family Medical Practice** (Diamond Plaza, 34 Le Duan, D1, tel. 08/3822-7848, www.vietnammedicalpractice.com, 24 hours daily) operates a 24/7 emergency hotline (tel. *9999) and medical staff are always on standby. Family Medical is also the only facility in town equipped with proper ambulances. **International**

SOS Clinic (167A Nam Ky Khoi Nghia, D3, tel. 08/3824-0777, www.internationalsos.com, 24 hours daily) also provides routine check-ups as well as emergency services. Both of these clinics are reputable and staffed by well-qualified doctors. The largest and most sophisticated facilities are located at **FV Hospital** (6 Nguyen Luong Bang, D7, tel. 08/5411-3333, www.fvhospital.com, 24 hours daily), which is reminiscent of a standard Western hospital. Due to its size, the facility is located farther from the city center, in District 7. The hospital operates a **24-hour emergency hotline** (tel. 08/5411-3500).

For non-emergencies, **Columbia Asia International Clinic** (8 Alexandre de Rhodes, D1, tel. 08/3823-8888, www.columbiaasia.com/saigon, emergency room 7:30am-9pm Mon.-Fri., 8am-5pm Sat.-Sun.) is located downtown between Notre Dame Cathedral and the Reunification Palace. The clinic also offers emergency services, though it closes at night.

Pharmacies *(nha thuoc tay)* are common throughout the city and carry all manner of prescription and over-the-counter drugs. Most pharmacies within District 1 have at least one English-speaking staff member. **Pharmacy 22** (214 De Tham, D1, tel. 012/8472-3669, 7am-9:30pm daily) on the corner of De Tham and Bui Vien is reliable and sells hard-to-find products like contact solution and tampons.

DIPLOMATIC SERVICES

The massive, heavily guarded **U. S. Consulate** (4 Le Duan, D1, tel. 08/3520-4200, www.vn.usembassy.gov) provides assistance in emergency situations such as arrest, destitution, or serious illness in addition to dealing with passport-related issues. Appointments are required, and the consulate keeps separate hours for specific non-emergency services, so check online for hours. The consulate is closed to the public on both Vietnamese and American holidays. In the event of an emergency, consulate officers will assist U.S. citizens 8am-5pm Monday-Friday using the phone number above. After 5pm, however, you should phone the embassy's **emergency hotline** (tel. 04/3850-5000).

Getting There

AIR

Ho Chi Minh City is connected to the rest of the world by **Tan Son Nhat International Airport** (SGN, tel. 08/3848-5383), located just four miles north of the city center. This is the country's largest airport, seeing over 30 million passengers per year and serving both prominent international carriers and regional budget airlines.

In recent years, overcrowding has become a problem at Tan Son Nhat. While immigration and processing lines move at a steady pace, be prepared to wait if you are receiving your visa stamp at the airport. Traffic around the airport has become increasingly congested in recent years, so it's important to budget enough time to get to Tan Son Nhat when you have a flight to catch. The evening rush hour is particularly busy, so you'll want to tack on an extra 30 minutes or so if you're leaving around this time.

Taxis from the Airport

This is the easiest way to get downtown. Outside the arrivals area are dozens of taxis waiting to ferry passengers into the city. Cab drivers can be persistent, so turn left down to the end of the sidewalk and find a dispatcher from either Mailinh or Vinasun companies. (There are occasional reports of tourists being overcharged or meters running faster than they should when using lesser-known companies.) Forming lines is an oft-ignored concept in Vietnam, so be proactive and let the dispatcher know where you're going. Getting to downtown District 1 takes about 30-40 minutes, depending on traffic, and costs VND150,000-180,000. Rides from the airport are metered, not flat rate.

Xe Om from the Airport

Though it requires a bit of a walk, you can take a *xe om* (motorbike taxi) directly from the airport. If you're a lone traveler, it's cheaper than grabbing a cab. Exiting the arrivals area, look for an overpass. (From the international terminal, it's ahead and to the right; for domestic arrivals, it will be ahead and to the left.) Follow the other people walking past this structure toward the road. There will be a parking garage on your right and, beyond it, bustling Saigon traffic. *Xe om* drivers will start to approach at this point. Agree upon your fare before you set off. A typical ride to the Pham Ngu Lao area should take about 25 minutes and cost no more than VND80,000. If you'd rather not haggle, you can also hail an **UberMOTO** or **GrabBike** (VND30,000-VND50,000) via smartphone, but you must leave the airport terminal first and head toward the road, as two-wheeled vehicles are not allowed at Tan Son Nhat.

Public Bus from the Airport

If you're up for traveling like a local, you can take the bright yellow **public bus 109** (5:30am-1:30am daily, VND20,000) from the airport directly to Ben Thanh Market, a stone's throw from the backpacker area. This is the cheapest transportation option and takes about 45 minutes to reach the market. Don't expect anyone on the bus to speak English.

TRAIN

The **Saigon Train Station (Ga Saigon)** (1 Nguyen Thong, D3, tel. 01/900-6469, www.dsvn.vn) sits just south of the Nhieu Loc Canal in District 3 and is the final destination for all domestic trains. The country's north-south Reunification Line runs along the coast from Hanoi with major stations in

Hue, Danang, and Nha Trang before reaching HCMC. Trains arrive from Nha Trang in the early morning or Phan Thiet in the evening. There are always taxi drivers and *xe om* drivers waiting outside the station's main entrance; it's about 15 minutes via taxi or *xe om* to downtown. Public bus 65 can also take you to the main bus station at Ben Thanh Market (30 min., 4:30am-8pm daily, VND5,000).

BUS

The majority of tourist buses coming from Can Tho, Nha Trang, Dalat, and Mui Ne drop off passengers in the Pham Ngu Lao area of District 1. Tour operators usually park their vehicles around 23-9 Park or on De Tham, right in the heart of Pham Ngu Lao. **Phuong Trang** (272 De Tham, D1, tel. 1900-6067, www.futabuslines.com.vn, 5am-1am daily) is a major bus provider, as is **Sinh Tourist** (246-248 De Tham, D1, tel. 08/3838-9593, www.thesinhtourist.vn, 6:30am-10:30pm daily).

There are three main stations used by local buses. To the northwest is **An Suong bus station (Ben Xe An Suong)** (Quoc Lo 22, D Hoc Mon, tel. 08/3883-2517), nine miles from the city center, just beyond the airport where Truong Chinh street turns into Highway 22. Also nine miles from the city center is the **Western bus station (Ben Xe Mien Tay)** (Kinh Duong Vuong, D Binh Tan, tel. 08/3877-6594), which sits farther south and serves the Mekong Delta. For all other destinations, Saigon's **Eastern bus station (Ben Xe Mien Dong)** (292 Dinh Bo Linh, D Binh Thanh, tel. 08/3899-1607) is a mere four miles from town. It is unlikely that you will need to visit any of these places, but if your bus drops you at one of these stations, the usual modes of transportation—taxis, *xe om*, ride-hailing apps, and the public bus—are all good ways to get downtown.

MOTORBIKE

The most direct—and congested—route into the city is National Highway 1, a gritty, chaotic road that runs into town from the Mekong Delta on the western side and Phan Thiet on the eastern end. Highway traffic is usually a mess, full of massive trucks, buses, cars, and motorbikes, and the flow of vehicles becomes more backed up as you approach the city, particularly during the evening rush hour.

Coming from the east, things start to get better once you reach the Saigon Bridge, which takes you out of District 2 and, from there, into the city center. If you're approaching from the Mekong Delta, Highway 1 curves north to avoid Saigon. Make a right onto Vo Van Kiet (look for signs), and follow the road straight into town, getting off at the Ben Thanh Market exit. If you go too far, you'll know it—the Thu Thiem tunnel leads right back out of town and into District 2.

Getting Around

When driving around town, there are essentially no rules. People drive while texting, neglect to use the correct turn signals (if they use them at all), routinely speed in the opposite direction down a one-way street, and generally disregard lane markings. Exercise caution on the road and obey stoplights and traffic laws as you would at home, even if others don't.

TAXIS

When traveling in the city, it's best to hail a green-and-white **Mailinh** (tel. 08/3838-3838) or green, white, and red **Vinasun** (tel. 08/3827-2727) cab, particularly at night. These vehicles are clean and well kept, the drivers are knowledgeable, and the meters correct. Other cab companies are okay to use during the day.

Cab drivers occasionally try to beat the system by taking a longer route than necessary. The most trusted cab companies in Saigon are Vinasun and Mailinh, so it's a safe bet to stick with them. Never bargain for a cab ride in Vietnam. All taxis are metered and it is always to your benefit to use the meter.

It's easier to hail a cab from the street rather than calling for one, but if it's late at night or no taxis are around, then ask a Vietnamese speaker to call for a Mailinh or Vinasun taxi.

RIDE-HAILING APPS

In the last couple years, both global giant **Uber** (www.uber.com) and regional app **Grab** (www.grab.com) have made their mark on Saigon traffic, much to the ire of both traditional *xe om* drivers and cabbies alike. Both apps offer riders dirt-cheap rates in both two- and four-wheeled vehicles. While Grab and Uber drivers can be a mixed bag—your driver might be a knowledgeable local, a whiz with the GPS, or someone who just moved to the city yesterday—the service is generally safe and the prices are unbeatable. Unlike some other cities, you can also opt to pay by credit card or in cash.

XE OM

As you wander around the city, you will hear cries of "You! Motorbiiiiiiiiike!" These are Saigon's *xe om* drivers, an impressive and eclectic fleet of motorbike drivers that ferry people from place to place. This is the most efficient way to get around town, though it is not for the faint of heart. *Xe om* drivers drive fast and are just as likely as the rest of the population to break traffic laws. Always agree on a price before embarking and stand firm on that agreement, as drivers sometimes attempt to glean extra cash from you later on.

The going rate for a *xe om* fluctuates depending on where you're headed, so ask a local what they might pay to get an idea of a fair price. At night, stick to taxis.

CYCLOS

Hopping on a cyclo can be a nice way to see the city. Muscular cyclo drivers will pedal you around the downtown area and past some of the city's most popular sights. Many drivers speak English well, as these pedal-powered vehicles are more likely to be used by visitors for tours of District 1 than by the local population, who prefer to get around on a motorbike. Prices are negotiable, though you should be prepared to pay more than you would for a *xe om*, as your driver will also be your guide around town and he is doing a lot more legwork than someone on a motorbike. The experience is fun and something that many visitors to HCMC enjoy, but this is not a method of transportation for someone in a hurry.

BUSES

An efficient army of bright green city buses roams Saigon's streets. Buses generally run 5am-7:30pm, but some may go as late as 9pm. It can be difficult to navigate the dizzying maze of bus routes that crisscross the city, though there is a handy interactive bus map online (www.saigonbus.net) that helps. Paper maps are available at the main **bus station** (Quach Thi Trang roundabout, tel. 08/3821-4444), across from Ben Thanh Market.

Buses vary in size from minibuses to large air-conditioned vehicles. Bus stops are either a small, navy blue sign listing that stop's buses, or full covered stops with a bench and route map.

A trip within the city limits will set you back about VND5,000. If you're heading farther afield, prices go up according to your destination.

VEHICLES FOR HIRE

Motorbikes are available for hire (VND100,000-120,000 per day) throughout the Pham Ngu Lao area. Before heading out, give the bike a short test-drive and check that you have the vehicle's registration card. **Chi's Cafe** (40/31 Bui Vien, D1, tel. 09/0364-3446, www.chiscafe.com, 9am-10pm daily, VND100,000-120,000) has good, reliable vehicles, both automatic and semi-automatic, and offers daylong and long-term rentals (only for visitors staying in the city). **Trung's Motorbikes** (185 Pham Ngu Lao, D1, tel. 09/0330-8466, trung_motorbike@yahoo.com, 7am-10pm daily, VND80,000-120,000), a tiny green shop on the corner of a small alley, also has rentals available.

If you're looking to buy a bike for a longer trip around the country, signs advertising heavy-duty vehicles for sale can be found in the backpacker area. Make sure to have the bike checked by a mechanic before finalizing the purchase.

GETTING AROUND

Cu Chi Tunnels

Considered one of the greatest tactical achievements of the southern insurgency during the American War, the **Cu Chi Tunnels** (Ben Dinh, Nhan Duc Commune, Cu Chi, tel. 08/3794-8830, www.diadaocuchi.com.vn, 7am-5pm daily, VND110,000) spiderweb beneath miles of rice paddies and fertile farmland all the way from Ho Chi Minh City to the Cambodian border. As early as the 1940s, members of the Viet Minh resistance army (later the National Liberation Front, or NLF) began digging out these cramped crawl spaces by hand. With technology and firepower far inferior to their French enemies, the tunnels allowed Ho Chi Minh's rebel forces to communicate with nearby villages and bases undetected. By the time the American War arrived in the 1960s, a 155-mile underground network existed.

Initially, the tunnels were meant to provide escape routes and shelter during American bombing raids. As soon as the skies were clear, guerrillas would emerge from their tunnels, cart away the unexploded ordnance left behind and use these weapons to create grenades and smaller explosives. These homemade weapons were then planted alongside other, more crude booby traps, such as sharpened bamboo sticks and iron spikes. In the thick and unfamiliar jungle, the NLF proved almost invisible.

The retaliatory acts further frustrated American and south Vietnamese troops. Bombing raids became more frequent and the area was deemed a free-strike zone, giving U.S. pilots permission to shoot at anything that moved. With the onslaught of explosives, the NLF moved underground, sometimes for weeks or even months at a time. Kitchens and bedrooms were constructed, as well as hospitals, meeting rooms, theaters, and concert halls. Children were born below ground and entire communities set up. The most shallow tunnels were at least five feet underground, but four different levels of passageways existed, with each progressively smaller than the last. Overall, the crawl spaces ranged 2.5-4 feet wide and 2.5-6 feet high.

exploring one of the tunnels at Cu Chi

For every effort the U.S. military made to defeat the NLF, rebels in Cu Chi were one step ahead. Until the very end of the war, the NLF fighters defended their land successfully against the Americans and south Vietnamese.

Today, the government-run tourist area encompassing the Cu Chi tunnels features exhibits, guided tours, and a variety of other attractions. Weapons displays illustrate the gruesome methods of the NLF and hint at the hardships of those who lived underground.

Park guides escort you through the tunnels, telling of the history and people of Cu Chi. At each of the two tunnel sites, Ben Dinh and Ben Duoc, the narrow passageways have been lit and widened to accommodate visitors. Larger subterranean rooms are occasionally furnished with mannequins and other items.

The history of the Cu Chi tunnels is more interesting than a visit to the tunnels themselves. The present-day memorial site is a bit of a circus. On the same land where an estimated 45,000 men and women gave their lives over the course of the war, visitors are able to fire machine guns, play paintball, or splash around in a swimming pool. While the significance of these tunnels during the war is a valuable part of local history, visiting Cu Chi tends to be polarizing among tourists: people either love it or hate it.

Visitors are welcome to watch a harsh anti-American propaganda film that depicts a rosy picture of life in Cu Chi during the war, with smiling NLF women plowing the fields, rifles slung across their backs. In reality, conditions beneath the ground were horrific: snakes and poisonous creatures were rampant within the tunnels, along with malaria and other diseases. Though collapses were uncommon, when they did occur, death was almost certain. Those who survived weeks and months below ground often emerged with health problems, largely from lack of oxygen and sunlight. For all these flaws, the film manages to provide some useful historical information.

BEN DINH TUNNELS

The **Ben Dinh Tunnels** are the more popular of Cu Chi's two underground sites. This area is more touristy than its counterpart up the road. While it can become congested in the late morning and early afternoon, guides and other park staff at Ben Dinh speak more English than those at Ben Duoc. The web of tunnels and exhibits at Ben Dinh is more compact, allowing for visitors to get around more easily.

A souvenir shop hawks mass-produced tchotchkes, and a handful of restaurants sit across the road from the Ben Dinh entrance. There are also vendors within the grounds selling snacks and light meals at slightly inflated prices.

BEN DUOC TUNNELS

Farther down the road, the older **Ben Duoc** site is less frequented than Ben Dinh. It contains near-identical tunnels and weapons displays but is significantly more spread out than Ben Dinh. If you wish to visit other parts of the Cu Chi tourist area—such as the AK-47 shooting range—you will be required to take an electric car, which is available for hire near the park entrance. There are a handful of on-site restaurants serving light meals (VND20,000-100,000) as well as a few souvenir vendors just beyond the entrance.

TAY NINH HOLY SEE

A colorful, sprawling complex in an otherwise sleepy town, the **Tay Ninh Holy See** (Ly Thuong Kiet, Hoa Thanh Town, tel. 06/6384-1193, www.cao-dai.com.vn, 6am-6pm daily) is the epicenter of Caodaism. Built in 1933 by a devout group of followers, the holy city's main temple stands at the end of a long, narrow parade ground, flanked on either side by banks of stadium-style seating. This is the most ornamental and visually interesting piece of architecture within the Cao Dai complex.

Leave your shoes at the edge of the raised sidewalk surrounding the building. The temple's exterior has an ornately decorated entrance and a long, three-tiered roof. Inside, the building is divided into three separate areas that pay tribute to the three main branches of Caodaism: the legislative branch, the administrative branch, and the spiritual branch. The small area at the front belongs to the three protectors and upholders of Caodaist law: Ho Phap at the center, and his right- and left-hand men, Thuong Sanh and Thuong Pham. These three men are represented by a set of colorful statues inside the main hall. On the opposite wall, facing the temple's main entrance, a painting depicting three of Caodaism's most famous saints, poet Nguyen Binh Khiem, Sun Yat-Sen, and Victor Hugo, shows the trio writing the phrases "God and humanity" and "love and justice" in French and Chinese.

The administrative branch of Caodaism is represented in the long, airy main hall where Caodaist followers, known as adepts, participate in

Tay Ninh Holy See

religious proceedings. This is the most colorful and decorative section of the temple. Wide-eyed, multi-hued dragons snake down the endless rows of pillars, while the ceiling is painted to reflect a bright blue sky with silver stars. The all-seeing eye, the central symbol of Caodaism, is featured heavily upon the walls, surrounded by lotus flowers and repeating up all nine of the main hall's steps to the altar. Here, a large blue orb adorned with stars and a single image of the all-seeing eye sits at the center of a large table, upon which offerings of fruit, tea, alcohol, and other items are presented.

Religious ceremonies take place four times a day: at 6am, noon, 6pm, and midnight. Most guided tours arrive at the temple in time for the midday procession, in which men and women file into the temple from separate sides and take their place within the main hall. The entire length of the building is divided into nine steps, each of which represents part of the hierarchy within Caodaism. Only about six steps are used, while the rest remain empty, including a series of red-and-gold lacquer chairs at the very front, which are reserved for the Pope and other high-ranking members of the religion. During prayer, men take the right side of the temple and women the left. The adepts complete a series of prostrations before the altar as well as several religious chants, usually accompanied by a band of traditional Vietnamese musicians, who sit on the balcony.

Due to the high volume of visitors at the temple, adepts usher you along after some time to allow for other visitors to watch the ceremony from above. You'll also be able to wander around the main entrance of the temple. If you stick around long enough, the adepts file out after prayer and a smaller group returns with another altar, this time filled with incense, fruit, and other offerings, which is blessed on each and every step up to the altar before being placed in front of the all-seeing eye.

On your way out of the building, take a look across the parade grounds into the distance to find another cluster of sparkling, intricate towers devoted to the trio of protectors who guard the laws of Caodaism. If you've got time and want to ask questions, local adepts are friendly and willing to chat, though few of them speak English.

There have been some reports of shoe theft outside the temple, so you can remove your shoes and carry them inside, though it's better to stick them in your bag and out of sight, or you may be told to leave them again.

TOURS

For dirt-cheap mass tours, **Sinh Tourist** (246-248 De Tham, D1, tel. 08/3838-9593, www.thesinhtourist.vn, 6:30am-10:30pm daily, VND109,000-169,000) offers half-day trips to the tunnels or full-day tours combining Cu Chi with a visit to the Cao Dai temple at Tay Ninh. Admission to the tunnels is not included in the price, but you are spared the hassle of navigating the public bus system and a tour guide is provided. Groups tend to be 30-40 people; get a spot at the front if you want to hear what your guide has to say.

Ho Chi Minh City Urban Adventures (tel. 09/0990-4100, www.hochiminhcityurbanadventures.com, VND800,000-1,500,000) runs a tour from the city to Cu Chi for a maximum of 12 people, allowing for additional one-on-one time with the guide and more than the cookie-cutter speeches provided by the guides at the park. The company offers a standard visit along with a couple flourishes, including a brief stop at a local farm en route to the tunnels, as well as a chance to learn how rice paper is made. HCMC Urban Adventures prides itself on creating tourism that benefits the local community, and so its tours often include extra, off-the-beaten-track stops, which allow travelers to see how the local population lives. Half-day tours to the tunnels are available as well as full-day excursions that go to both the Cu Chi tunnels and the Cao Dai temple at Tay Ninh. The company books its tours via Internet or through telephone reservations; travelers can call at any time to book a tour.

More expensive but also more relaxing is a tour with **Les Rives** (Me Linh Point Tower, Ste. 2105, 2 Ngo Duc Ke, D1, tel. 012/8592-0018, www.lesrives-experience.com, 10am-10pm daily, VND1,899,000-3,599,000), a company that provides on-the-water excursions to a handful of nearby sights, including the tunnels. The company offers half-day tours to Cu Chi in both the morning and afternoon with an array of extra features, from an additional bicycle trip to a "hidden HCMC" tour that includes a trip to the tunnels. Meals are served, along with unlimited fruit and refreshments, and the hour-long boat ride to the tunnels eliminates the stress of inching through the bumper-to-bumper traffic that often crowds the outskirts of the city. Hotel pickup and all park entrance fees are included in the tour price.

TRANSPORTATION
Bus

Public buses run regularly to Cu Chi District from the city's main bus station (Quach Thi Trang roundabout, opposite Ben Thanh Market). Take the number 4 bus to An Suong bus station, right on the outskirts of town (1 hour, VND6,000). From there, bus 122 will bring you to Tan Quy junction, where you can catch the number 70 to Ben Duoc. You will carry on for some time in this direction before arriving at the Cu Chi tunnels stop (1.5 hours, VND13,000). It should be easy to spot, as there are large signs announcing the tunnels as soon as you enter the area. The last bus from Cu Chi leaves at 6:30pm.

It is also possible to take bus 13 from the 23-9 Park bus depot (Pham Ngu Lao, near Nguyen Trai) out to the Cu Chi bus station, where you can transfer to bus 79, which takes you directly to the tunnels. Confirm your destination with the driver or fare collector before setting off.

Motorbike

The Cu Chi tunnels are located along Provincial Road 15. From Saigon, take Truong Chinh street in Tan Binh District out past An Suong bus station on

Highway 1, labeled QL22 on the kilometer stones. Roughly three miles past the bus station, make a right onto Ba Trieu street. Once you reach the Hoc Mon Market, this road changes names a few times, from Trung Nu Vuong to Do Van Day, but will eventually turn into Provincial Road 15. Stay on this route for another 20 miles and you'll find yourself at the tunnels. The drive takes 1.5-2 hours.

While it is possible to reach the tunnels on your own, this trip is not recommended for novice drivers, as it involves a stretch along Highway 1, the nation's busiest and most dangerous road. Unless you have a hired driver at your disposal, save yourself the hazard and the headache and hop on a tour or a public bus instead.

Vung Tau

Stretching out into the ocean, Vung Tau was not always the buzzing tourist town it has become. Well before droves of domestic visitors began to flock here for weekend getaways and summer vacations, Vung Tau played a significant role in the military history of most powers to occupy Vietnam. For centuries, its view of Can Gio, the entryway into the Saigon River, made it a valuable strategic outpost for several different armies, from the Vietnamese battling against colonial invasion in 1859 to the French army, a brief occupation by the Japanese during WWII, and an extended presence of the Australian military throughout the American War.

In the 19th and 20th centuries, French colonists identified this sleepy beach town as the ideal spot from which to keep an eye on Saigon. It was armed with artillery cannons and military forts, hidden deep in the thick tangle of jungle, which still obscure many of its mountainsides today. Later, when the NLF and Communist forces were battling against Western troops, the Australian military, who had come to assist their American allies, set up a logistics base in the area, stationing its soldiers all over Ba Ria-Vung Tau province. Throughout the region, tunnels were dug, forts built, and several significant battles played out within the mountains.

Years of missionary proselytizing created a strong Catholic following alongside Buddhist traditions. Every other building is a bright, eye-popping decorated pagoda or a towering, stark white statue of Jesus Christ or the Virgin Mary. One of Vung Tau's most famous attractions is the gigantic Christ of Vung Tau, believed to be among the largest statues of Jesus Christ in the world.

Vung Tau is regarded as a weekend tourist hot spot, packed with domestic visitors and overpriced goods. Avoid Vung Tau on Saturdays, Sundays, and public holidays. Its beaches have a reputation for being on the seedy side, due to some harassment of women in revealing swimsuits. Focus on the town's sights and you'll be fine.

CHRIST OF VUNG TAU

Vung Tau's most famous monument, the enormous **Christ of Vung Tau** (2 Ha Long, main gates 6:30am-5pm daily, statue 7:30am-11:30am and 1:30pm-4:45pm daily) is among the largest statues of Jesus Christ in the world. Nestled partway up Small Mountain, this sculpture is 105 feet tall, with a 60-foot wingspan. Vung Tau's statue is taller than the Christ the Redeemer statue in Rio de Janeiro. Visitors can ascend the narrow interior, going 133 steps up for a stunning 360-degree view of Vung Tau and the ocean.

Construction began in 1974, before the end of the American War. A year later the statue was complete, but the 800-odd steps from the base of Tao Phung to the base of the statue had yet to be finished. Construction was suspended over the next decade, and the statue sat partially hidden in the thick brush of the mountain. When it was discovered that the statue's lightning rod system—the metal points of the halo—had been stolen, the Catholic church was allowed to complete the project. In 1994, the statue and walkway were opened to the public.

Make the long hike to the statue in the early morning or late afternoon, as the sun can be brutal. There is also a back passage up to the statue. It begins from alley 220 of Phan Chu Trinh and ends at the last 200 steps up to the statue. This is no less challenging for hikers, but a skilled motorbike driver could take the narrow path up here.

Before entering the statue, take your shoes off and leave all bags at the door. On either side of the main monument are two massive French artillery cannons. Beyond the statue, small bridges arch over a waterless canal:

Christ of Vung Tau

This is where the French transported ammunition to the cannons, loading the magazines from below.

Anyone wearing short shorts or a tank top will be turned away from the statue.

FRENCH FORT RUINS

A lesser-known but equally fascinating relic of Vung Tau's history are the **French Fort Ruins** scattered across Big and Small Mountains. From as early as the late 19th century, the French colonial government recognized Vung Tau as a valuable military outpost, affording them a clear view toward the mouth of the Saigon River. Several separate forts were built, each extensively armed. Soldiers kept watch from their on-site living quarters, and underground rooms were built to accommodate ammunition stores. During WWII, the Japanese also made use of these posts. Following the end of French colonial rule, many of the military forts were abandoned. Several of these hidden forts remain forgotten, covered in plant life and crumbling on the mountainsides of Vung Tau. The local authorities have done little to maintain these sites, giving the old forts an eerie feel.

One of these military forts exists on the back passage from Christ of Vung Tau, which begins on **alley 222 of Phan Chu Trinh street.** At the entry to the ruins is a battery of artillery guns as well as the remains of a well and some living quarters. Below, the dark, cave-like opening leads beneath the guns. If you've got a flashlight handy, you can venture inside (though it's more than a bit spooky) and see where and how the guns were loaded, feeding ammo up through a metal chamber at the center of the back room. If you visit the statue of Christ of Vung Tau on foot, it is also possible to hike down to these ruins, as they're not too far from the stone steps. From the statue, drive across the stone path and down to the left. The ruins will be on your left but are barely visible from the path, appearing as only a bit of stone wall and a hollow doorway. Park your bike and walk up the steps beside the darkened entryway.

The other, more easily accessible fort ruins exist off **alley 444 of Tran Phu street.** The trip up the mountain is pleasant, passing by brightly hued houses and locals raking out their catch of shrimp to dry in the sun. Scenic views abound. There is a plaque providing some general information about the fort, and then two batteries of weapons, one with six artillery guns, the other with three. The road up to these ruins is paved the entire way, making the trip a much easier feat, whether on foot, on a motorbike, or via a hired *xe om* driver.

These historical sites are free to visit and open to the public.

WORLDWIDE ARMS MUSEUM

The extensive collection within the **Worldwide Arms Museum** (98 Tran Hung Dao, tel. 06/4381-8369, 8am-5pm daily, VND100,000) comes as something of a surprise. Featuring weapons and military uniforms from across the globe, the museum's mannequins don the colors of China, Japan, Mongolia,

England, Scotland, and France, while every wall of the space is covered in intricately detailed weapons dating back centuries. Englishman Robert Taylor has spent years cultivating both his collection of military memorabilia.

VUNG TAU LIGHTHOUSE

Though the **Vung Tau Lighthouse** (end of Hai Dang on Small Mountain, 7am-11am and 2pm-6pm daily) is rather unimpressive on its own, its views of the town and the beach, as well as of the Christ of Vung Tau statue, make this a nice spot to visit. Perched 170 meters above sea level atop the summit of Small Mountain, this modest white tower was built in 1910 in order to guide ships leaving and entering the Saigon River. Visitors are not allowed inside the lighthouse, but the views from the ground are pleasant and the breeze is refreshing.

WHITE VILLA

Perched atop a small hill between Front Beach and Big Mountain, **White Villa (Bach Dinh)** (4 Tran Phu, tel. 06/4351-1608, 7am-5pm daily, VND5,000) was built as a holiday residence for the Governor General of Cochinchina, Paul Doumer, in 1898. The six-hectare plot of land originally housed Phuoc Thang Fort, a military base. After colonization, Phuoc Thang was destroyed to make way for the two-story structure that exists today. During its heyday, Bach Dinh served as the living quarters of not only Governor General Doumer but also Emperors Thanh Thai and Bao Dai, Vietnam's final king. With its intricate mosaics and detailed ceramic accents, the grounds surrounding Bach Dinh are surprisingly lush for being so close to the center of town.

A lasting relic of Vietnam's colonial history, the house is most impressive from outside. Inside, the ground floor exhibit is filled with late 17th- and early 18th-century Chinese ceramics and porcelain discovered from a shipwreck bound for Europe that sank just off the Con Dao Islands. Upstairs is a preserved version of the house's former glory, though the solid wooden furniture and moldy drapes are worse for wear. Upstairs is also a nice spot to take in a sea view.

A long, well-covered path runs out to a headstone honoring Emperor Thanh Thai. Thanh Thai became emperor at the ripe age of 10 and, in his later years, grew unpopular with the French on account of his resistance toward colonial powers. In 1907, he was placed under house arrest at Bach Dinh, living under the watchful eye of the French government until 1916, when he was sent away to Reunion Island, another French colony off the eastern coast of Madagascar. The stele, emblazoned with a dragon at the top, bears one of the emperor's poems, written in Vung Tau.

BEACHES
Front Beach

Situated right along a bend between the ferry port and Big Mountain, **Front Beach** (Quang Trung and Ha Long streets) is directly at the center of the action. Front Beach Park acts as a buffer between the main road and the water, which comes all the way up to the sea wall. The park makes for a nice place to stop and relax in the shade with swaying palm trees blocking out the midday sun. While Front Beach is fine for swimming and markedly less crowded than Back Beach on the weekends, its flaw is its lack of sand. In the early morning and late afternoon, when the sun is less fierce, this is a lively spot full of local vendors and patrons.

Back Beach

For sunbathing and as much R&R as can be gleaned from the well-touristed shores of Vung Tau, **Back Beach** (Thuy Van between Phan Chu Trinh and Nguyen An Ninh) is the place to go. Spanning two miles—longer than Vung Tau's other main beaches—and boasting plenty of room to lay down a towel, this is a quieter spot during the weekdays and sees more of the foreign tourist crowd, though you are still likely to receive a few stares. The beach itself is nothing stunning, but its close proximity to the rest of town make it a nice escape. There are several tourist areas based on the beach, including **Bien Dong Ocean Park** (8 Thuy Van, tel. 06/4381-6318, www. khudulichbiendong.com, 6am-10pm daily), which features a restaurant, swimming pool, and beach chairs and is free to enter.

SPORTS AND RECREATION
Golf

Part of a larger resort complex, **Paradise Golf Vung Tau** (1 Thuy Van, tel. 06/4385-3428, www.golfparadise.com.vn, 5:30am-4:30pm daily, VND1,400,000-2,100,000 for 18 holes) is the town's only golf course. Located about two miles from the town center, the seaside course features three separate areas with a total of 27 holes and offers caddies, golf carts, and rental equipment. Guests can call to book a tee time for 18 holes; fees go up on weekends.

Dog Racing

A lesser-known attraction in Vung Tau takes place every weekend at **Lam Son Stadium** (15 Le Loi, tel. 06/4380-7309, www.duachovietnam. net, 7:30pm-10:30pm Fri.-Sat., VND60,000), the country's only venue for greyhound racing and one of the few places where gambling is legal for Vietnamese. Every Friday and Saturday, a few thousand people flock to the stadium to watch the races and wager bets. Purchase a cheap ticket and hang out with the masses, or spring for an air-conditioned balcony view. Drinks and snacks are available inside.

SHOPPING

If you're in need of good beach clothing or a bathing suit, the ultra-modern **Imperial Plaza** (159-163 Thuy Van, tel. 06/4352-6688, www.imperial-plaza.vn, 9am-9:30pm Mon.-Fri., 9am-10pm Sat.-Sun.) is the place to go. The shopping center has several floors of well-priced local and foreign brand-name clothing, swimsuits, and souvenirs, as well as a small food court on the top floor with mainly Vietnamese food and a café out front. Only Vietnamese sizes are offered here.

FOOD

Being a beach town, Vung Tau is known for its seafood. However, the main culinary specialty is a dish called *banh khot,* which is something like a miniature version of the large, hang-over-the-plate southern-style Vietnamese pancakes you might find in Saigon, or their smaller cousins up in the central region. Bite-sized and accompanied by all the same fixings, these fried morsels of rice flour are often topped with shrimp but can also be served with meat or other seafood, usually squid. A healthy serving of fresh greens, pickled veggies, and fish sauce are added to the mix, making for a delectable, authentic Vung Tau meal.

Famed throughout Vung Tau and beyond, the *banh khot* at ★ **Banh Khot Goc Vu Sua** (14 Nguyen Truong To, 7am-2pm Mon.-Fri., 7am-8pm Sat.-Sun., VND36,000) is considered the best in town. Packed at all hours, this restaurant is just a few metal tables and plastic stools tucked into an outdoor space with pale-blue chain-link "walls." Fresh greens and veggies come standard with every order, as well as fish sauce and as much crushed chili pepper as you can stomach. Grab a lettuce leaf; toss in your *banh khot;* add some pickled carrots and daikon, mint leaves, and other herbs; wrap; dip; and enjoy. Order a refreshing *nuoc mia* (sugarcane juice) to go with your meal.

For more variety, **Co Ba Vung Tau** (1 Hoang Hoa Tham, tel. 06/4352-6165, www.cobavungtau.com, 7am-10pm daily, VND45,000-180,000) serves equally delicious *banh xeo* (Vietnamese pancakes) as well as *banh khot,* the Vung Tau specialty, and *banh beo,* a steamed rice flour cake similar to its fried counterpart, all in an open-air setting. All meals are reasonably priced and the open kitchen allows diners to watch the food being prepared.

Right in the thick of the cafés and restaurants that surround the cable car to Big Mountain, **Co Nen** (20 Tran Phu, tel. 09/0709-0606, www.quannuongconen.com, 4pm-11pm Mon.-Fri., 10am-11pm Sat.-Sun., VND60,000-280,000) is a spot-on barbecue joint serving a variety of seafood and meat as well as hotpot dishes. Its decor is limited to the bare essentials, with metal tables and creaky chairs, but the grilled octopus here is incredible and well worth enduring the loud music blaring from the café nearby and the flashing lights of the smoothie and snack stands across the way.

Excellent seafood and views of the water can be found at **Ganh Hao** (3 Tran Phu, tel. 06/4355-0909, www.ganhhao.com.vn, 10am-9:30pm daily, VND95,000-900,000), located past the cable car to Big Mountain. The restaurant's huge menu includes everything from squid, fish, shrimp, snails, and several types of crab to Vietnamese meat and vegetable dishes. The restaurant's outdoor dining area is perched right at the edge of the sea. Dishes at Ganh Hao are affordable, with a few higher-cost items available.

★ **Pizzeria David** (92 Ha Long, tel. 06/4352-1012, 9am-10:30pm daily, VND145,000-235,000) turns out top-notch classic pies, including a delicious quattro formaggi as well as prosciutto and mushroom. Two floors of open-air indoor and outdoor seating are available, with cozy low tables and patio furniture reminiscent of a European café. Add to this the exposed brick exterior and you might forget you're on the other side of the world. David's also boasts an impressive wine list as well as pasta dishes, ice cream, and Italian desserts.

Not far from the beach but down a quiet street, **Tommy's 3 Restaurant & Bar** (3 Le Ngoc Han, tel. 06/4370-7845, www.tommysvietnam.com, 7am-late daily, VND60,000-320,000) has an extensive menu of reasonably priced Western dishes, from hamburgers and pizza to steaks and savory pies, not to mention the self-proclaimed "coldest beer in town." Televisions broadcast international sports channels and a live band performs Fridays and Saturdays. Owners Glenn and Trang Nolan offer travel tips and help visitors with visas, motorbike rentals, or tours to historical sights.

A cozy little spot near Tran Hung Dao Park, **Good Morning Vietnam** (6 Hoang Hoa Tham, tel. 06/4385-6959, www.goodmorningviet.com, 10am-10pm daily, VND85,000-210,000) is another anomaly among Vung Tau cuisine, serving up unexpectedly delightful Italian food at affordable prices. Its menu runs the spectrum from standard pastas and pizzas to dishes like gnocchi, risotto, and authentic fish and poultry fare, all accompanied by a healthy wine list. Add to that linen tablecloths and its breezy corner real estate and this tiny Italian eatery is worth a visit.

Overlooking the sea, **Ned Kelly's** (128 Ha Long, tel. 06/4351-0173, 7:30am-midnight daily, VND60,000-270,000) is a ramshackle, little Aussie expat bar with cold beers and an assortment of Western dishes. The open-air watering hole serves breakfast, lunch, and dinner as well as a variety of drinks and is open later than most bars in town.

ACCOMMODATIONS

Vung Tau is a small town. Most accommodations are within 5 or 10 minutes' drive of its major sights and beaches. The majority of budget accommodations are located on or around Back Beach, while you'll find fancier, more expensive digs near the Front Beach area. Visiting Vung Tau on the weekend is not a great idea, as the city is flooded with local tourists. If you visit on a Saturday or Sunday, book your hotel in advance, as rooms fill up quickly. Many hotels increase their room rates on the weekends.

VND210,000-525,000

No-frills but clean and adequately appointed, the **Dai An Hotel** (151A Hoang Hoa Tham, tel. 06/4352-5439, weekdays VND350,000-900,000, weekends VND450,000-1,100,000) is minutes from Back Beach and a decent value for the money. Each room includes a fan, air-conditioning, hot water, and a television. Bathrooms are spacious and the hotel staff are kind and easygoing.

Ha Thanh Hotel (137 Phan Chu Trinh, tel. 06/4352-5848, sales.hathan-hhotel@gmail.com, VND400,000-950,000) is a decent place to base yourself, not far from the south end of Back Beach. Rooms are clean, with a decent amount of space and light. There aren't many amenities in the hotel beyond hot water and air-conditioning. Breakfast is included in the room rate, though you can get a better deal if you skip the breakfast and just pay for the room.

VND525,000-1,050,000

Slightly removed from the beachfront tourist zone, ★ **Maccas Place** (31 Lac Long Quan, tel. 06/4352-7042, maccasplacevietnam@gmail.com, VND520,000-VND1,200,000) more than makes up for its lack of ocean-front property by providing comfortable, tidy rooms with high ceilings and plenty of light. Bruce, the proprietor, is a genial Australian expat full of local knowledge and always willing to chat about the history and sights in the surrounding area. The rest of the staff at this family-owned guest-house are equally friendly and help give the place a homey feel. Each room comes equipped with a fan and air-conditioning, a television, hot water, and minibar; larger rooms have a balcony. There is a small café downstairs that serves light meals and drinks. Maccas Place rents out motorbikes and is willing to help with travel arrangements for sightseeing around Ba Ria-Vung Tau province.

Overlooking the enormous Martyrs' Memorial roundabout, the decor of the **Kieu Anh Hotel** (257 Le Hong Phong, tel. 06/4356-3333, www.kieuan-hhotel.vn, VND400,000-1,000,000) is nothing special, but its large rooms offer a beautiful view of the monument at the center of the roundabout as well as the manicured grounds. Beds are generously sized and rooms are clean and quiet. Though the hotel seems isolated, the beach is just a short walk down Le Hong Phong street on the other side of the roundabout.

A beautiful building with well-appointed rooms, the **Ocean Star Hotel** (45 Thuy Van, tel. 06/4358-9589, www.oceanstarhotel.vn, VND650,000-1,450,000) is located right in the heart of Back Beach and offers pleasant views of the ocean. The hotel offers great value for money, as its staff are particularly friendly, and each room comes equipped with modern facilities such as a minibar, hot water, air-conditioning, and a large bathroom.

VND1,050,000-2,100,000

For a step above average, the **Ky Hoa Hotel** (30-32 Tran Phu, tel. 06/4385-2579, www.kyhoahotel.com.vn, VND900,000-2,000,000), just beyond the cable car to Big Mountain, boasts large, modern rooms and excellent views of the sea. All rooms feature air-conditioning, hot water, a TV, and large beds, and the hotel has an on-site restaurant and a pool where guests can soak up the sun just opposite the sea. Built into the mountainside, Ky Hoa has plenty of rooms with a view. Superior-level and higher rooms have better views and include a small balcony.

With peaceful, shaded grounds, stunning rooms, and a stellar view of the sea, it's hard to believe that a resort like **Binh An Village** (1 Tran Phu, tel. 06/4351-0016, www.binhanvillage.com, VND2,200,000-5,250,000) exists so close to town. Each spacious room features opulent traditional Vietnamese decor and plush beds along with a sitting area and large bathroom. While the smaller rooms are spacious well beyond your average accommodations, Binh An's larger guest suites include a private garden as well as a separate bathtub and shower. Beyond its lodgings, the resort boasts both freshwater and saltwater swimming pools, with the latter built into the ocean and naturally maintained by the ebb and flow of the sea.

VUNG TAU

INFORMATION AND SERVICES

For medical emergencies, the **International SOS Clinic** (1 Le Ngoc Han, tel. 06/4385-8776, www.internationalsos.com, 8am-5pm Mon.-Fri., 8am-11:30am Sat.) keeps physicians on-site 24 hours a day. The clinic has regular hours for non-emergency medical consultations.

GETTING THERE
Boat
A handful of high-speed boat companies in HCMC offer daily departures from **Nha Rong Wharf** (1 Nguyen Tat Thanh, D4) just over the bridge from District 1, with boats leaving roughly every two hours from 8:30am to 3:30pm. **Greenlines DP** (tel. 09/8800-9579, www.greenlines-dp.com, 8am-5pm daily, VND200,000 adults, VND120,000 children) makes the trip from Saigon to Vung Tau at 9:30am and 11:30am daily, departing for the return trip from Vung Tau at 1pm and 3:30pm. The trip takes about an hour and 20 minutes and drops you at the centrally located **Ferry Terminal** (Tran Phu) in Vung Tau, just a stone's throw from Front Beach.

In most cases, it is possible to show up at the wharf a half-hour or so beforehand and purchase the ticket then, but if you're visiting Vung Tau on a holiday or weekend then it's best to reserve your seat ahead of time, as this is a popular destination for city folks taking a long weekend. Fares sometimes go up on weekends and holidays. If you plan to buy a ticket on the day of departure, check the website to confirm that the time you want is still available.

Bus
From HCMC, tourist buses heading to Vung Tau depart regularly from the Pham Ngu Lao area and the **Eastern bus station (Ben Xe Mien Dong)** (292 Dinh Bo Linh, D Binh Thanh, tel. 08/3899-1607). Several reputable companies make the trip, including **Phuong Trang** (272 De Tham, D1, tel. 1900-6067, www.futabuslines.com.vn, 5am-1am daily, VND95,000) and **Kumho Samco** (239 Pham Ngu Lao, D1, tel. 08/3511-2112, www.kumhosamco.com.vn, 4:30am-7pm daily, VND90,000). The trip takes 2.5-3 hours and buses

arrive at the **Vung Tau bus station** (192 Nam Ky Khoi Nghia, tel. 06/4385-9727), about a mile from both Front and Back Beaches.

The return trip can also be made from the Vung Tau bus station via **Mailinh** (192 Nam Ky Khoi Nghia, tel. 06/4357-6576, hourly 5am-7pm daily, VND95,000) and **Kumho Samco** (192 Nam Ky Khoi Nghia, tel. 06/4361-1111, 4:15am-6pm daily, VND90,000) bus lines, which have on-site offices.

GETTING AROUND

On account of all the tourists that pass through this town, taking a cab in Vung Tau is notably more expensive than in HCMC. If you're in a larger group it may still be cost-effective to hop in a **Mailinh** (tel. 06/4356-5656) or **Petro** (tel. 06/4381-8181) taxi when getting around town; opt for a *xe om* if you're traveling solo or in smaller numbers.

It's necessary to bargain for *xe om* rides in Vung Tau. The town is small, so a ride around town should set you back roughly VND30,000-40,000, though be prepared to pay more if you go farther out of the town center.

Most hotels in town can arrange a motorbike for hire. Prices should range VND100,000-175,000 per day.

Con Dao Islands

Arriving in Con Dao is a surreal experience. After the claustrophobic cities of Vietnam's southern coast, the sight of lush, wild green hills and rocky precipices appear like something out of a postcard. Made up of 16 individual islands, Con Dao is one of the best-guarded secrets in Vietnam, a spectacular combination of white sand beaches, thick forests, and sharp, sun-bleached cliffs plunging into the turquoise sea. With 80 percent of Con Son, the main island, a protected national park, there are dozens of opportunities for the adventurous traveler, from hiking to diving and snorkeling.

fishing boats off Con Dao

Endemic species such as the giant black squirrel and bow-fingered gecko **101** can be found along national park trails alongside monkeys and several species of birds.

Con Dao was once the site of several of the nation's most brutal prisons, built by the French during the colonial era and used all the way through the American War to house political prisoners. These horrific places claimed the lives of roughly 20,000 Vietnamese from 1862 until the late 1970s. A look at the surviving prisoners turns up a veritable who's who of the Communist party. Only a handful of the country's prime ministers since reunification did not see the inside of a Con Dao prison. Though locals also venture here for the stunning natural scenery, a visit to the prison cemetery and the shrine of Vo Thi Sau, the first Vietnamese woman to be executed by the French, is all but required for Vietnamese.

Con Dao's relative isolation from the tourist crowds of the mainland means that some initiative is required on the part of visitors to make their own fun. English speakers on Con Son are few and far between. Locals are friendly, and good humor and a few charades go a long way in communication. As a result of its remoteness, certain costs differ from the mainland. Accommodations tend to be cheaper—though more limited—than you might find elsewhere, but food is usually more expensive. Unless you're willing to fork over an arm and a leg at Six Senses, the island's sole five-star resort, restaurants serve only Vietnamese cuisine. The main town on Con Son is very small. It makes little difference where you stay, and most resorts are located on the coastal road; budget options are set farther back into town.

SIGHTS

With the exception of the prison complex, most of the sights around Con Dao are located within the national park.

Museums

Set amid a large clearing just north of Vo Thi Sau Park, the **Con Dao Museum** (10 Nguyen Hue, tel. 06/4383-0517, 7am-11am and 2pm-5pm Mon.-Sat., free) is a modern take on the islands' older Revolutionary Museum. This museum possesses decent English signage and takes visitors through the history of the islands, from its first European settlers in the early 1500s through the brutal Con Dao prison system and into the present day. While these exhibits encompass all of Con Dao's past, it is the island's penal history that features most heavily within the museum. In-depth displays cover everything from the daily lives of inmates to the facility's development as a revolutionary school and the harsh mistreatment suffered at the hands of Con Dao's prison guards. If you have the time and interest, this location does an admirable job of providing visitors with detailed information on one of the darkest eras in modern Vietnamese history.

The older, more abridged version of Con Dao's prison history resides at the **Revolutionary Museum** (Ton Duc Thang opposite Quay 914, tel.

The Island Prison of Con Dao

Vietnam is eager to cast off the darker days of the 20th century, opting instead to look toward the future. Many of its wartime sites have been transformed into tourist attractions. While there are plenty of past hardships that the nation seems ready to shrug off, Con Dao still weighs heavily upon Vietnam's collective psyche.

In 1862, a few years after the French wrested control from Vietnam's emperors, the colonial government went to great pains to suppress political dissent among the Vietnamese. Outspoken locals were imprisoned on the small island of Con Son, 111 miles away from mainland Vietnam. Up until the end of the American War, inmates were mercilessly beaten, tortured, starved, and worked to death. The French guards were ruthless, enacting cruel and severe punishments. Forced labor built many of the island's roads and structures, including Quay 914, whose name comes from the 914 prisoners who died over the course of its construction. The miserable living conditions and meager rations were so bad that diseases like leprosy spread rapidly, killing some and leaving others permanently disfigured. The Con Dao prisons claimed 20,000 Vietnamese lives.

Though widely regarded as the most terrible of the prison facilities, the island's infamous tiger cages were but one of a wider array of punishments handed down to the Vietnamese, along with solitary confinement units, in which prisoners were forced to exist in ghastly and unsanitary conditions. Built in 1907 to accommodate the offenders of a student uprising, the tiger cages allowed guards to survey their prisoners from above and permitted inmates very little light or space to move. Those who managed to survive these dank, narrow cells often left with debilitating physical injuries, their muscles atrophied from being shackled in the same place for weeks or months at a time.

After the French left, an American-backed south Vietnamese government took over the prison, maintaining the policies of torture and abuse. American officials swore throughout the 1960s and '70s that Con Dao's tiger cages were no longer in use. That is, until 1970, when photographer Tom Harkin and two American congressmen, Representatives Augustus Hawkins and William Anderson, visited the prison on a government-led tour. Armed with a map drawn by a student who had just been released from the tiger cages,

06/4383-0517, 7am-11am and 2pm-5pm Mon.-Sat., VND20,000), where exhibits feature more photos and historical write-ups than actual artifacts. The majority of these images appear at the newer Con Dao Museum as well, so a visit to both venues is unnecessary. If you're looking for a more condensed version of the island's history, this is the place. Entry tickets for this museum are also valid for the prison complex, so hang onto your receipt to show the guides at each respective location.

Con Dao Prison Complex

Perched on the northeastern edge of town, the mossy, crumbling stone exterior of the **Con Dao Prison Complex** (Le Van Viet, tel. 06/4383-0517, 7am-11am and 2pm-5pm Mon.-Sat., VND20,000) serves as a reminder of the island's grim history. From as early as 1862, the cells within these

the Con Dao Prison Complex

the men discovered the prison's entrance, masked by a vegetable garden. Harkin's photos were published in *LIFE* magazine in July 1970 and served as another blow against American involvement in Vietnam.

Con Dao's overcrowded facilities fast became a de facto training school for the opposition. Shackled side-by-side for hours at a time, the prisoners studied Communist theory and, during the American reign, even published several news magazines, with the written materials smuggled out of the prisons, printed, and then returned to the grounds, where they were disseminated among the inmates. Many of the Communist party's most famous players did time at Con Dao. In a country where most streets and public spaces are named after national heroes, nearly all of the island's roadways bear the name of a former prisoner who went on to greatness.

When the American War ended in 1975, word traveled quickly to Con Dao, where frightened prison guards fled at the news, leaving the island to the Communist captives. On May 4, 1975, nearly 7,500 prisoners walked out of their cells, free at last, to greet the arrival of the Vietnamese navy. Today, visiting the prisons is a rite of passage among locals, who come to pay their respects to the collective ancestors who struggled for national independence.

high-walled structures housed Vietnamese political prisoners banished to the island for acting out against the French colonial government. Miles away from the mainland and the general public, guards quickly became known for their harsh treatment and torture of prisoners, which included forced labor, beatings, and starvation. The conditions of the prison's dank cells were equally miserable, with dozens of inmates crammed into dimly lit rooms and often shackled at the ankles, unable to move. As the number of political dissidents grew, so did the number of facilities on Con Dao. At its height, the island contained no less than eight separate facilities, each as cruel and unforgiving as the next.

While it is still possible to visit most of the prisons on the island, the main facilities are Phu Hai and Phu Son, located beside one another on Le Van Viet street, as well as the infamously brutal tiger cages a little farther out of town on Nguyen Van Cu. Phu Hai, Con Dao's original prison, is the largest of these buildings and depicts the harsh living conditions of its former inmates with the help of mannequins, which are shackled in the same place where many prisoners once sat. Next door, Phu Son is similar but holds added notoriety as one of the main centers of Communist training within the prison system. Farther afield, the tiger cages sit eerily empty; guests are free to wander around on their own, treading the catwalk above these dark, isolated cells, just as the prison guards would have done.

Entrance tickets can be purchased at any of the prisons or at the **Revolutionary Museum** (Ton Duc Thang opposite Quay 914, tel. 06/4383-0517, 7am-11am and 2pm-5pm Mon.-Sat., VND20,000) and are valid for all locations so long as you keep the ticket handy to show the gatekeepers. There is little to no signage in most of these places, which is why a visit to either the Revolutionary Museum or the Con Dao Museum is recommended in order to have a better understanding of the history associated with these aging buildings.

Vo Thi Sau Park

The island's most famous revolutionary in a long list of revolutionaries, Vo Thi Sau was just 14 years old when she joined a Communist volunteer police outfit. Despite her youth, the girl became involved in plots to attack and kill French officials, some of which succeeded. In 1950, at 17 years old, Vo Thi Sau was arrested by the French. Due to her age and the harsh public reaction an immediate execution was sure to produce, officials waited until she was 19 before carrying out the young woman's death penalty in 1952. This made Vo Thi Sau the first Vietnamese woman to be executed by the French. Today, she is deeply revered by locals and nearly every Vietnamese visitor to the island pays their respects at her grave. Though the **Vo Thi Sau Park** (in front of Con Dao Museum, Ton Duc Thang and Nguyen Hue) is small and far less ornamental, there is a small building on the grounds dedicated to offerings for the young revolutionary.

Quay 914

At the center of town, a long sandy walkway protrudes out into the harbor just beyond Saigon Con Dao Resort. This is **Quay 914** (intersection of Ton Duc Thang and Le Duan), not an impressive sight but a historical one. During the brutal years of French rule, prisoners were forced to construct this pier, beginning in 1873 and carrying on for decades. When prisoners faltered or refused to continue work they were beaten severely, causing 914 deaths during the pier's construction. Today, the quay still functions as an integral part of the harbor. A small plaque honoring the fallen prisoners stands at the entrance.

Hang Duong Cemetery

Though it wasn't constructed until after reunification, the **Hang Duong Cemetery** (Nguyen An Ninh, tel. 06/4383-0517), just outside of town, serves as a final resting place for many of Con Dao's deceased prisoners. In the same spot where, years before, French and American guards had carelessly disposed of Vietnamese bodies, the manicured grounds of Hang Duong are now a peaceful green space with winding pathways.

A walk up the main road brings you to the cemetery's large martyr's monument, a towering stone structure. Hang Duong's most famous resident resides to the left of the main path. Amid a sea of modest red-and-yellow headstones, the large black tomb of Vo Thi Sau, the first Vietnamese woman to be executed by the French, lies in sharp contrast to the other graves in the area. Its sleek exterior is laden with offerings, from fruit and drinks to flowers, incense, and prayers. Beyond the young revolutionary's resting place, the sight of so many headstones in one area helps to illustrate just how many prisoners succumbed to the harsh conditions on Con Dao.

Con Dao National Park

The largest attraction on Con Son, **Con Dao National Park** (visitors center 29 Vo Thi Sau, tel. 06/4383-0669, www.condaopark.com.vn, 7am-11:30am and 1:30pm-5pm daily, free) is home to approximately 160 species of animals, including three endemic creatures found only on the islands, as well as over a 1,000 marine species. The park boasts hiking trails, snorkeling beaches, camping, and bird-watching excursions. Stop by the visitors center to arrange guides, hire boats, or book tours to the different areas of the park. Make your booking at least a day in advance. Given the temperamental weather of the island and the limited organization of the park offices, guides and tours are subject to sudden changes or cancellations; head to the national park office as soon as you arrive in order to allow enough time for any scheduling hiccups that may occur. At the time of writing, there was no entry fee to the park for hikers. This is expected to change in the near future.

BEACHES

While there are a handful of sandy stretches along the main drag that are largely used by fishermen, the crème de la crème of the island's beaches lie farther afield. Wherever you lay out your towel and catch sun, there is little chance you'll be disappointed: with far fewer people and far less pollution than its mainland counterparts, Con Dao's beaches live up to the hype. Locations range from easily accessible to a few hours' trek. Always bring insect repellent, as the sand flies can be a major detractor from your stay in paradise. If you don't have repellent, swing by the **Dive! Dive! Dive!** shop on Nguyen Hue and ask Larry to set you up.

Dat Doc Beach

Stretching along the southern coast just before you enter town is **Dat Doc Beach**, a beautiful patch of white sand framed by dramatic cliffs and rocky precipices. Hidden from view by a wall of shaggy trees and underbrush, this quiet beach comes in just close enough to make it easily accessible from town but remains far enough away that the harbor is invisible from here, and so you are left with the company of blue skies, turquoise seas, and a glimpse of the ultra-swanky interior of Six Senses, the island's only five-star resort.

Nhat Beach

Rounding out the other end of town, **Nhat Beach** sits just beside Con Son's ferry docks, slightly rocky and more visible from the road but still gifted with the same awe-inspiring views of the sea and the sharp rise and fall of the island's cliffs. This is a beautiful place from which to take in a good island vista, but not the best for swimming on account of its terrain.

Ong Dung Beach

The most easily accessible beach on the northern shore, **Ong Dung Beach** is a 20- to 30-minute hike from the end of Vo Thi Sau street, just past the national park office, and is a popular spot among visitors. Follow the path down to the water, where you can pay the national park entrance fee. From there you are free to swim, snorkel, and enjoy the beach. This particular stretch of water is not ideal for sunbathing, as the sandy area is small. But, it does make for great snorkeling farther out, where an array of colorful sea creatures mill about among the reef. Snorkeling gear can be rented from the national park outpost here; the more adventurous traveler can make a full loop from the thick jungle of So Ray down to the beach and then back around into town on Vo Thi Sau street.

Dam Trau Beach

Popularly known as Airport Beach, **Dam Trau** is the pristine white-sand ribbon you see stretched across the north shore when approaching Con Dao from the sky. Picture-perfect and surrounded by emerald green palm trees, this beach is the ideal oasis for travelers hoping to lay out a towel and catch some rays. Stunning and secluded, Dam Trau is a more peaceful option than Ong Dung—with the exception of a small number of daily plane departures. It has a beautiful area for swimming, though don't bother snorkeling here, as you'll find the fish are few and far between.

SPORTS AND RECREATION
Diving

Though the islands themselves are quiet, Con Dao is known as the best diving spot in Vietnam. Even so, the slow-but-steady trickle of visitors have only managed to keep three diving outfits in business, and with a recent dip in tourists to the island, even those are struggling. All of Con Dao's diving outfits require you to have comprehensive dive insurance before going out, as the islands are remote and any serious medical treatment means an airlift to Saigon. If you don't have insurance purchased beforehand, it is possible to buy coverage on-site. Given the temperamental weather of the

Dive! Dive! Dive! (Nguyen Hue, tel. 06/4383-0701, www.dive-condao.
com, VND970,000-5,660,000) provides both top-notch diving excursions
and sound travel advice. Headed up by American expat Larry and his wife
Quynh, the small PADI-certified shop on Nguyen Hue takes divers out to
some of Vietnam's best spots, including the only dive-able shipwreck in
the country. Snorkeling trips also run from here. Larry and Quynh have
a stack of free tourist maps complete with hiking recommendations for
visitors. The pair also rents out motorbikes and bicycles and are a wealth
of information when it comes to hotels, guesthouses, and restaurants. Due
to the lower volume of tourists on Con Dao, the shop's hours are not set
in stone. You may find Larry and Quynh available at 6am one day and not
until 9am or 10am the next. If you drop by any time from mid-morning to
early evening you will catch someone hanging around.

Hiking

From the center of town there are several hiking trails that you can take
through the national park area that allow for wildlife-spotting and beach
time. Most treks can be done without hiring a guide. Wear decent shoes and
stick to the trails. Hikes to So Ray, where monkeys, birds, and the endemic
black squirrel can be seen, take about 45 minutes and require a moderate
level of fitness, while the trek to Ong Dung Beach is an easy, 20- to 30-min-
ute walk. Farther afield near the airport, a two-hour hike to Dam Tre Bay
is possible, though it is required that you hire a guide for this journey, as
changing tides and weather conditions make it necessary to have a local on
hand. Guides can be hired at the **national park office** (visitors center 29
Vo Thi Sau, tel. 06/4383-0669, www.condaopark.com.vn, 7am-11:30am and
1:30pm-5pm daily) for VND300,000-400,000. Most don't speak English
but are knowledgeable about the terrain and conditions along these routes.

Wildlife-Watching

Turtle- and bird-watching trips can be booked through the national park
office. The best time for bird-watching is in the summer months. It is recommended that you steer clear of Con Dao's turtle-watching excursions, as
there have been reports of animal rights abuses within the park.

FOOD

Con Dao has little in the way of proper eateries, and the only cuisine served
is Vietnamese. There are a cluster of **street food vendors** selling broken
rice, pho, *banh mi* sandwiches, rice porridge, and other cheap local meals
around the intersection of **Ton Duc Thang and Nguyen Hue** streets as
well as near the market. Many of the nicer hotels, including Saigon Con
Dao, have restaurants attached, which you can patronize even if you're
not a guest, and the **local market** (corner of Vo Thi Sau and Tran Phu)

sells fruit and snacks from the wee hours of the morning, though there is a noontime siesta.

With very few restaurants in town and even fewer that offer a decent selection, **Thu Ba Restaurant** (Vo Thi Sau, tel. 06/4383-0255, 10am-10pm daily, VND70,000-350,000) stands out as a more diverse eatery than most. Though the small restaurant serves only Vietnamese fare, its menu goes beyond the standard-but-delicious seafood options that occupy most menus on the island to include pork, beef, chicken, and vegetarian dishes. Servers speak some English and are friendly and easygoing.

At the far end of the Saigon Tourist line of properties, **Hoa Bien Restaurant** (Ton Duc Thang, tel. 06/4383-0155, 6am-10pm daily, VND80,000-400,000) has a nice view of the ocean and decent Vietnamese fare. Seafood features heavily on the menu, but other options are also available. Open-air dining looks out onto the picturesque Con Dao harbor and portions on the family-style menu are generous.

A more diversified option, **Thu Tam** (Nguyen Duc Thuan, tel. 06/4360-8040, nhahangthutam@yahoo.com.vn, 8am-10pm daily, VND50,000-300,000), located directly opposite of Con Dao Seatravel Resort, features a plethora of breakfast, lunch, and dinner items alongside friendly service. The dining room is a large, open-air area where those who opt for seafood dishes are able to choose their meal from a series of small fish tanks lining the far wall. Prices are reasonable and the restaurant is open late.

Directly across from Quay 914 is **Con Son Cafe** (Ton Duc Thang, 7am-11pm daily, VND20,000-50,000). No more than a couple of plastic tables and chairs, this outdoor-only spot offers nice views of the harbor and main coastal drag. While the menu lists items like smoothies and fruit juices, they are not always on offer; be prepared to make second or third choices.

ACCOMMODATIONS

There is a large divide between high-end resorts and dirt-cheap budget hotels on the island. Some accommodations have less-than-stellar business practices and, with so few options available, it's easy to wind up with a bad apple. Larger hotels have information listed online and arrange airport pickup for guests. Smaller, more inexpensive guesthouses tend to have fewer reviews and recommendations, though there are a handful of reliable places in town.

VND210,000-525,000

Just beyond the main coastal road is ★ **An Khanh Mini Hotel** (Nguyen Hue, tel. 06/4390-8089, VND350,000-500,000), a small guesthouse with clean, spacious rooms and high ceilings. Prices vary depending on the number of guests, but two-person lodgings should set you back VND400,000. Each room has Wi-Fi, a fan, air-conditioning, and a TV.

VND525,000-1,050,000

Farther from the beach and closer to the national park office, **Hai An**

Hotel (10 Ho Thanh Tong, tel. 06/4350-8077, haianhotelcondao@gmail. com, VND500,000-800,000) is clean, quiet, and affordable. Rooms are basic, featuring Wi-Fi, TV, air-conditioning, and a fan; the beds are large. The hotel assists with additional travel arrangements, such as tour bookings and ferry tickets.

Clean, if a bit cramped, rooms at the **Red Hotel** (17B Nguyen An Ninh, tel. 06/4363-0079, VND530,000-800,000) feature two twin beds apiece, decent bathrooms, Wi-Fi, cable TV, and plenty of light. Rates vary depending upon the number of people. The hotel staff assist guests with tour arrangements and motorbike hires.

VND1,050,000-2,100,000

Housed in a beautiful, expansive set of colonial-style villas, **Saigon Con Dao** (18-24 Ton Duc Thang, tel. 06/4383-0336, www.saigoncondao.com, VND1,590,000-3,390,000) resort is a property of the mammoth Saigon Tourist company. Featuring a large swimming pool, two restaurants, and a tropical garden, the hotel has rooms that are a little dated but nice and spacious with large bathrooms and, in some cases, a sitting room. Breakfast is included in the room rate, as is airport pickup and drop-off. The hotel offers motorbike rentals, tour information, and flight ticket services.

Beyond the shore-hugging street of Ton Duc Thang, **Con Dao Resort** (8 Nguyen Duc Thuan, tel. 06/4383-0979, www.condaoresort.vn, VND1,500,000-4,200,000) features tasteful rooms with enclosed showers and private balconies as well as a pool, tennis courts, and a pristine private beach that runs along the far edge of the harbor. Breakfast and airport pickup are included in the room rate and the staff speak decent English.

ATC Resort (8 Ton Duc Thang, tel. 06/4383-0456, www.atcresort.com, VND730,000-7,200,000) boasts a friendly and conscientious staff on top of its spacious, well-appointed rooms, which include standard amenities such as air-conditioning, cable TV, Wi-Fi, breakfast, and airport pickup. ATC is located across the street from the harbor beach. There is a private outdoor pool hidden by the surrounding buildings for guests to use. Each room comes with a private balcony with a view of the pool, garden, or sea.

Over VND2,100,000

The island's sole luxury accommodation, **Six Senses Con Dao** (Dat Doc, tel. 06/4383-1222, www.sixsenses.com, VND13,000,000-62,000,000) is a secluded beachfront property whose lavish rooms and exclusivity are second to none. Each split-level villa comes with a private infinity pool and panoramic ocean views as well as high-end amenities, including satellite TV, BOSE sound system, and a butler service. Six Senses also counts a spa, several restaurants, and activity services in its offerings.

INFORMATION AND SERVICES

Though their primary business is as a dive shop, **Dive! Dive! Dive!** (near corner of Nguyen Hue and Ton Duc Thang, tel. 06/4383-0701, www.

dive-condao.com) is the unofficial tourism office of the island. Quynh and Larry are exceptionally friendly, easygoing folks who are happy to offer advice, hotel and restaurant recommendations, and tourist maps free of charge. They are also your go-to spot for sand fly repellent—a necessity if you visit the beach—and can offer safe, reliable motorbikes and bicycles for rent.

There is a **Vietnam Airlines ticketing office** (44A Nguyen Hue, tel. 06/4383-1831, condaobranch@vasco.com.vn, 7:30am-11:30am and 1:30pm-5pm Mon.-Fri.), which helps arrange and confirm flight reservations.

There are two ATMs on the island, a **Techcombank ATM** (corner of Vo Thi Sau and Tran Phu, opposite the market) and one beside **Vietin Bank** (2 Le Duan, tel. 06/4383-0162, www.vietinbank.vn, 7:30am-11:30am and 1:30pm-4:30pm Mon.-Fri., 8am-11am Sat.). These ATMs are prone to malfunction or technical issues, so bring enough cash for your entire stay. Foreign currencies cannot be exchanged on the island; bring Vietnamese dong.

Con Dao's only **hospital** (corner of Le Hong Phong and Pham Van Dong, tel. 06/4383-0128, 7am-11:30am and 1:30pm-5pm daily) is located just north of the town's only roundabout, and facilities are about as rudimentary as they come. The staff do not speak English. While minor injuries and illnesses may be treatable here, anything beyond that will require a trip to the mainland.

GETTING THERE
Air
Despite its growing popularity, Con Dao is still a very difficult place to reach. **Vietnam Airlines** (ticketing office 44A Nguyen Hue, tel. 06/4383-1831, condaobranch@vasco.com.vn, 7:30am-11:30am and 1:30pm-5pm Mon.-Fri.) is the only carrier to serve the small **Con Son Airport** (VCS, Khu Dan Cu 1, Con Dao). Flights run several times a week, with fewer options than you might have for other destinations. Tickets cost VND1,000,000-1,700,000 each way. The flight is 45 minutes and arrives at Con Dao airport, nine miles from town. Most hotels on the island offer airport pickup if you book in advance. You can also jump on several of the hotel minibuses for VND50,000 and they will take you where you want to go. Don't bother with hailing a taxi—a fare from the airport into the center of town runs about VND300,000.

Boat
If you've got a more flexible schedule and don't mind traveling like a local, an overnight ferry (VND250,000) runs from Cat Lo port (973 30 Thang 4) about seven miles north of downtown Vung Tau to Ben Dam port on Con Son, the main island. This option is much cheaper than a plane ticket, but it is unpredictable. Boats do not run on a set schedule and are subject to changes depending on the weather, so it is imperative that you book your ticket in advance and check regularly to ensure that the ferry is still

GETTING AROUND

Since the island is so small, the best way to explore is on two wheels. Hiring
a bicycle or motorbike gives you the freedom to head out on your own and
appreciate the island scenery. Due to the island's size, most roads are easy
to navigate both in and out of the main town. Due to its location, weather
on Con Son is very temperamental and strong gusts can be dangerous when
driving. Especially during the last few months of the year, when Con Dao is
at its windiest, pay special attention on the roads, as accidents do happen.

Taxi

There are a handful of **taxis** (tel. 09/1438-0816) that make their rounds on
the island at a much higher cost than the ones you'd find on the mainland.
Base rates are roughly double what you'd pay elsewhere in Vietnam, starting at VND25,000 just to enter the taxi.

Rentals

Once on the island, the easiest and most cost-effective way to get around
is by hiring a motorbike or bicycle. Most guesthouses rent out either vehicle for a daily fee; check the quality of your bike before setting out on a
long trip.

Con Son has only one **gas station** (corner of Nguyen Hue and Ngo Gia
Tu, 6am-11:30am and 1:30pm-8pm daily). Also beware that driving on
the coastal roads can be a challenge in strong winds, especially if you're
traveling by pedal power. Proceed with caution and always take it easy on
the turns.

Phu Quoc Island

A world apart from the Mekong mainland, Phu Quoc has fast become one
of Vietnam's most sought-after island escapes. Blessed with pristine white-
sand beaches, turquoise waters, shaggy palm trees, and an abundance of
sunshine, the island's postcard-perfect coast sees droves of visitors during
the high season, particularly December and January.

Phu Quoc's shoreline is its main attraction. But beyond the sun and
sand is an island crisscrossed with dozens of winding red dirt roads and
unspoiled landscapes waiting to be discovered. To the north, Phu Quoc's
sprawling national park and deserted coast pack a full day's adventure,
while the pepper farms and freshwater streams of the interior provide
further opportunities for exploration. Avid divers will appreciate the island's underwater scenery. Though some of these untamed areas are sure
to change as more high-end resorts and chic beach bungalows crop up,
for now the island offers an exceptional combination of adventure and

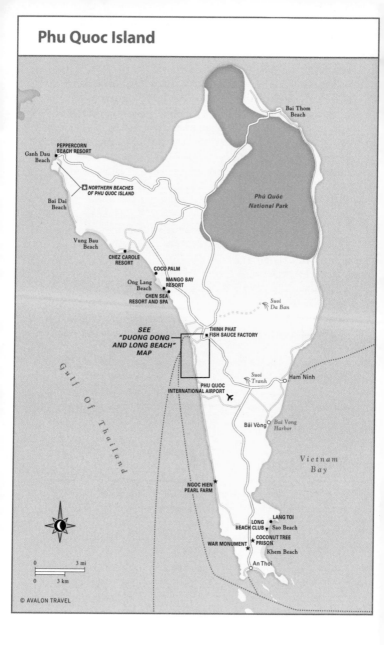

Phu Quoc Island

Bai Thom
Beach

Phú Quốc
National Park

PEPPERCORN
BEACH RESORT

Ganh Dau
Beach

NORTHERN BEACHES
OF PHU QUOC ISLAND

Bai Dai
Beach

Vung Bau
Beach

CHEZ CAROLE
RESORT

COCO PALM

Ong Lang
Beach

MANGO BAY
RESORT

CHEN SEA
RESORT AND SPA

Suối
Da Ban

SEE
"DUONG DONG
AND LONG BEACH"
MAP

THINH PHAT
FISH SAUCE FACTORY

Suối
Tranh

Ham Ninh

PHU QUOC
INTERNATIONAL AIRPORT

Gulf Of Thailand

Bãi Vòng

Bai Vong
Harbor

Vietnam
Bay

NGOC HIEN
PEARL FARM

LANG TOI

LONG
BEACH CLUB

Sao Beach

COCONUT TREE
PRISON

WAR MONUMENT

Khem Beach

An Thới

0   3 mi

0   3 km

© AVALON TRAVEL

relaxation, allowing visitors to enjoy a lazy outing at the beach one day and a backroads adventure along Phu Quoc's dusty, rutted forest trails the next.

Most visitors to Phu Quoc turn up between November and April, outside of the rainy season when temperatures are at their best. Depending upon the extent to which you plan to explore the island, a trip here could last as little as three days or as long as three weeks and chances are you'd still have some discovering left to do. Travelers get the gist of the island in 3-4 days, but many people tack on extra beach time. On account of its growing popularity, you'll find that Phu Quoc's prices—from food to accommodations to basic services—are more expensive than those on the mainland. These costs are easily split between two or more people; solo travelers might find themselves shelling out more, as the island tends to be a destination that sees more couples and families than individual visitors.

ORIENTATION

The majority of Phu Quoc's accommodations, restaurants, and other services are located along the western side of the island near the main town of **Duong Dong. Long Beach,** where most travelers base themselves, sits just south of Duong Dong on the western coast. There are smaller settlements in **An Thoi** on the southern tip of the island and east at Ham Ninh, a village near Bai Vong Harbor, where speedboats from Rach Gia and Ha Tien arrive. Most areas beyond Duong Dong and Long Beach have little in the way of services and amenities, except for resorts.

SIGHTS

There is plenty to see in Phu Quoc beyond the beach, from the historical Phu Quoc prison near Ham Ninh town to the local fish sauce factories or the freshwater streams hidden deep within the island's interior. If you're comfortable behind the wheel, the best way to explore the island is by grabbing a map, renting a motorbike, and setting out on your own, as this gives

beach on Phu Quoc Island

The Dogs of Phu Quoc

a Phu Quoc ridgeback

As you make your way around the island you'll spot dogs trotting along the roadside or napping in the midday heat. This isn't particularly unusual for Vietnam, but take a closer look and you may notice that some of these animals have a long, spiked ridge of hair running along their backs. The Phu Quoc ridgeback (*cho xoay* in Vietnamese) is one of only three species of dog in the world that has this backward-running ridge, not unlike a cowlick. Though its history isn't terribly well-documented—some say the dogs were brought to the island by the French, while others believe that the Phu Quoc Ridgeback is actually an offshoot of the Thai Ridgeback—these canines have a local reputation for being intelligent and affable and they make excellent hunters.

you the freedom to move around and discover all the island's narrow dirt paths. However, if you're not yet a master of the motorbike then you may feel more at ease in the passenger's seat, as Phu Quoc's roads are constantly under construction. A handful of local tour companies provide trips to some of these places, but you may also be able to track down a local guide or *xe om* driver through your hotel who can take you around the island.

Duong Dong
DINH CAU

Perched on the edge of the harbor, **Dinh Cau** (end of Bach Dang street, 6am-9pm daily) is a small temple dedicated to the protection of all those who travel by sea. Its colorful red-and-gold doorway has looked out over the mouth of the town's narrow, meandering river since 1937 and sits just beside a miniature blue-and-white lighthouse. In the late afternoons, this is a popular gathering spot for locals and it offers a nice view of the northern end of Long Beach.

Duong Dong and Long Beach

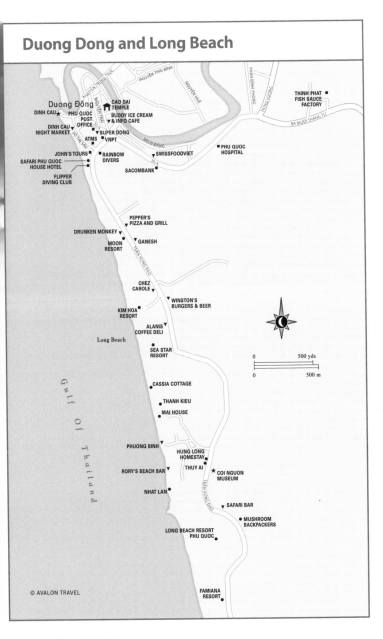

CAO DAI TEMPLE

In case you missed Tay Ninh's Holy See or some of the other mainland branches, Phu Quoc's very own **Cao Dai Temple** (near corner of Nguyen Trai and Nguyen An Ninh, 6am-6pm daily) bears the same architecture as its other Delta counterparts, emphasizing yin and yang in its symmetrical design. Inside, the signature blue-and-white swirls of cloud and all-seeing eye emblems fill up the main hall.

FISH SAUCE FACTORIES

Something of an unusual attraction, the **Thinh Phat Fish Sauce Factory** (30 Thang 4, tel. 07/7398-0224, www.nuocmamthinhphat.com, 7am-7pm daily) and most other producers on the island are eager to share with Phu Quoc's visitors the finer details of the nation's favorite condiment: fish sauce. If you've eaten any local cuisine, chances are you've tasted this salty, reddish sauce, which is used in preparing everything from soups to noodle dishes to meat and veggies. On the island, fish sauce is something of a specialty. Each individual batch is unique in both strength and color. Heaps of anchovies are mixed with salt, piled into enormous wooden barrels that reach nearly as high as the ceiling, and left to sit for at least one year before the oily red sauce is dispensed from a tap at the bottom of the barrel, then bottled and sold. Though some batches can sit for longer, no less than 12 months is required, and each gargantuan container produces 3,000 liters of fish sauce. If you pay a visit to any of the island's countless factories, you'll be allowed to look around and possibly even sample their product, however it may be difficult to ask questions, as factory employees rarely speak English. Whatever happens, one thing you'll remember is the smell. Thankfully, fish sauce tastes infinitely better than it smells.

SUOI TRANH

About six miles from Duong Dong town en route to Ham Ninh and Sao Beach, the freshwater stream at **Suoi Tranh (Khu Du Lich Suoi Tranh)** (Suoi May Hamlet, no phone, 7am-5pm daily, VND3,000) runs during the rainy months from May to November. Hidden amid the lush cover of the forest, many tourists visit Suoi Tranh's rushing waters to take in the area's charming natural scenery and have a picnic or a swim. There is also **Suoi Da Ban** (Ap Ben Tram, no phone, 7am-5pm daily), another stream located farther into the island's interior. Suoi Tranh is the more scenic and more accessible of the two.

Long Beach
COI NGUON MUSEUM

The first privately owned museum in the Mekong Delta, the **Coi Nguon Museum** (149 Tran Hung Dao, tel. 07/7398-0206, www.coinguonphuquoc. com, 7am-9pm daily, VND20,000) is not unlike most provincial museums, featuring exhibits on the geography, history, and revolutionary activities of the island, but it restricts its scope solely to Phu Quoc. In an unusual building chock full of small alcoves and religious shrines, the five-story exhibition hall includes English signage and an interesting collection of Oc Eo artifacts, natural souvenirs from the surrounding waters, and also a few displays dedicated to Phu Quoc's most famous visitors, including Mac Cuu, considered a major player in the island's development, and Nguyen Trung Truc, a revolutionary hero who was captured in the island's eastern town of Ham Ninh in 1868. From its many balconies Coi Nguon offers a nice view of Long Beach and the main drag along Tran Hung Dao.

Up a stone path behind the museum, a sanctuary houses several very large, very noisy sea birds. Though the sanctuary could use a facelift, the birds are worth a look, if only to pass the driftwood sculpture carved into a fire-breathing dragon on the way up.

PEARL FARMS

On the road from Long Beach south to An Thoi are a string of massive jewelry companies that harvest local pearls. While some bill these mega-centers as a tourist attraction, they are, for the most part, reserved for serious shoppers only. Long, unending showrooms of pearls are tended to by eager sales assistants. A few times a day, someone will cut open an oyster from the small pool out front to show tourists how the pearls are collected. Many day tours make a stop at one of these places for a brief show and then leave ample time for shopping. There are several pearl farms stretched along the southern end of Long Beach, including **Ngoc Hien** (Duong Bao Hamlet en route to An Thoi, tel. 07/7398-8999, www.ngochienpearl.com, 8am-5pm daily), which has a showroom full of both high- and low-quality local pearls. Do your homework when purchasing jewelry on the island, as there are plenty of legitimate pearl companies but also several impostors.

An Thoi
COCONUT TREE PRISON

Hidden near the southern tip of the island, Phu Quoc's infamous **Coconut Tree Prison (Di Tich Lich Su Nha Tu Phu Quoc)** (tel. 07/7384-4578, 7:30am-11am and 1pm-5pm daily) is a faded, unassuming collection of iron stockades that is easily missed when following the road to Sao Beach. During

a pearl showroom in Long Beach

the American War, this crumbling, shadeless complex claimed the lives of nearly 4,000 prisoners, as Communist supporters and prisoners of war were exiled to the confines of its high barbed-wire gates and subjected to harsh conditions, starvation, and torture.

Though the prison had existed as early as the 1950s, its worst horrors came to pass between 1967 and 1973, during which time more than 40,000 men and women suffered the brutality of south Vietnamese soldiers. A variety of punishments were used. The worst of the bunch were the prison's tiger cages: low barbed-wire pens used to confine as many as five people in one small space near the main entrance of the prison. Left outdoors with no food or shelter and crammed into an area barely large enough to squat, inmates in the tiger cages often succumbed to the heat and dehydration and were unable to properly stand, sit, or lie down. Those who survived often remained permanently handicapped, unable to walk after extended periods of confinement.

Despite—or perhaps because of—this ruthless treatment, the cramped quarters of Phu Quoc Prison became a training ground for revolutionaries, and several jailbreaks occurred over the course of the prison's worst years. Inside the corrugated iron stockades, jailers covered the original dirt floors with tile in an effort to prevent further escapes, but a handful of detainees still succeeded in fleeing the prison and making it back to the island's revolutionary base.

Today, visitors to the complex roam the enclosed area dotted with low stockade buildings, where several eerily lifelike displays depict the harsh realities of the prison. Plenty of English signage helps travelers navigate each exhibit, and there is a small gallery of photographs and artifacts housed in the aged colonial building beside the prison grounds, which features some graphic evidence of the south Vietnamese army's brutality. Many visitors to the Coconut Tree Prison combine this sight with a stop at Sao Beach. You can also visit the sky-blue **War Monument** just down the road opposite the prison.

AN THOI ISLANDS

A trail of rocky islands scattered off the southern point of Phu Quoc, the **An Thoi Islands** are most often visited on snorkeling or diving trips, as the area is known for its colorful underwater scenery and wildlife-watching. Check with local diving outfits or tour providers about visiting the area. Trips to the islands are usually a day-long affair from Long Beach, with boats casting off from An Thoi Harbor and dropping anchor just offshore to explore the nearby reefs.

BEACHES
Long Beach

Long Beach is the island's most popular stretch of sand. Most of Long Beach has been chopped up by individual resorts and other businesses, but there are still a few bits and pieces left for the budget traveler, and it is walkable from any of the accommodations along Tran Hung Dao. Thanks to its location, Long Beach has dozens of bars and restaurants right on the shoreline, making it easy to grab a quick bite or a seaside drink. Though prices are steeper here, it's worth it to buy a drink if only for the beach chairs offered. There are also plenty of women advertising beach-side spa and massage services at low prices.

Sao Beach

Tucked in a shallow cove on the southeastern coast, **Sao Beach (Bai Sao)** has earned enough attention from travelers to house a handful of seaside restaurants and basic services. About a half-hour from Duong Dong town over dirt tracks and partially paved roads, development in the area has been rather slow, but this contributes to Sao Beach's atmosphere of peace and quiet.

Most people visit the beach park at the inaccurately named **Long Beach Club** (Hamlet 4, An Thoi, tel. 07/7399-7789, www.longbeachvn.com, 7am-10pm daily), a tourist complex that rents out lounge chairs and other beach-going equipment in addition to housing a restaurant and small souvenir shop, though this is the most expensive of the beach-side businesses.

A quick wander down the shore brings you to **Lang Toi** (Bai Sao, tel. 07/7397-2123, langtoi_restaurant@yahoo.com.vn, 8am-8pm daily), a restaurant and guesthouse combo where the beach chairs are free for paying customers and prices are more reasonable. The folks at Lang Toi also rent out four guest rooms (VND630,000-1,029,000). Rooms are fan-only and minimal (no more than a bathroom, bed, and bug net), but accommodations are comfortable and include a massive bathtub as well as a balcony. You will almost certainly be bound to the place for breakfast, lunch, and dinner, as it is the only restaurant around for miles.

Day-trippers can try to access the nearby **Khem Beach,** just south of Sao Beach, however it does take some work and is occasionally closed, courtesy of the military. If you're looking for more beautiful, deserted beaches, head up north.

★ Northern Beaches

While Sao Beach is hailed as one of the most beautiful spots on the island and Long Beach is equipped with everything you could ever need, Phu Quoc's northern beaches give both spots a run for their money. The more tranquil sands of the northwest are as idyllic as can be, though time will surely change this. Indeed, resorts are beginning to take hold along the coast all the way up to Ganh Dau port. For now, the ravishing shores of the island's north are peaceful, picturesque, and accessible to anyone with a motorbike. Navigating Phu Quoc's northern roads can be tricky, as most of them are still red dirt tracks and you'll be lucky to find a street sign of any kind north of Duong Dong. It's best to bring a map and remain patient, as you're likely to get lost a few times before reaching your destination.

ONG LANG BEACH

Not far from town, **Ong Lang Beach** is a quiet stretch of sand that is beginning to see more private resorts. Though its ocean-side real estate is hemmed in by a sea wall, the grassy field around the beach turns this area into something of a park where regular weekend visitors turn up for picnics and fresh air. The end of a narrow, rutted path leads onto the beach's public access area, where visitors can park and walk farther along the sand. Though you won't find any snack or drink vendors, the restaurant at **Coco Palm Resort** is open to non-guests. There's plenty of space for visitors to camp out in the public area of Ong Lang as well.

VUNG BAU BEACH

A small cove protected by Fingernail Cape, **Vung Bau Beach** is one of the most isolated stretches of sand on the island. There is nothing here but for an endless expanse of white sand and turquoise seas. You'll catch a glimpse of passing fishermen or the odd motorbike. Most visitors simply appreciate the emptiness of the area. With complete seclusion comes a lack of services; you won't find many restaurants or drink shops, so come prepared.

BAI DAI

Looking out over the vast cerulean waters of the Gulf of Thailand, **Bai Dai** is Phu Quoc's northern answer to Long Beach and far less populated than its southern counterpart. Stretching over nine miles along the western edge of the island, Bai Dai's breezy, sun-bleached shores see only a handful of visitors who are willing to navigate the rugged dirt track that runs along the coast. As a result, this area is pleasantly devoid of vendors or massive resorts, instead affording visitors ample space to stretch out and enjoy the view. While Bai Dai is equally off the beaten path as Vung Bau, its neighbor to the south, there are a few small snack and drink shops here that cater to visitors, offering a little more ease for travelers who have trekked all the way here.

Ong Lang Beach

Perched on the northwestern edge of Phu Quoc and extending towards Cambodian shores, **Ganh Dau** is a small corner of the island still untouched by locals and resort developers, though that is sure to change with time. From this stunning, pristine white-sand beach, you can see across the border to the southern coast of Cambodia. As one of the most remote parts of the island, the dusty paths that lead into Ganh Dau tend to weed out all but the serious beach-goers. Getting to this area takes effort; so if you head this far north, make a day of it and your efforts will be duly rewarded.

A handful of burgeoning mini-resorts and restaurants are around for food and drink. One of the nicer spots is **Peppercorn Beach** (Ganh Dau, tel. 07/7398-9567, www.peppercornbeach.com, 10am-9pm daily, VND50,000-250,000), a resort that offers drinks and food as well as brand-new beachfront bungalow accommodations (from VND2,940,000). Rooms are basic, and electricity on more remote parts of the island tends to cut out. If you're looking to get away from it all, this is the place to go.

BAI THOM

One of the most remote beaches on the island, **Bai Thom** hides on the northeastern edge of Phu Quoc just beyond the boundaries of the national park. Thanks to its location, this area sees few visitors; the small amount of usable coastline and a rubbish problem may account for this, too. While the trip itself is a fun jaunt through the island's less-charted interior territory and a nice, newly paved road makes access to Bai Thom far easier than places like Sao Beach and Bai Dai, Bai Thom is the kind of place to visit for a quick drink, a rest in the hammock, and a look at the waves rolling into shore. It's a nice spot to incorporate on a loop around the northern half of Phu Quoc and the drive offers a brief respite from the bumpy, rocky dirt paths that line most of the rest of the island's north.

TOURS

With no provincial tourism office on the island, homegrown tour providers are springing up by the day. Trips to the southern An Thoi islands are popular, whether for fishing, snorkeling, or sightseeing, and often include a quick stop at a pearl farm. In most cases, your hotel will be able to recommend a particular company or book a tour through their own outfit. Ask the specifics of these tours first—from the itinerary to the number of people who will be joining you—as several different outfits band together and send their customers on the same mass ventures around the island.

Easily the largest and most well-represented company on the island is **John's Tours** (143 Tran Hung Dao, tel. 07/7399-0111, www.johnsislandtours. com, 8am-5pm daily), which offers affordable large-group excursions and is often featured in hotels and guesthouses across the island. These tours don't allow for much down time and visit very popular tourist spots. Other operators, such as **Jerry's Jungle & Beach Tours** (106 Tran Hung Dao, tel. 09/3822-6021, http://jerrystours.wix.com/jerrystours), arrange personalized

PHU QUOC ISLAND

trips around the island and run overland tours to snorkeling destinations as well as to the more uncharted parts of the island on the back of a motorbike.

NIGHTLIFE

As a destination that caters mostly to couples and families, there isn't much in the way of nightlife on Phu Quoc, however a handful of laid-back beach hangouts and bars advertising European sports channels exist along Tran Hung Dao. In truth, most restaurants and other businesses close their doors by 10pm or 11pm, but anyone who's out later than that can still find a place to relax, as bars stay open until the last patrons go home.

The only spot on the waterfront open late, **Rory's Beach Bar** (118/10 Tran Hung Dao, tel. 09/1933-3250, 9am-late daily, VND30,000-100,000) is an easygoing place that serves food during the day and rents out paddleboards before carrying on with its festivities at night. Up on deck, a long wraparound bar serves beer and cocktails as well as other beverages and still leaves some room for a dance floor. Down in the sand, low tables and chairs are lit by colorful overhead lanterns. The amiable and outgoing Rory is always around for a chat, too, and DJs are regularly featured here.

Farther down the Long Beach road, **Safari Bar** (167 Tran Hung Dao, tel. 09/0522-4600, 5:30pm-late daily, VND25,000-200,000) is home to a pool table and a nightly selection of beers and cocktails. Like most spots on the island, this is a fairly laid-back joint, with a patio area and rows of red lanterns hanging from the ceiling. The owner likes chatting and offering travel information and recommendations to patrons.

The sign above the bar at **Drunken Monkey** (82 Tran Hung Dao, tel. 09/0925-9605, 5pm-late daily, VND25,000-110,000) says it all: "Monkey to man: 1 million years. Man to monkey: 10 beers." Along with sports TV, a pool table, and several other cheeky slogans, the friendly bartenders at this roadside watering hole prepare a variety of cocktails and also serve beer. Grab a seat at the bar, at one of the cocktail tables around the interior, or out front on the patio.

SPORTS AND RECREATION
Snorkeling and Diving

In the years before divers caught wind of Con Dao, Phu Quoc was known as home to the best underwater scenery in Vietnam and, by some accounts, still holds that title. The ample reef surrounding the southern An Thois and a handful of smaller northern islands make them prime spots for snorkeling and diving, though the reef has taken a hit in recent years due to the high number of tourists visiting the island. Several outfits run day trips to each of these locations a few times a week, with the southern An Thois being the best of the bunch.

If you're interested in snorkeling and don't mind spending more cash, opt for a trip through one of the dive shops, as they are guaranteed to have less people on board as well as high-quality equipment, and the amount of time you spend in the water will be far greater than it is on cheaper excursions.

The longest-running PADI-certified dive center in the country, **Rainbow Divers** (11 Tran Hung Dao, tel. 09/1340-0964, www.divevietnam.com, 8am-9pm daily, VND630,000-2,800,000) is far and away the island's best-known brand. Like most outfits, Rainbow alternates day trips to the northern and southern islands of Phu Quoc each week, as well as offering night dives, snorkeling, and full-fledged diving certification for first-timers. All gear is included in the company's fees, and additional rental gear (such as Go Pros and other underwater gadgets) can be rented from the shop.

One of the fastest-growing outfits on the island, **Flipper Diving Club** (60 Tran Hung Dao, tel. 09/3940-2872, www.flipperdiving.com, 8am-9pm daily, VND675,000-3,375,000) is also PADI-certified and organizes trips to both the northern islands and the An Thoi area. A variety of supplementary PADI courses are available.

Massages and Spas

Many of the island's resorts offer massage and other spa treatments in-house, though these are often expensive. For budget travelers, local masseuses set up shop on Long Beach, offering cheap spa services. There are one or two independent outfits on the waterfront that operate out of a proper shop, but these seem to provide a level of service that doesn't match the higher price.

FOOD

When it comes to dining on the island, Phu Quoc offers a much wider variety of cuisines than most destinations in the Mekong Delta. All along Tran Hung Dao, you'll find dozens of restaurants offering European and Asian dishes. These eateries are more expensive than their mainland counterparts, but their variety and the quality of the food usually make up for this increase. The cheapest option is local fare, with the Dinh Cau Night Market being a popular spot to enjoy delicious local cuisine and fresh seafood. Thanks to the island's many foreign visitors, travelers will find plenty of vegetarian options available.

Cafés and Bakeries

The quiet, air-conditioned paradise at **Alanis Coffee Deli** (98 Tran Hung Dao, tel. 07/7399-4931, alanis.deli@yahoo.com, 8am-9pm daily, VND20,000-140,000) is home to Phu Quoc's best pancakes as well as a variety of European coffee, sandwiches, and other Western breakfast options. Add to that a solid Wi-Fi connection and friendly service and the place is a hit.

International

Located right on the main drag, with a narrow storefront that opens onto a long, well-lit dining area, **Ganesh** (97 Tran Hung Dao, tel. 07/7399-4917, www.ganeshphuquoc.com, 10am-10pm daily, VND70,000-160,000) is the island's one and only Indian restaurant. Owned by the same folks responsible for Ganesh eateries in Saigon, Nha Trang, and other Vietnamese cities, the food here is just as good as any of their locations.

Formerly known as Mermaid's Dive Bar and several other incarnations, **Winston's Burgers & Beer** (121/1 Tran Hung Dao, tel. 012/6390-1093, 11am-11pm daily, VND155,000-385,000) serves a short but creative list of burger combinations. Its fixings include blue cheese and bacon, avocado, pineapple, and ham. The friendly owner is always around for a quick hello or a chat, giving the place a pleasant, laid-back feel. With tasty food and superb service, there's a strong chance that Winston's will become a popular name among travelers.

Pepper's Pizza and Grill (89 Tran Hung Dao, tel. 07/7384-8773, 10am-10pm daily, VND75,000-255,000) does a fair turn in pizza, pasta, and, inexplicably, German sausage. Its elevated open-front dining area looks out onto the traffic of Tran Hung Dao, a less scenic view than the ocean. The staff are friendly and the restaurant also does delivery.

Claiming the best burgers in town, **Swissfoodviet** (81 30 Thang 4, tel. 07/7399-4941, 8am-10pm daily, VND35,000-270,000) is a small shop in Duong Dong town that is giving some of the other more conveniently located Western eateries a run for their money. Serving breakfast, sandwiches, *rosti,* and even a cheese fondue in addition to its burgers, the modest restaurant may not appear to be much from the outside, but its mouthwatering meals prove your first impressions wrong.

One of Long Beach's more upmarket restaurants, the Duong Dong extension of **Chez Carole** (127C Tran Hung Dao, tel. 07/7384-8884, www.chezcarole.com.vn, 10am-midnight daily, VND80,000-320,000) is a garden restaurant with plenty of palm trees and a peaceful setting. During dinner hours, a large wooden cart laden with the catch of the day greets visitors at the entrance, while the Filipino band keeps diners entertained from 7:30pm to 11pm. Chez Carole's menu features a variety of both Western and Vietnamese dishes, counting seafood among its specialties.

Vietnamese

One of the most affordable options by far is the **Dinh Cau Night Market** (near Dinh Cau, 6pm-11pm daily), a bustling open-air affair where vendors roll out cartloads of fresh seafood—some of it still swimming—and diners are able to select their meal. With everything from fish and squid to prawns as big as your head, the market features mostly seafood but also offers a handful of other choices.

From morning to night, the beachside restaurant at **Phuong Binh** (Alley 118 Tran Hung Dao, tel. 07/7399-4101, www.phuongbinhhouse.com, 7:30am-10:30pm daily, VND30,000-150,000) offers a menu of mostly Vietnamese dishes with a few Western options and sees a steady crowd throughout the day. It's located beside the public beach entrance off Alley 118 and is one of the more affordable spots right on the water.

ACCOMMODATIONS

Like most other services on Phu Quoc, you'll find that accommodations here are notably more expensive than the mainland. While several smaller dorms and other budget lodgings are available, local developers recognize Phu Quoc's immense potential as a tourism destination, and so there is no doubt that prices will continue to climb. Most resorts are already charging upwards of VND1,000,000 a night for a spot on Long Beach. High season on the island falls around December and January. These months invariably bring higher rates and booked-up rooms, so reserve your place early and allot extra cash.

While there are dozens of beautiful, tranquil beach resorts stretched along the western side of the island, Phu Quoc is very much in its early stages of development. As the area continues to grow, construction is a constant along Long Beach and up to Cua Can. For light sleepers and late-risers, check with your hotel or resort before booking whether or not there is construction going on nearby, as workers begin around the same time the sun comes up. Electricity on the island is not always a given. Power outages are common during the day and, while higher-end resorts have a back-up generator on hand, budget hotels may be without electricity for a few daylight hours.

Resorts are scattered across the island, not only on Long Beach but as far away as Ganh Dau and Sao Beach. For budget travelers, Long Beach is without a doubt the place to go, as this is where you'll find a wider range of accommodations. The coast along Ong Lang Beach and up to Cua Can is filled with smaller boutique resorts that are more expensive but also live up to their added value. Travelers can base themselves in more remote locations, too, however escaping the relative bustle of Long Beach means that you will most likely be bound to whichever resort you choose, as even places in Cua Can are far enough removed from town that the on-site restaurant often becomes your only option.

Duong Dong
OVER VND2,100,000

The rustic rooms at **Coco Palm Resort** (Ong Lang, tel. 07/7398-7979, VND1,200,000-2,500,000) are simple but offer a quiet, scenic location right on Ong Lang Beach. A collection of bungalows frame the resort's pleasant garden area and you'll find air-conditioning, hot water, and a refrigerator in each room. Coco Palm's seaside restaurant serves complimentary breakfast daily as well as other meals and the peaceful, secluded beach is steps away.

Chez Carole (Hamlet 4, Cua Can, tel. 07/7653-4679, www.chezcarole. com.vn, VND1,580,000-2,260,000, breakfast included) is an out-of-the-way boutique resort boasting a private beach and ocean-side pool. Each bungalow features rustic decor, bathrooms with stone bathtubs, and a private sun terrace with views of unspoiled scenery. Snorkeling tours, Jet ski rentals, and kayaking can be arranged through the resort. The on-site restaurant and bar is open to non-guests. Chez Carole has an additional restaurant near Duong Dong town on Long Beach that features fresh seafood and nightly live music.

One of Ong Lang's most posh and exclusive accommodations, **Chen**

Sea Resort and Spa (Bai Xep, Ong Lang, tel. 07/7399-5895, www.chensearesortandspa.com, VND10,200,000-24,000,000) is a sprawling, all-inclusive retreat nestled in a beautiful natural cove. Its sloping grounds boast private beach access, an infinity swimming pool, a restaurant, and a bar. Each spacious villa is constructed in the style of a traditional Vietnamese house but features modern touches such as flat-screen TVs, DVD players, an in-room safe, and a minibar. Depending upon your accommodations, a private pool or whirlpool tub is also included, as well as a terrace overlooking the sweeping white-sand coastline. Water activities, such as kayaking, sailing, and windsurfing, are available, as are massage and spa services, a tennis court, and an open-air exercise area.

Bordered by lush wilderness and crystalline ocean, charming **Mango Bay Resort** (Ong Lang Beach, tel. 07/7398-1693, www.mangobayphuquoc.com, VND3,900,000-11,000,000, breakfast included) is an eco-friendly resort that emphasizes conservation and low-impact tourism. The thatched-roof bungalows feature fans and mosquito nets rather than air-conditioning. All rooms come with sturdy four-poster beds, an electricity-free icebox, and Wi-Fi. The resort's on-site restaurant serves appetizing fare throughout the day. Activities like snorkeling, kayaking, and tours around the island are available.

Long Beach
UNDER VND210,000

Though it's a bit farther along Tran Hung Dao, backpackers looking for a budget bed will appreciate **Mushroom Backpackers** (Tran Hung Dao, tel. 09/3794-2017, www.mushroomsphuquoc.com, VND136,000-273,000). With a large communal area and a constant flow of travelers hoping to do Phu Quoc on the cheap, this place draws a younger, livelier crowd and offers dirt-cheap, fan-only dorm accommodations, complete with individual lockers, Wi-Fi, and shared bathrooms. The staff are easygoing, and someone is always hanging around the garden out front.

VND210,000-525,000

Sitting in a nice central location along Long Beach not far from town, **A74 Guesthouse** (74 Tran Hung Dao, tel. 07/7398-2772, a74hotelphuquoc@gmail.com, VND300,000-600,000) offers decent rooms and good value. All accommodations come with air-conditioning, hot water, a television, and a minibar. Staff are notably helpful with arranging motorbike rentals, tours, and transportation around the island.

Though there are only three rooms available, the owners at **Hung Long Homestay** (147B Tran Hung Dao, tel. 07/7652-4468, VND380,000-600,000) go to great pains to make their guests feel welcome. Rooms are basic but clean and include Wi-Fi, TV, hot water, and air-conditioning, all of which is solar-powered, a fact that allows electricity to run throughout the day—something that most other budget accommodations can't offer with the regular daytime power cuts on Phu Quoc in order to conserve

energy. The family runs a restaurant at the front of the building, serving **127**
decent local meals.

Right next door to Hung Long is the **Phu Quoc An Guesthouse** (122
Tran Hung Dao, tel. 07/7247-8555, VND340,000-460,000), another excellent budget option that offers your choice of fan or air-conditioning as well
as TV, hot water, and Wi-Fi access. The guesthouse rents out motorbikes
to guests and is just a short walk from Alley 118, which has public access
to Long Beach.

VND525,000-1,050,000

Moon Resort (82 Tran Hung Dao, tel. 07/7399-4520, www.moonresort.
vn, VND560,000-1,200,000) is a series of bungalows dotting a stone path
to Long Beach. These are a decent value for the location. Rooms are basic
but include hot water and your choice of fan or air-conditioning. A small
restaurant and bar are set up right on the beach. Opt for the cheaper garden view rooms, as the beachside rooms can be up to double the price and
don't provide much extra.

The bungalows at **Nhat Lan Resort** (118/16 Tran Hung Dao, tel. 07/7384-
7663, nhanghinhatlan@yahoo.com, VND900,000-VND1,700,000) may not
be out of this world, but their beachfront location makes up for the wear
and tear on the rooms. Accommodations are basic but clean and include
both fan and air-conditioning options, as well as your choice of garden or
beach view. Nhat Lan counts a restaurant and bar in its services, and staff
can assist guests with travel arrangements.

VND1,050,000-2,100,000

The ocean views from the top floor of the **Kim Hoa Resort** (88/2 Tran Hung
Dao, tel. 07/7384-8969, www.kimhoaresort.com, VND1,125,000-2,500,000)
would make for a good reason never to leave your room. This ocean-side
property boasts private beach access, a restaurant, and a swimming pool
in addition to a variety of room options, from standard hotel rooms to
beach and garden bungalows (from VND1,470,000 a night). All accommodations include air-conditioning, television, Wi-Fi access, hot water, a
minibar, and complimentary breakfast. The resort arranges tours around
the island through their own outfit and offers airport pick-up upon request.

One of the best value accommodations on Long Beach, **Thanh Kieu
Resort** (100C/14 Tran Hung Dao, tel. 07/7384-8394, www.thanhkieuresort.
com, VND1,805,000-2,370,000) is a collection of pleasant thatched-roof
beach-side bungalows. Featuring a fridge, an in-room safe, mosquito net,
and a fan, the place is more rustic than some of its Long Beach counterparts, but the private terraces and excellent sea views more than make up
for this. Breakfast is included in the room rate, and staff can assist guests
with renting vehicles or booking tours to explore the island.

Near the north end of Tran Hung Dao not far from Duong Dong town,
the **Safari Phu Quoc House Hotel** (40 Tran Hung Dao, tel. 07/7399-9797,
www.thesafari.com.vn, VND1,160,000-4,200,000) is a lovely little boutique

hotel with pleasant views of Long Beach and the ocean. Decked out in an eco-chic decor, rooms at the Safari Phu Quoc feature tiled floors and wood accents as well as balconies in some accommodations. Television, air-conditioning, hot water, Wi-Fi, and a fridge are all standard amenities, and breakfast is included in the room rate. The hotel staff are a friendly, outgoing bunch who offer free travel advice. There is a café and bar downstairs.

One of the island's more popular accommodations, **Sea Star Resort** (98/2 Tran Hung Dao, tel. 07/7398-2161, www.seastarresort.com, VND1,200,000-2,000,000) offers resort-level accommodations at affordable prices. Private bungalows and double rooms are simple yet sophisticated in their decor and the staff assists with airport pick-up as well as arranging day trips around the island. Sea Star has its own stretch of Long Beach, complete with lounge chairs as well as a restaurant on-site. Book ahead as rooms fill up fast.

OVER VND2,100,000

The wide-open grounds of **Mai House** (112/7/8 Tran Hung Dao, tel. 07/7384-7003, www.maihousephuquoc.com, VND2,300,000-2,852,000) offer a pleasant break from the close quarters that make up most Vietnamese accommodations. Set around the perimeter of a grassy lawn peppered with palm trees, these plush beach bungalows are minimally furnished but have generous bathrooms, comfy beds, and modern decor. Amenities include hot water, air-conditioning, Wi-Fi access, tea- and coffee-making facilities, and in-room safety deposit boxes, as well as complimentary breakfast. Staff assist with motorbike rentals or in arranging tours around the island. Guests have easy access to Mai House's private beach.

Though its rates are higher than some, the exceptional service and top-notch accommodations at ★ **Cassia Cottage** (Tran Hung Dao, tel. 07/7384-8395, www.cassiacottage.com, VND4,500,000-9,200,000) are well worth the additional investment. From its stunning garden, featuring a variety of local foliage, to the pristine shoreline out front, the environment at Cassia is a cut above the rest, a fact that is only made better by the friendliness and charm of its staff. Inside each room, beautiful wooden furnishings opt for simplicity over ornamentation and guests will appreciate the great attention that is paid to detail, with added touches like tea sets and cinnamon-scented rooms, not to mention the "welcome" greetings carefully spelled out in palm leaves on each bed. Both garden and sea view options are available, and breakfast at the resort's excellent beachside restaurant is included in the room rate. There are also massage services on-site as well as a private beach and two swimming pools.

Styled in the design of a traditional Vietnamese village, the impressive **Long Beach Resort** (Tran Hung Dao, tel. 07/7398-1818, www.longbeachphuquoc.com, VND2,450,000-5,500,000) is lined with cobblestone pathways and towering palm trees. All rooms, from deluxe accommodations to semi-detached bungalows, are furnished in beautiful, detailed solid wood and come with air-conditioning, hot water, television, DVD player, minibar, and complimentary breakfast. Overlooking the resort's private beach is a stunning lotus pond topped with a stone footbridge, which serves as the backdrop for its ocean-side restaurant. A swimming pool is located a few steps back from the water and on-site spa services are available.

Famiana Resort (Tran Hung Dao, tel. 07/7398-3366, www.famianaresort.com, VND2,800,000-13,900,000) is a trendy modern retreat situated near the southern end of Long Beach. Its monochromatic Asian-inspired rooms boast plush beds and open-plan sitting rooms, as well as kitchenettes in the beachside villas. Guests can choose from garden or sea-view accommodations, and both breakfast and dinner are included in the nightly rate. Famiana offers private beach access and a swimming pool as well as spa services, a fitness center, mini golf facilities, and a playground for young kids.

INFORMATION AND SERVICES
Tourist Information

Your go-to spot for a decent island map and sound travel advice, **Buddy Ice Cream & Info Cafe** (6 Bach Dang, tel. 07/7399-4181, www.visitphuquoc. info, 8am-10pm daily) is more or less Phu Quoc's unofficial tourist information spot. Beyond doling out useful tips about visiting the island, the amiable staff at Buddy provide proper New Zealand ice cream in a variety of flavors as well as coffee, smoothies, and some small meals. Both Wi-Fi access and use of the café's desktop computers are available for paying guests.

Banks

For fast cash, there are several **ATMs** located at the intersection of Tran Hung Dao and Vo Thi Sau, just beside the entrance to the Dinh Cau Night Market, as well as a few near the top of Alley 118 on Tran Hung Dao. For currency exchange, many hotels offer this service, though check the rate against the local **Sacombank** (52B 30 Thang 4, tel. 07/7399-5118, www. sacombank.com.vn, 7:30am-11:30am and 1pm-5pm Mon.-Fri., 7:30am-11:30am Sat.), where you can also switch currencies.

Internet and Postal Services

The island's only **post office** (10 30 Thang 4, tel. 07/7384-6038, 7am-6pm daily) is located right in the center of Duong Dong. For Internet, you can either grab a coffee at **Buddy Ice Cream & Info Cafe** (6 Bach Dang, tel. 07/7399-4181, www.visitphuquoc.info, 8am-10pm daily) and take advantage of their free computers and Wi-Fi or visit **VNPT** (2 Tran Hung Dao, tel. 07/7399-4888, 7am-6pm daily), just around the corner from the post office.

Medical Services

Phu Quoc's main **hospital (Benh Vien Phu Quoc)** (128 30 Thang 4, tel. 07/7384-6074) is located in Duong Dong town, not far from the top of Tran Hung Dao, and has 24-hour emergency services; facilities are very basic.

GETTING THERE

Air

Phu Quoc International Airport (San Bay Quoc Te Phu Quoc) (PQC, www.phuquocinternationalairport.com), opened in 2012, receives multiple daily flights from Saigon (1 hour, VND300,000-1,720,000 one-way), Can Tho (50 min., VND1,100,000 one-way), and Hanoi (2 hours, VND1,300,000-3,500,000). Both Vietnam Airlines and its budget competition—namely VietJet and Jetstar—fly between Saigon and Phu Quoc.

The airport is six miles northeast of Duong Dong. Taxis from the airport to Duong Dong and Long Beach cost around VND100,000-120,000.

Boat

While there are high-speed boat services which run from two Mekong Delta towns—Rach Gia and Ha Tien—to Phu Quoc, catching a ferry to the island would require you to extricate yourself from Saigon's congested outer districts, a feat that winds up being more time than it's worth. As such, it's recommended that short-term vacationers travel by air in order to maximize beach time.

If you should choose to go by boat, high-speed vessels arriving from both Rach Gia (2.5 hours, VND350,000) and Ha Tien (2 hours, VND230,000) dock at the **Bai Vong harbor,** about eight miles from Duong Dong, the largest town on the island. If you book ahead, many hotels and resorts will arrange pick up for you. You can also hop on a minibus (30 min., VND50,000) from the harbor. Be clear about where you want to go, as drivers will sometimes insist on bringing you to a particular guesthouse or hotel.

GETTING AROUND

Taxis and *Xe Om*

At both the harbor and the airport, *xe om* are sure to find you before you find them. Throughout the rest of the island these drivers are harder to come by, as accommodations are fairly spread out. If you can't track anyone down, call a **Mailinh** (tel. 07/7397-9797) or **Hoang Long** (tel. 07/7398-8988) taxi.

Vehicles for Hire

For complete freedom, many travelers prefer to rent motorbikes to get around the island. The going rate for an automatic is around VND150,000 and for a semi-automatic vehicle is VND120,000. Driving yourself is the most cost-effective and efficient option, but construction is everywhere, so novice drivers might want to stick to the passenger's seat. You can usually ask your hotel for driver recommendations, or chat up the drivers that hang around the harbor. Some places will also rent out bicycles to travelers, though with little shade you may find yourself wilting before you make it to your destination.

PHÁT HUY TRUYỀN THỐNG YÊU NƯỚC
VÀ ANH HÙNG CÁCH MẠNG, QUYẾT TÂM XÂY DỰNG
TỈNH KHÁNH HÒA GIÀU MẠNH, VĂN MINH

Background

The Landscape

Covering a total area of 127,880 square miles, Vietnam is a skinny, S-shaped country that snakes its way from the southern border of China all the way down to the mouth of the mighty Mekong. While there is no official nickname for the country, its shape is sometimes likened to a dragon, a moniker which locals are happy to accept, as this mythical creature has ties to the origin story of the Vietnamese people. To the west, Vietnam shares a frontier with both Cambodia and Laos, while the north is bordered by China. Along the southern and eastern edges of the country is the East Sea, also known as the South China Sea.

GEOGRAPHY

While Vietnam's rice paddies seem to go on for miles across the Mekong and Red River Deltas, only about 20 percent of the country's land area is actually flat. The rest of Vietnam, from low, rolling hills along the southern coast to the soaring peaks of the far north, spans a range of elevations. Near the sea, white-sand beaches are dotted with clusters of tropical foliage. The dense jungle of Vietnam's mountainous regions, including the Central Highlands and much of the area north of Hanoi, is all but impenetrable.

Down south, the low-lying Mekong Delta is an unusual combination of water and land. This is largely a result of the region's namesake river, a mammoth waterway that begins in eastern Tibet and flows through several Southeast Asian nations before splintering into nine separate tributaries across the Vietnamese border. Moving along the coast, the shores east of Ho Chi Minh City bear an odd climate that lends itself to a coupling of tropical beaches and barren sand dunes. The country's interior is comprised of undulating mountains and lush jungle that extend all the way to the western border. Up north, the Red River Delta creates a similar effect to its southern counterpart, with an expanse of pancake-flat rice paddies around Hanoi extending toward the coast, punctuated only by limestone karsts, the same rocky outcroppings you'll see in Ha Long Bay and around Phong Nha-Ke Bang National Park, which rise unexpectedly out of these level landscapes. Along the northern border, the terrain becomes mountainous once again, rising and falling dramatically all the way from the East Sea west through Ha Giang and Lao Cai provinces to Laos. This region is also home to Vietnam's highest peak, Mount Fansipan (10,311 ft.).

CLIMATE

While the majority of Vietnam never really gets cold, the northern and southern halves of the country experience two very different weather patterns. Residents in Hanoi and the surrounding region see four seasons

---

throughout the year, though they are not as distinct as North American seasons. Up north, a cold, damp winter and a sweltering hot summer are separated by a few months of mild weather on either side. Temperatures in this part of the country fluctuate from a brisk 50°F in January to 100°F in July and August. Pack warm clothes if you plan to visit in winter, as Hanoi does not have heaters and the bone-chilling humidity can be deceptive. In the extreme north, some areas along the border even experience snow, though this is never more than a light dusting on mountain peaks and rooftops.

In the southern and central regions, temperatures remain more consistent, varying only a few degrees between the rainy and dry seasons. Rainy season begins when temperatures are highest, breaking the heat with heavy rainfall for a few hours each day. These rains remain consistent until the end of the season, at which time a constant downpour ushers in slightly cooler weather. Dry season still sees some precipitation, though significantly less, as well as lower temperatures and occasional winds, with the heat building over time until rainy season returns. Depending upon your location, these seasons come at different times of year, with the rains arriving in May down south and ending in late October, while the central region experiences rainy season from September to January. For southern Vietnam, temperatures usually change no more than a few degrees, holding steady around 90°F, with varying levels of humidity depending upon the season. While central Vietnam's climate is more similar to the south than the north, this region experiences a wider range of temperatures, from a cool 65°F to around 85°F in the summer, as well as more intense storms. Danang, central Vietnam's most cosmopolitan city, is also the mainland's easternmost point. As a result, the surrounding area experiences yearly typhoons, which bring heavy rainfall and high winds, which have been known to destroy homes and farmland near the coast.

ENVIRONMENTAL ISSUES

Vietnam has a poor track record on both conservation and clean-up efforts. A handful of NGOs and other independent organizations do their part to help protect the country's natural resources. Despite enacting laws to safeguard its forests and waterways, environmental regulations are only sometimes enforced to protect the country's natural resources, leading to issues such as water shortages and deforestation. In the Central Highlands, scores of hydropower plants harness the strength of the region's rivers for economic benefit, but the dams that come with these facilities often dry up riverbeds below, eliminating a valuable water source for downstream communities.

Industrial pollution has become a hot-button issue in recent years. In April 2016, a Taiwanese steel company dumped large amounts of toxic wastewater into the East Sea, killing an estimated 70 tons of fish and other marine life along a 124-mile stretch of central Vietnam's coast. The mass fish death affected the region's many fishermen and brought the country's seafood industry to a grinding halt. Though this incident was the largest and most publicized case, smaller instances of industrial pollution continue to take place elsewhere in the country, affecting local waterways and the people who rely on them to survive.

Along the coast, specifically in urban areas, air pollution is also a growing problem. Though Vietnamese cities are not as bad as some of their East Asian counterparts, rapid industrialization and expanding metropolitan areas are cause for future concern as nearby suburbs are devoured by modern development and increased pollution from traffic and factories leaves air quality diminished.

While none of the urban rivers, canals, or lakes you see may look like a nice place for a swim, officials in cities like HCMC and Hanoi have done a tremendous amount of work to rehabilitate these heavily polluted waterways. Garbage collection takes place on a daily basis and younger generations are more conscious of how their individual actions can affect Vietnam's urban pollution.

Beyond these issues, the country's greatest challenge is bringing attention to the value of its natural resources and encouraging its citizens to clean up. More than a few breathtaking landscapes in Vietnam are clouded by reckless littering. While urban centers employ hundreds of street cleaners to remedy this, rural areas and smaller towns are often left to languish in their own garbage, and there is a general expectation that someone else will clean up a person's litter.

Plants and Animals

Stretching over 2,000 miles along the East Sea, Vietnam is home to countless varieties of flora and fauna. From the peaks of Sapa all the way down to the watery Mekong Delta, the country's range of climates and habitats lends itself to an equally diverse array of plant and wildlife. However, with an ever-growing population and a rapid pace of development, many of Vietnam's plant and animal species are in danger. Deforestation and the overuse of natural resources threaten to erase natural habitats, while several species, some of which are unique to Vietnam, have become critically endangered in recent years due to the illegal wildlife trade. Today, Vietnam is home to nine "death row" species, or critically endangered animals endemic to Vietnam, according to the International Union for Conservation of Nature (IUCN). High demand for animal parts, such as rhino horn, has also forced a handful of primates, turtles, and other creatures onto the IUCN Red List, which documents the world's most endangered flora and fauna. Vietnam is the leading market for the illegal rhino horn trade.

While Vietnam boasts 30 protected national parks, not all are strictly supervised. Authorities have stepped up their punishment of poachers in recent years, but the wildlife trade continues to be a problem in Vietnam. In 2011, WWF confirmed that the country's small population of Javan rhino, an extremely rare animal, was officially extinct after the last of its kind was likely killed by poachers. Additionally, nearly one-third of the country's protected lands are in and around the Mekong Delta, a region already straining under high population density. While the forests and jungles of Vietnam contain countless fascinating creatures, the country still has a ways to go in protecting its natural resources and bringing the 77 species of flora and fauna currently listed as critically endangered on IUCN's Red List back to a healthy number.

PLANTS

According to the World Bank's World Development Indicators, over 45 percent of Vietnam's land area is covered by forest. These woodlands can be broken down into several categories, from the dry lowland forests of southern Vietnam, largely made up of tropical hardwood, to the flooded forests of mangroves and cajuput trees in that same region. Highland forests cover the northern region under a dense canopy of broad-leaved trees and moss. Inland, cooler climates like that of Lang Biang Plateau, are home to pine forests, which coexist alongside groves of bamboo. Fruit trees are common in the Mekong Delta, with jackfruit, durian, longans, rambutans, and papayas aplenty. Commercially prized woods like teak, rosewood, and ebony are raised here, as is bamboo. Rattan, an extremely durable wood used in basket-weaving, particularly by the minority communities of the north, is also prevalent.

ANIMALS

A growing number of people are flocking to the country's seaside areas, pushing many animals out of their natural habitats. In a region with many endemic species, Vietnam's fauna holds its own array of endangered creatures. Larger species like the Indochinese tiger, moon bear, and Asian elephant often take center stage thanks to their size and prominence around the world, but Vietnam is also home to a host of native species that are found only within its borders. Even today, scientists continue to discover rare creatures, like the thorny tree frog, an amphibian that lives only among the highest peaks of Vietnam in its remote northern region, and as late as the 1990s, large mammals were still being found in the dense forests of central and northern Vietnam. The most elusive of these is the saola, an ox-like creature with long horns that is sometimes called the Asian unicorn due to its rarity.

Chances are you won't get a glimpse of Vietnam's more exotic animals during your visit. Travelers are more likely to encounter domestic creatures during their trip: chickens are common even in urban centers like Ho Chi Minh City, where they are sometimes kept as pets; pigs and water buffalo are abundant in the countryside.

Those eager to see Vietnam's more exotic creatures, particularly its many varieties of primates, are encouraged to view these animals in the wild rather than at a zoo or tourist attraction, as the creatures in these centers tend to be mistreated and sometimes aggressive. The majority of Vietnam's wildlife lives in national parks and nature reserves. National parks in Con Dao and Cat Ba have wild populations of different primates, including macaques, langurs, and gibbons, while both Cuc Phuong National Park and the Cu Chi Wildlife Rescue Center rehabilitate endangered primates, turtles, and other animals captured in the wildlife trade, providing a closer look at these creatures in an environment where they are safe and well looked after.

Mammals

While, in name, Vietnam continues to boast incredible biodiversity, today many of its mammal species exist only in protected wildlife areas. Fast-paced development and growing populations have encroached upon the natural habitats of many species, including the country's array of primate species. Macaques are far and away the most common and can be found in national parks and nature reserves from north to south. Endemic species like the Cat Ba, Ha Tinh, and douc langurs, also found in government-protected forests, are trickier to spot given their smaller numbers. Still, there's a chance you might catch a glimpse of these creatures in their respective habitats. Beyond primates, Vietnam's mammals include Asiatic black bears, banteng, gaur, deer, pangolins, and dugongs.

Reptiles and Amphibians

Reptiles are one of Vietnam's more visible categories of fauna, and you're likely to spot a few geckos on the walls, even in urban areas. Several species of turtle, a revered animal in Vietnamese lore, exist throughout the country, from the massive Yangtze softshell turtle, of which just one remains in Vietnam, to several smaller varieties, such as the Chinese three-striped box turtle and the Indochinese box turtle, both of which appear on Vietnam's endangered species list. While the future of these animals is precarious, new species are still being discovered in some of Vietnam's more remote areas. As recently as 2014, scientists came upon a previously unknown variety of tree frog living in the mountainous central region. Along the coast, snakes are equally elusive thanks to the country's growing population. There are over 200 different varieties of snakes in Vietnam, including 60 venomous species, many of which appear in the wilder interior regions.

Birds

Vietnam's wealth of feathered friends are a birder's dream. Over 850 different varieties of bird live within the country's borders, including the highest number of endemic species in mainland Southeast Asia. The rarest of these is the Edwards' pheasant, among the most endangered species in the world. There are also several varieties of laughingthrush that are endangered. Southern Vietnam, namely the Mekong Delta, is a prime location to catch a glimpse of the country's array of bird species. With endless flooded fields and high trees, sanctuaries such as Tra Su and Tram Chim National Park, home to the sarus crane, the world's largest flying bird, afford travelers a rare glimpse of local wildlife in its natural habitat.

History

From the earliest days of the Dong Son to a thousand-year occupation by the Chinese, centuries of dynastic rule, French colonialism, the rise of Communist revolutionaries, and a tragic war that captured the attention of the world, Vietnam's history has been one of struggle and resilience. The 20th century alone included wars against France, the United States, Cambodia, and China. As a result, nationalism runs deep in Vietnam. Regardless of age, gender, religion, or political opinion, Vietnamese take great pride in their cultural identity and in their perseverance against foreign invaders.

After years of post-war poverty followed by an incredible economic boom, Vietnam has transformed from a small, war-stricken nation into one of Southeast Asia's most promising economies in little more than a few decades. As the country continues to prosper, the government struggles to reconcile its values with the rampant capitalism of Vietnam's urban centers, as well as the environmental impact of its fast-paced development.

ANCIENT CIVILIZATION

While most Western accounts of Vietnamese history tend to focus on more recent events, the earliest inhabitants of the S-shaped country arrived several thousand years ago. In the Mekong Delta, an ancient civilization known as Funan existed from around AD 100 up until the 6th century. The south-central coast was once occupied by Champa, a matriarchal Hindu civilization now remembered for its famous red-brick architecture. From the 2nd century AD to as late as the mid-1600s, the Cham

temple carvings from the ancient Champa era

held an ever-decreasing foothold in the region, farming rice, making pottery, trading with other civilizations, and often engaging in armed conflicts with their neighbors, a fact that led to their eventual demise at the hands of the Vietnamese.

Today's Vietnamese originated in the Red River Delta where, as far back as the first millennium BC, a highly evolved culture known as the Dong Son ran a thriving trade port, developed a complex irrigation system for rice farming, and is now remembered for its intricately patterned bronze drums. Hung Vuong, the first ruler of the Vietnamese people, is believed to have been a Dong Son ruler, though it is difficult to discern exactly when he lived, as the true origins of the Vietnamese people are intertwined with mythology. This dynasty reigned over northern Vietnam and parts of southern China for 18 generations before the throne was usurped by An Duong Vuong in the 3rd century BC.

ONE THOUSAND YEARS UNDER THE CHINESE

In 208 BC, the Chinese invaded northern Vietnam, marking the start of a thousand-year occupation that would deeply influence Vietnamese traditions and culture. At first, the Han dynasty was lax, allowing its colony to function in much the way it always had. But, once the Chinese began to impose high taxes and force the Vietnamese to adopt their traditions and style of dress, resentment flourished among the general population. Across the northern reaches of the country, rebellions were routinely suppressed. The most famous of these, an AD 39 insurrection led by the Trung sisters, drove the Chinese out of Vietnam for just over two years before the northern power returned to reclaim its colony. Following this semi-successful revolt, the Han dynasty gave up all pleasantries, removing Vietnamese lords from power and permitting local aristocrats to occupy only the lowest rungs of the political ladder.

Eventually, after centuries of rule, things began to come undone in China. Growing unrest along the border made it difficult for the northern empire to keep its colony in check. In the far north, minority hill tribes rebelled against Chinese rule, while several Vietnamese aristocrats began claiming a right to the throne. Ultimately, the Tang dynasty fell in China in 907, creating a weakened empire, and Vietnamese general Ngo Quyen swooped in to take independence for his country.

AN INDEPENDENT VIETNAM

Despite Ngo Quyen's victory over the Chinese, his own reign was brief. In less than three decades, the emperor was overthrown. A handful of other short-lived rulers took his place, but it wasn't until the Ly dynasty that the kingdom was able to grow. In 1075, royal officials in Vietnam wrote examinations for the first time, following in the footsteps of the Chinese empire. By 1089, the practice was required, creating a fixed hierarchy of

The Trung Sisters

Two of Vietnam's most celebrated figures, the Trung sisters were a pair of aristocratic women born in Giao Chi, as the country was then called, in the early AD years. Like many at the time, Trung Trac and Trung Nhi opposed Chinese rule, but it wasn't until the husband of the elder sister, a Vietnamese nobleman named Thi Sach, was put to death by Giao Chi's Chinese ruler that the women took action.

In order to avenge Thi Sach's death, the Trung sisters launched a rebellion that unified anti-colonialists against the Giao Chi administration, driving its Chinese ruler out of Vietnam in AD 39. Trung Trac became the nation's queen, her sister a high-ranking second, and the pair briefly held sovereignty over the kingdom until the Chinese returned in AD 42, armed to the teeth and with enough warriors to defeat their enemy. When it became clear that the fight was over and defeat inevitable for the Vietnamese, the sisters jumped into a river and committed suicide. To this day, their name, Hai Ba Trung, appears on street signs across the country and they are revered as an example of fierce nationalism and powerful Vietnamese women.

public officials. At the same time, the Ly dynasty adopted Buddhism as its royal religion, which in turn encouraged Vietnamese subjects to convert.

Southward expansion also began, with the Dai Viet marching out to conquer the Cham kingdom of Vijaya in 1079. An arranged marriage in 1225 ended the Ly dynasty, transferring power from its last remaining princess to the Tran family, who carried on a similar tradition of success. During this time, Kublai Khan and his Mongol army began to eye northern Vietnam, thrice attempting to take over the empire. One of the Tran dynasty's most famous heroes is Tran Hung Dao, the celebrated general who thwarted the Mongols' final attempt at Bach Dang River by impaling his enemy's ships with wooden spikes during low tide.

Following the defeat of the Mongols, the Tran dynasty entered a steady decline. They managed to get in a few more victories over the Cham before a power shift came in 1400, when General Ho Quy Ly overthrew the king and claimed Dai Viet for himself. General Ho's policies proved unfavorable and local landowners appealed to the Chinese for help. China's Ming dynasty promptly returned and reasserted its authority in 1407. This second occupation lasted roughly two decades, with the Chinese exerting their unrestrained power over the Dai Viet. All local customs and traditions were banned, citizens were required to wear Chinese dress, and a particularly harsh forced labor policy came into effect, all of which had a significant impact on local culture for years to come. In 1428, colonization ended thanks to Le Loi, a scholar who had rejected the Ming dynasty's rule and amassed an army to defeat the Chinese. In an attempt to remain civil, he provided the losers with ships and supplies to sail home rather than putting them to death.

THE NGUYENS AND TRINHS

Throughout the 15th century, Vietnam's Le dynasty continued to move south, conquering any kingdom that stood in their way. However, as Vietnam's territory expanded, its rulers struggled to maintain control over the newer settlements, which were far-removed from the capital. When a high-ranking official usurped the throne in 1527, two aristocratic families, the Trinh and Nguyen lords, backed the Le dynasty in hopes of sharing their power once the kingdom had been retaken. After 1545, Vietnam found itself divided: the Nguyens controlled the southern half of the country, while the Trinhs took charge of the north.

During this time, European missionaries began to appear in Vietnam, hoping to convert the local population. One of the most famous was French priest Alexandre de Rhodes, who arrived in Indochina in 1619, picked up the local language, and promptly began espousing the benefits of Catholicism to the Vietnamese. By the time he was kicked out of the country in 1630, de Rhodes had converted over 6,000 Vietnamese. He is also credited with the development of the Romanized *quoc ngu* script used by the Vietnamese today.

Down south, the Nguyens ran an agricultural society, keeping uneducated peasants at bay, while the northern Trinh emphasized education and intellectual development. Neither gained a strong following among the masses, as ongoing war, natural disasters, and taxes left the general population frustrated and disillusioned. Rebellions were common, though they were often small and concentrated to a single area, making it easy for both ruling families to silence their opponents. That is until a trio of brothers from Tay Son appeared on the scene.

TAY SON REBELLION

Nguyen Hue, Nguyen Nhac, and Nguyen Lu were three brothers from central Binh Dinh province whose ancestry actually traced back to the short-lived reign of General Ho Quy Ly in 1400. Like many subjects at the time, the brothers were thoroughly displeased with the Nguyen Lords and unimpressed by imperial bureaucracy in general. Initially siding with the Trinhs of the north, the brothers launched a revolt in 1771, intending to overthrow the Nguyen Lords on their own. By the following year, they had successfully taken Binh Dinh and Quang Nam provinces and, with growing support, managed to extend the takeover to all of southern Vietnam by 1778. Operating on a Robin Hood-style mantra, the brothers nixed taxes, set prisoners free, and gave out food to the peasant population. Their progressive policies later moved north, turning on the Trinh Lords and once again fending off the Chinese to rule the entire country, with each brother presiding over a region of Vietnam.

In defeating the southern rulers, the Tay Son rebellion had failed to kill all heirs to the throne: Prince Nguyen Anh, the only remaining Nguyen Lord, fled to Gia Dinh, now known as Ho Chi Minh City, and sought the assistance of Pigneau de Behaine, a French bishop. Shortly thereafter, Pigneau de Behaine sailed to Pondicherry in French India and, later, back to Europe to request the aid of the French king in restoring Nguyen Anh to the throne. Louis XVI agreed, so long as Vietnam would offer up the port of Danang and the Con Dao islands, then known as Poulo Condore, in exchange. But, upon Pigneau de Behaine's return to Pondicherry, the French delegates refused to help. The bishop raised his own funds to hire ships and soldiers, returning to Vietnam in 1789 with enough ammunition to wipe out the Tay Son rebels by 1801, creating a unified Vietnam for the first time in 200 years.

Under newly crowned emperor Gia Long, the country returned to a more conservative imperial rule, with the king undoing many policies enacted by the Nguyen brothers in order to assert his authority. Opposition was strictly punished and many of the previously erased taxes returned. Though there was occasional dissent, it wasn't until the death of emperor Gia Long that France's intention to invade solidified. Gia Long's son Minh Mang, an austere ruler and staunch believer in Confucianism, expelled all European missionaries from Vietnam and set about killing Vietnamese Catholics and any missionaries caught preaching the Bible.

FRENCH COLONIALISM

Convinced that invasion was the best course of action, the French stormed the shores of Danang in 1858, advancing south to take Gia Dinh the following year. Armed with a religious cause—to protect its missionaries—the French had hoped that Vietnamese Catholics would rush to their aid, but no one appeared. Instead, it became clear that the motives for this invasion had nothing to do with Catholicism and everything to do with business and military might. Over the next decade or so, the French managed to acquire all of Vietnam's territory, wresting power from then-emperor Tu Duc by 1874, though the country's colonization wasn't official until 1883.

The Vietnamese were caught between two evils: the French were unpopular for having taken the country by force, but the poor government of emperor Tu Duc and his failure to protect the people from harm had lost him a great deal of public support. In the beginning, some were open to the idea of a new governmental system. But, as it became clear that economic exploitation was part of the plan, the French fell out of favor. Under colonial rule, most Vietnamese were overtaxed, overworked, and abused. While rice exports soared in the colonists' new open economy, all profits went to the European power. Many high-ranking Vietnamese scholars and officials refused to play a part in the colonial government for this reason.

By the turn of the 20th century, dissent sparked rebellions across the country. As World War I raged in Europe, Vietnamese troops were sent abroad in the name of France. Shortly thereafter, Ho Chi Minh arrived in Guangzhou, China, where he founded the Revolutionary Youth League in 1925, attempting to wrangle all of Vietnam's disparate Communist and anti-French parties together. A 1930 conference solidified the main aims of the resistance from abroad, while, in Vietnam, the people of Nghe An and Ha Tinh provinces rioted against colonial rule. As a response, the French bombed the area and sent many of its citizens to jail.

WORLD WAR II

Toward the end of the 1930s, trouble was brewing in Europe on the eve of World War II, and dissent in its Southeast Asian colonies had France on edge. In 1941, Ho Chi Minh returned to Vietnam after 30 years abroad and was welcomed with open arms. When France fell to the Nazis in 1940 and Japanese troops arrived in Vietnam, demanding safe passage of their military and weapons through the country, Ho Chi Minh's now-famous resistance army, the Viet Minh, took note of the colonial government's weakness.

By March 1945, Uncle Ho felt confident enough that he offered the French an ultimatum: relinquish power or face the consequences. Japan didn't wait for a response and wrested the country from European hands that same month, claiming it a free state under Japanese occupation. But while their Asian neighbors had removed authority from the Europeans, Vietnam recognized Japan's increasingly dire circumstances on the world stage and prepared to swoop into the anticipated power vacuum that would occur when they left. Sure enough, when Japan retreated from Vietnam in 1945, the Viet Minh launched its now-famous August Revolution across the country, stepping into power for the first time, just as Bao Dai, Vietnam's last emperor, relinquished his crown. Ho Chi Minh declared independence on September 2, 1945, in Hanoi.

FRANCO-VIETNAM WAR

The French refused to go quietly. Though Ho Chi Minh's declaration was met with an overwhelmingly positive response, the Europeans returned to Vietnam after World War II in hopes of regaining their colonial foothold. By 1946, it was clear that there would not be a peaceful resolution and both sides prepared for war. Over nine years, the French and the Viet Minh duked it out across the country, the former well-armed, the latter boasting heavy manpower. Though France had many Vietnamese cities within its grasp, the countryside belonged to the Viet Minh, who set up training camps and recruitment centers within its territory. After the People's Republic of China was officially established in 1949, the Viet Minh were able to source weapons from the north, a move which gave them the upper hand. As Vietnamese forces took back northern Vietnam, opening up supply lines and enabling them to attack the Red River Delta, the French began to lose heart.

Still, by the end of 1953, colonial forces took Dien Bien Phu, a far-off town in the mountainous northwest, hoping to turn the tide of war by interfering with their enemy's access to supplies. Instead, this was the move that sealed their fate. In March 1954, two months before diplomatic talks were set to begin in Geneva, the Viet Minh laid siege to Dien Bien Phu, bringing in ample artillery and over 100,000 troops to cut off all access to the outside world. By the time the Geneva talks began on May 8, France had surrendered and Ho Chi Minh's army was victorious.

In the resulting accords, which were signed by both Vietnam's Communist government and France, the country was divided in half at the 17th parallel with the promise of reuniting both sides in a 1956 election. While this agreement brought temporary peace and the exodus of Vietnam's colonizers, few—if any—of the parties present during the Geneva talks actually believed that Vietnam would be reunited so seamlessly.

With northern Vietnam now staunchly Communist and the southern Republic of Vietnam in limbo, the United States began to take a vested interest in the country's political situation. Hoping to keep the Communists out of power, they backed Ngo Dinh Diem, a Vietnamese Catholic with little political experience. Over the next two years, Diem exercised strict control over religious groups in the Mekong Delta and quashed any dissent in Saigon. By 1955, Diem openly rejected the elections meant to reunify Vietnam and instead held his own rigged referendum, winning the presidency by a landslide.

Using his own family and connections, Diem fashioned himself a cabinet of leaders and began to rule, making little effort to win over public support. As the 1950s drew to a close, the southern government had become so careless with its power that many of the Communists who had opted to go north after the Geneva Accords returned in order to stage attacks against Diem's government. In the city, regular protests took place. Diem attempted to resettle all south Vietnamese into what he termed "strategic hamlets," an effort to separate average civilians from the NLF rebels fighting against him. These villages turned out to be a breeding ground for NLF converts, as south Vietnamese did not take kindly to leaving their homes and rebel fighters were able to tunnel beneath the hamlets, establishing access to this increasingly disgruntled population.

VIETNAM WAR

By 1963, tensions in south Vietnam had reached a fever pitch: across Saigon, civilians routinely demonstrated against Diem's corrupt government. For his part, the president showed no interest in appeasing his public and carried on in the same disconnected fashion. When the Venerable Thich Quang Duc, senior monk of a Saigonese pagoda, lit himself on fire in the middle of a downtown intersection one morning in June, photos of the scene were splashed across front pages worldwide. In the face of an international outcry, Diem and his cronies remained flippant. Madame Nhu, the wife of Diem's brother and a powerful behind-the-scenes player, famously referred to the event as a "barbecue." However, the military arm of Diem's government saw the writing on the wall and discreetly approached the U.S. government in order to gauge their receptiveness to a coup. They were hardly met with resistance.

By November, the generals of south Vietnam realized their plan, assassinating Diem and his brother, Nhu. The Americans remained neutral on the subject and, less than a month later, President John F. Kennedy met the same fate, shaking up the stability of the American-backed south once more. Newly installed President Johnson took a different approach to his predecessor, sending increased military aid to Vietnam. In 1964, north Vietnamese forces exchanged fire with an American naval ship, prompting the Gulf of Tonkin Resolution, which granted President Johnson the power to take "necessary measures" against the Vietnamese Communists. Air strikes were ordered against the north, but American planes alone could not keep the enemy from advancing. Eventually, ground troops began to pour into Vietnam, their numbers swelling to 485,000 by the end of 1967. Defoliants like Agent Orange were used to destroy the dense jungles where NLF and north Vietnamese forces hid, and heavy bombing ravaged the countryside. Americans at home, meanwhile, began to express their growing disapproval of the war, questioning the role of U.S. troops in the conflict and the increasing civilian casualties.

The 1968 Tet Offensive proved a turning point for the war. On January 31, the eve of the country's biggest holiday, north Vietnamese and NLF forces launched a coordinated attack. Five major cities, 36 provincial capitals, 64 district capitals, and over two dozen airfields were targeted and some taken over by Communist forces. Though U.S. soldiers ultimately regained the territory lost during these attacks, the event did major damage to public sentiment at home, where Americans were being told that victory was imminent. Instead, footage of the Tet battles broadcast on news channels around the world showed a far more dire situation.

In 1969, with troop numbers already exceeding 500,000, President Nixon began to withdraw American soldiers from Vietnam, a move that was met with approval at home but only worsened the low morale of troops left behind. The new president pushed for "Vietnamization," handing over control to south Vietnamese forces. Peace talks were arranged in Paris. But, by 1971, little progress had been made. Meanwhile, news of the My Lai massacre, in which U.S. troops killed hundreds of unarmed Vietnamese in Quang Ngai province, was made public, as were Nixon's secret bombings of Communist bases in Cambodia, both of which fueled public outrage in the United States. Over the next two years, the United States and north Vietnam's Communist government went back and forth at the negotiating table, using military attacks to encourage their adversaries to bargain. On January 27, 1973, the Agreement on Ending the War and Restoring Peace in Vietnam was signed by north Vietnam, south Vietnam, and the United States and a cease-fire went into effect the following day.

By the end of March, the last American military units left Vietnam. Over the next two years, the country continued to suffer casualties as an ineffective south Vietnamese government aimed to win over civilians while its military, with a soaring number of deserters and the NLF hot on their heels, rapidly came undone. The following year, north Vietnamese forces made a push to reclaim the areas they had lost. On April 30, 1975, north Vietnamese tanks crashed through the gates of Saigon's Independence Palace, marking the end of the 30-year conflict.

AFTER 1975

At peace for the first time in 30 years, Vietnam's Communist government found itself faced with a new challenge: how to take a ravaged, war-stricken nation and bring it out of poverty. Still reeling from the after-effects of war and deeply paranoid about the possibility of any more foreign invaders, the country closed itself off from the world. This proved to be a justifiable concern, as brief border skirmishes with China and a two-year war with Cambodia followed; both conflicts were resolved by the end of 1979. Meanwhile, South Vietnam supporters were sent to study sessions and re-education camps, essentially hard labor outfits, in order to restructure southern society to match the wishes of the northern government. Surveillance was heavy throughout the country, as the new government worked hard to squash any and all dissent. A central economy, built on austerity, steered people forward over the next decade or so, but it soon became clear that this government-run system was doing nothing to bring the average Vietnamese out of abject poverty.

For this reason, the government instituted *doi moi* in the mid-1980s, a series of economic reforms which eventually transitioned Vietnam to a market economy. As 1990 approached, the country began to open itself up again to the world. These reforms became the saving grace of Vietnam: in just two decades, *doi moi* took Vietnam's poverty rate from 60 percent of the population to 17 percent.

Government and Economy

GOVERNMENT

The Socialist Republic of Vietnam is a one-party Communist state. Its legislative body, the National Assembly, consists of 500 representatives who meet twice a year and are elected for five-year terms by popular vote. This organization has the power to both make and amend the country's laws, as well as its constitution, and is responsible for voting in the government's highest officials, including the president and prime minister. Both of these offices belong to the Politburo (executive branch) and are among the highest positions of power in the country. In addition to the president, the highest office in Vietnam, and the prime minister he appoints, several other ministers are proposed by the prime minister for specific areas such as finance, education and training, foreign affairs and public security, and later approved by the National Assembly, rounding out the rest of the high-ranking cabinet. Both the president and the prime minister can serve up to two terms.

Elections

Elections for National Assembly delegates are held once every five years. This is the only governmental body to be selected by popular vote, but due to the fact that Vietnam is a one-party state, there is little difference from one candidate to another. Still, these elected officials—Party members who have been chosen for the public to select—are responsible for voting in a president, who later has the power to select a prime minister.

ECONOMY

While Vietnam's economy took a rocky turn after the American War, stifled by strict centralized policies, the *doi moi* economic reforms of the mid-1980s opened the country up to international trade and industrial development. Once a solely agricultural society, industry has made its way into the country, with plenty of foreign enterprises setting up offices in major cities, particularly Ho Chi Minh City. Vietnam has become an especially attractive destination for foreign firms to outsource work in garment and textile production, as well as electronics and food processing. Though growth has slowed somewhat in recent years the country continues to make economic gains, albeit at a slower rate.

Today, much of Vietnam's wealth is concentrated in urban areas along the coast. The majority of Vietnam's rapidly growing middle class lives here, where greater work and educational opportunities are available. Rural areas remain at a disadvantage. Family members who move away from the countryside or overseas often remit part of their salary back to these rural communities as financial assistance—Vietnam is one of the top-10 remittance-receiving nations in the world. As economic growth slows in Vietnam, its poorest citizens remain in very remote areas where infrastructure is weak and access to education, job opportunities, and even basic necessities is limited. In the mountainous northern and interior regions, this lack of infrastructure and opportunity tends to affect minority communities more heavily than their ethnic Vietnamese counterparts. Meanwhile, a select group of urban Vietnamese are considered ultra-wealthy, boasting a net worth of USD$30 million or more, highlighting the country's growing income disparity.

DEMOGRAPHY

Though Vietnam is composed of 54 separate ethnic groups, the Kinh (ethnic Vietnamese) make up an overwhelming 87 percent of the population, which is now an estimated 91.7 million. Thanks to this rapid growth, a two-child rule is loosely in effect throughout Vietnam; while it is seldom enforced, you'll see signs across the country encouraging families to stop at two babies. Vietnam is an incredibly literate society, with over 90 percent of the country able to read and write.

The majority of Vietnam's population lives on or near the coast, leaving the more remote mountain areas for the country's ethnic minorities, once known to the French as *montagnards,* an array of small, tight-knit groups that still lead traditional farming lives and practice many of the same customs as their ancestors. In the Mekong Delta, a healthy Khmer community lives among the region's Kinh farmers, practicing their own brand of Buddhism, as do small, isolated groups of Islamic Cham. The mountainous areas of the Central Highlands are inhabited by the Gia Rai, E De, and Churu, among other groups, while the soaring peaks around Sapa and the rest of the northwest are home to the Dao, Giay, Thai, and H'mong people, each with their own language, culture, and traditions. While these are some of the most diverse areas in the country, they are also the least developed and, in many cases, the poorest.

RELIGION

Vietnam is a largely Mahayana Buddhist country, with most people paying a visit to the local pagoda every few weeks. The country's religious beliefs are deeply influenced by Chinese beliefs, with traces of Taoism and Confucianism. Thanks to its former European ties, a strong Catholic following also exists, though their numbers are nowhere near as great as the Buddhist community. Several smaller, homegrown religions were invented in the 20th century in the Mekong Delta area, including Caodaism, a syncretic faith in which Victor Hugo and Elvis are considered saints, and Hoa Hao, which amassed a large following in the mid-1900s but later faded out after its military involvement in the Franco-Vietnam War.

Vietnamese culture includes a strong spiritual aspect, and most locals believe in worshipping their ancestors. In addition to the many pagodas and Catholic churches throughout the country, the vibrant Caodaist temples, and even a small collection of local mosques, Vietnam boasts several temples in honor of national heroes and those considered collective ancestors of the Vietnamese people.

Death Rituals

Vietnam's approach to death is different than that of the Western world. Regardless of religion, Vietnamese believe in ancestor worship. These include blood relatives as well as collective national ancestors like Ho Chi Minh or Tran Hung Dao. When a Vietnamese person passes away, it is believed that one's life does not end but that the afterlife begins. The afterlife requires basic necessities, such as food, clothing, and money, all of which a family must provide for its deceased loved ones. In most homes, shops, and businesses, you'll find a small altar where local residents put food, beverages, and occasionally cigarettes for the dead. These offerings are often accompanied by prayers and incense. On holidays and certain Buddhist festivals, Vietnamese burn paper money and clothing for their ancestors to use in the afterlife. While it's bad luck for the living to keep these items, you'll likely spot stray hundred dollar bills on the sidewalk or in the streets. Though they're flimsier than the actual currency, these paper notes are surprisingly accurate—until you turn them over to find the phrase "Bank of the Dead" instead of "In God We Trust."

Beyond these ongoing rituals, Vietnamese funerals are a multi-day affair meant to usher a loved one into the afterlife. When a Vietnamese person dies, his or her family will mourn for several days, inviting friends and family as well as a religious leader to say goodbye. Mourners often wear white headbands. The funeral, held at home, usually includes a large tent set up in front of the building for guests to visit. An altar, complete with offerings and portrait of the deceased, is set up inside. At the end of the mourning period, the body is placed in a coffin and carried to its final resting place in a large, truck-like hearse, usually decorated with colorful symbols; some Vietnamese are cremated. This final procession begins before sunrise, sometimes as early as 4am or 5am, and often involves music. Don't be surprised if you wake up in the wee hours of the morning to trumpets and crashing cymbals—this is simply someone on their way to the afterlife.

Once the funeral is complete, Vietnamese carry on providing the essentials for their ancestors through offerings. The day of a person's death, rather than his or her birth, is remembered and celebrated as a holiday. This occasion, called *dam gio*, is a family event, in which members of that particular house come together and give offerings to their deceased relative, visit with family and friends, and often make trips to the local pagoda or church to commemorate the individual. Contrary to Western ideas of death, *dam gio* is not a somber occasion but rather a celebration of that individual and his or her life.

LANGUAGE

Vietnamese is the nation's official language and features a mind-boggling six tones and 11 vowel sounds. Though it was originally written in a modified version of Chinese characters, known as *chu nom*, European missionary Alexandre de Rhodes developed a Roman script for the language that is now used throughout the country, making Vietnam one of the only nations in mainland Southeast Asia to use a Roman alphabet. Throughout Vietnam, three major regional dialects are spoken, with the northern

Vietnam is one of the only nations in Southeast Asia to use the Roman alphabet.

Hanoian dialect considered the most authentic Vietnamese thanks to its short, succinct tonal pronunciation. The southern and central regions of the country also have their own respective dialects: You'll find a slower, more fluid accent in Ho Chi Minh City and the Mekong Delta, while central Vietnam is known for its creative pronunciation and a slew of unique regional vocabulary. Among Vietnamese, the central accent is considered the most difficult to understand, with many native speakers straining to converse with those from cities like Hue or Hoi An.

Beyond Vietnamese, an array of languages are spoken among the country's ethnic minorities in their respective homelands. These languages are rarely heard on the coast, and all public transactions are conducted in Vietnamese. Ethnic minority citizens must learn Vietnamese as a second language in order to participate fully in society.

The Arts

VISUAL ARTS

Vietnamese visual art draws upon an interesting variety of mediums and influences, thanks to its past relationships with China and France. Particularly over the last century, traditional handicrafts like lacquer painting and enamel have been combined with both Asian and European ideas to create uniquely Vietnamese artwork. While many of the masterpieces displayed in forums like the local fine arts museum are prime examples of traditional Vietnamese artwork, both Hanoi and Saigon have small but deep-rooted contemporary art scenes and plenty of up-and-coming artists whose work is shared in local cafés and smaller galleries.

MUSIC

Traditional Vietnamese music is often closely linked with theatrical performance: *cheo,* a centuries-old satirical form of theater, uses music to communicate its messages, as does *cai luong,* a similarly operatic form of music from the south that had its heyday during the 20th century. For most locals today, famous revolutionary composers such as Trinh Cong Son, one of Vietnam's most prolific songwriters, and Pham Duy remain favorites among many Vietnamese, both old and young. Their songs are regular fixtures during karaoke sessions.

Beyond traditional music, the younger generation is following its Asian neighbors, eager to develop a V-Pop phenomenon similar to Japan or Korea, with plenty of doe-eyed young songstresses and flashy music videos making the rounds on the Internet. Music-related television shows like *Vietnam Idol* and *The Voice of Vietnam,* knock-offs of their American counterparts, are also popular, as is the famed program *Paris By Night,* a much-loved musical revue filmed in France, Canada, and the United States.

Essentials

Getting There

FROM NORTH AMERICA

Travelers may enter Vietnam by air through its three largest airports: **Tan Son Nhat International Airport** (SGN) in Ho Chi Minh City; **Noi Bai International Airport** (HAN) in Hanoi; and **Danang International Airport** (DAD) in Danang. From there, plenty of smaller regional airports serve the more remote areas of Vietnam.

The most expensive part of your trip to Vietnam will be the plane ticket. Even bargain fares across the Pacific are not cheap. Still, there are a couple of strategies to make your airfare as affordable as possible. Websites like **Kayak** (www.kayak.com), **Sky Scanner** (www.skyscanner.com), and **Expedia** (www.expedia.com) offer travelers a comprehensive range of airlines. When booking through these sites, monitor airfare prices 6-8 weeks in advance. While prices may fluctuate to some degree, USD$100-200 either way, round-trip tickets hover at about USD$1,000. Those leaving from the West Coast of the United States will find slightly cheaper fares; East Coasters and anyone traveling from the middle of the continental United States should expect four-figure prices.

It is sometimes possible to save money by flying into Los Angeles International Airport (LAX) with a budget airline and then heading for Asia from there. When traveling to Vietnam, most routes pass over the Pacific, connecting to Ho Chi Minh City or Hanoi in major hubs like Seoul, Hong Kong, Tokyo, or Taipei. A few airlines go the opposite direction, passing through Europe and the Middle East.

While dirt-cheap fares are offered by carriers like China Eastern and China Southern, these companies are not known for their service or safety ratings. Carriers like EVA, Japan Air, Emirates, Cathay Pacific, United, Singapore Airlines, and Qatar Airlines all serve Vietnam's major airports and, for a few extra dollars, are reliable, professional, and usually more comfortable (particularly important for a 14-hour flight).

FROM NEIGHBORING COUNTRIES

Vietnam shares several foreigner-friendly overland border crossings with its neighbors: five with Cambodia, six with Laos, and three with China. These crossings are fairly straightforward but, like any point of entry into Vietnam, you are required to obtain a valid visa prior to arrival. With the exception of e-visa processing, which is only available at the country's three largest airports, no crossing in Vietnam will supply you with a visa at the border gate. Regularly scheduled buses pass through the country's frontier

---

Previous: colorful lanterns in a shop; traffic on a rainy day.

areas on a daily basis and often provide service to major cities in neigh- boring countries. There are no international railways linking Vietnam to
its neighbors.

Several budget airlines fly to and from Vietnam. Direct flights depart
from major regional airports in Bangkok, Kuala Lumpur, Hong Kong,
and Singapore, as well as Yangon and Taipei. For other destinations, connecting flights go through the aforementioned hubs from dozens of destinations within Southeast Asia. Airfare from neighboring countries is
usually reasonable.

DISCOUNT TICKETS

Regional budget airlines such as **VietJet** (www.vietjetair.com), **Air Asia**
(www.airasia.com), **Jetstar** (www.jetstar.com), and **Tiger Air** (www.tiger-
air.com) serve Southeast Asia's major airports, including those in Thailand,
Cambodia, China, Laos, Malaysia, Myanmar, and Vietnam. VietJet, the
country's only homegrown budget airline, covers even the most remote
destinations in Vietnam as well as an ever-expanding network of international destinations throughout Asia. Air Asia's network is also extensive,
providing connecting flights from across the region, while Tiger Air and
Jetstar both fly to Australia and a handful of Southeast Asian nations.
These are the most affordable of the bunch, but most budget airlines within
the region tack on additional fees for just about everything; read the fine
print when booking these fares.

ORGANIZED TOURS

In any given tourist destination, there are dozens of companies offering
organized day trips and multi-day tours. The majority of Vietnam's cheaper
travel outfits follow the same tourist trail, offering cookie-cutter itineraries
that present little in the way of authenticity or spontaneity. Larger companies have day trips for as little as VND100,000; these trips provide an easy
way to meet other travelers, but the tours themselves are not groundbreak-
ing. In most cases, if you're up for the challenge it's more worthwhile to
make the trip on your own. For certain excursions (treks in Sapa, for example), hiring a guide and paying the extra cash is recommended to make
the most of your time.

More independent tour outfits are popping up all the time. Many of these
private companies have done great things for the country's tourism image,
providing foreign travelers with exciting, worthwhile experiences that also
benefit the local community. While prices are higher, these customized
tour outfits are usually affordable when split between several people and
the level of service is a cut above what you would find in a larger, corpo-
rate tour company.

Getting Around

AIR

Within Vietnam, there are three main airlines with domestic routes: the national carrier **Vietnam Airlines** (www.vietnamairlines.com); as well as two budget ventures, Australian company **Jetstar** (www.jetstar.com) and local outfit **VietJet** (www.vietjetair.com). For cheap fares, VietJet is a touch more reliable than Jetstar. Vietnam Airlines, though more expensive, serves the widest range of destinations, including some of the more remote airports in Vietnam. The national carrier also has exclusive access to certain areas, such as the remote Con Dao Islands.

RAIL

Vietnam's main railway runs from Saigon to Hanoi along the coast, with major stops in Nha Trang and Danang. While some of these trains have seen better days, the sleeper cars are reasonably comfortable, though more expensive than sleeper buses, which, while slightly less safe, run more frequently. Trains are a great way to complete any long-distance journey, particularly with so many overnight routes offered, as you can spend a bit more money on train fare in exchange for saving on a hotel bill. There are a handful of destinations to which a train ride is even preferable over other options, particularly in the mountainous north, where winding roads make for a less-than-pleasant bus ride. The website **Man in Seat 61** (www.seat61.com) is an indispensable source of information on train travel within Vietnam and Southeast Asia.

BUS

The cheapest way to get around in-country is by bus. Vietnam has an extensive system of roadways and dozens of tourist bus companies featuring both seated and sleeper vehicles, which run regularly along the length of the coast, from Hanoi and its surrounding areas all the way south to the Mekong Delta and into neighboring countries. Many tourists get around on buses, though certain routes—from Hue to Hanoi, for instance, or the drive up to Sapa—are more dangerous than others. In these cases, it's better to travel via train, motorbike, or hired vehicle.

In most major cities there is a bus station serving both nearby and long-distance destinations. Safe and reliable tickets are available through many of the more well-known travel companies, like **Sinh Tourist** (www.thesinhtourist.com) and **Phuong Trang** (www.futabuslines.com.vn). When booking tickets, deal with the larger, more reputable bus lines rather than smaller, cheaper companies, as the few dollars you may save on a local bus could wind up costing you time as a result of breakdowns or other troubles.

While buses are an affordable and convenient way to travel within Vietnam, theft sometimes occurs, particularly on overnight buses. Take care when traveling to keep your belongings with you at all times, either in your lap or very close to your person. Sadly, more than a few travelers have taken an overnight bus only to wake up at their destination with one or more of their possessions missing.

TAXI

Even many of Vietnam's smaller cities are equipped with taxi services, and cabs are usually so abundant that it isn't necessary to call an operator or arrange a pick-up unless you're in a remote area. Travelers should have no problem flagging down taxis in the street. The most reputable nationwide company is **Mailinh,** though there are dozens of smaller independent companies in various cities. While some of these cabs are more reliable than others, always check for a proper meter. Base rates for taxis in most major cities run VND10,000-15,000, with fares increasing incrementally based on the distance traveled. Never bargain with a driver for your fare, as this is not to your advantage.

RIDE-HAILING APPS

In recent years, transportation apps have come on the scene in urban Vietnam, upending the local taxi industry, not to mention the widespread use of traditional xe oms. These services are mainly available in Hanoi and Saigon, where you'll find both **Uber** (www.uber.com) and Malaysian transportation app **Grab** (www.grab.com) in operation. These services are safe and reliable, though few drivers speak English. Still, it's worth booking a Grab or an Uber if you're trying to keep costs down: A motorbike ride on either of these services can go for as little as VND10,000. On both apps, you can hail either a private car or a motorbike.

XE OM

Xe om (motorbike taxis) are a popular and inexpensive means of transportation used throughout the country. Drivers—usually men—perch atop their vehicles on street corners near public parks or in busy tourist areas, waiting to ferry passengers to their preferred destinations around town. As a foreigner, you'll no doubt come into contact with at least a few of these two-wheeled vehicles and their drivers, as *xe om* drivers often call out to passing pedestrians in order to drum up business. Don't be surprised if you hear a "YOU! Motorbiiiiike!" or *"Xe om! Xe om!"* as you approach a street corner, even if you're not looking for a ride.

While *xe om* are an easy and affordable way to get around, most foreign visitors also find them to be a hair-raising experience. *Xe om* drivers, like Manhattan cabbies, move at their own pace, which is usually breakneck, and defy most of the laws of physics, not to mention traffic. *Xe om* are a good way to experience the true pulse of major cities like Saigon or Hanoi and a much faster alternative to cars, thanks to their ability to weave deftly through traffic. While the "helmets" provided by *xe om* drivers would probably prove useless in an accident, it's required by law to wear one. Even if you are advised otherwise, it's important to insist upon some headgear, at least when in the city. Voice your concern if you feel unsafe aboard a *xe om*.

When taking a *xe om*, have the address of your destination written down, as not every driver speaks English, and always agree upon a price before you set off. *Xe om* fares are open to negotiation. Feel free to haggle, but once you've settled on the price stand firm. Drivers will sometimes continue to negotiate their fee once you've already hopped on. If you stand your ground and stick to the original agreement then your *xe om* driver will usually lay off.

With few qualifications required beyond a motorbike license and a full tank of gas, *xe om* drivers are a mixed bag: There are many honest, hard-working men who make a living this way, but, like any profession, there are also a few bad apples. For this reason, it is strongly recommended that you opt for taxis over *xe om* when traveling at night, as it's not unheard of for passengers to be robbed or even thrown off a motorbike after dark, and the *xe om* driver is sometimes in on the deal. Be careful when heading back to your hotel after a night on the town, as it's also possible that your *xe om* driver has had as much to drink as you have. Never hop on a motorbike with someone who appears to be intoxicated—the streets of Vietnam can be dangerous enough as it is.

MOTORBIKE RENTALS

Affordable motorbike rentals are available in major tourist destinations throughout Vietnam. Rates usually hover around VND80,000-200,000 per day, depending on the vehicle. All motorbike rentals should come with a helmet. Stick to recommended rental companies or ask around to find a reliable business. Rental companies often require some type of collateral—a down payment or, in some cases, a passport—before loaning out a bike in order to guarantee that their vehicle will be returned in good condition. This is usually not a problem, but beware that businesses have been known to tack on additional fees after they have your passport in their possession. To save yourself a headache, stick to recommended businesses only, check the brakes and gas gauge of your vehicle before you go, and, like any transaction in Vietnam, make sure that both you and the rental company are clear on the terms of your agreement before setting off.

In most cases, daily rentals are intended for use in or around the city. Barring certain exceptions, like the short trip between Hoi An and Danang or the drive from Nha Trang to Dai Lanh beach, you should not take a daily rental outside the city limits. If you plan to travel on the highway, inform the rental company of your intentions, as you may find yourself in hot water should anything happen to the bike while you're on the road.

When traveling long distances, such as the trip from Hanoi to Saigon (or vice versa), it's also possible to purchase a motorbike. Indeed, many travelers come to Vietnam, buy a heavy-duty vehicle, drive the length of the country, and then sell the motorbike once they've reached their destination. Particularly in Saigon and Hanoi, road-ready vehicles are often on sale in the backpacker neighborhoods, and you should have no trouble buying or selling a motorbike in these destinations.

HIRED CARS

Cars and minibuses can be hired in Vietnam and are widely available. These rental vehicles come with a driver, as foreigners are not permitted to operate a vehicle without a local license. The going rate for a hired car varies depending on the vehicle and its provider. Wherever you rent a car or minibus, be clear about the exact terms of the rental agreement, including which fees are included and which are not, before driving off.

DRIVING IN VIETNAM

Vietnamese law requires all motorists to have a local license, essentially making it illegal for tourists to drive. Though enforcement of the law varies, it is illegal to drive in Vietnam without a Vietnamese license. Most expats don't have a license and many Vietnamese people also operate a vehicle without one. Traveling in the countryside, you can see boys as young as 11 or 12 zipping by on a Honda Wave.

People drive while texting, fail to use the correct turn signals (if they use them at all), routinely speed in the opposite direction down a one-way street, and generally disregard lane markings. Vehicles must drive on the right side of the road, with motorbikes staying in the far right lane at all times. Turning right on a red light is illegal—though it's a common practice in Saigon and seldom enforced by police in the southern hub. While the noise is unpleasant, honking is often a means of defensive driving, an announcement of the vehicle's presence. Beyond that, pay extra attention to larger vehicles when driving, as public buses, taxis, and transport trucks will not hesitate to play chicken with a motorbike.

While it is less likely for foreign drivers to be pulled over by law enforcement (except in large cities like Hanoi and HCMC), it does happen. Most traffic police don't usually go to the trouble of fining foreigners, though this has become more common in Saigon as local authorities become more fluent in English. If you are stopped by the police, remain calm and polite. The proper legal course of action for an unlicensed driver is to impound the motorbike and fine the individual, but this almost never happens. Instead, money often changes hands.

VISAS

All foreign visitors to Vietnam are required to obtain a visa prior to arrival, a process that can be completed up to six months in advance of your trip. For non-American passport holders, tourist visas are available in one- and three-month increments and offer both single- and multiple-entry options. Prices for these visas range from US$25 to US$50.

For Americans, the same visa options are available, though with added complexities. In 2016, Vietnam introduced a **one-year visa** for American passport holders at a cost of USD$135-220, which accompanies the preexisting one- and three-month visa options. Depending on the duration of your visa and where you apply for it—whether through your local embassy or consulate, or via an online service—costs run USD$75-180 for visas in one-, three- and six-month increments, while the yearlong visa will set you back as much as USD$220.

If you are entering the country by land, you can arrange a visa through one of Vietnam's many embassies or consulates in neighboring countries (there are several in Laos and Cambodia) in a matter of a few business days. Visa fees tend to vary depending upon the specific office providing the paperwork, so it's best to inquire about costs at your local embassy or consulate.

Things are simpler for non-Americans, who are able to apply for either a 30- or 90-day tourist visa. Thirty-day visas cost around USD$75-80 for a single-entry stamp and roughly USD$120-135 for a multiple-entry stamp. Ninety-day visas run around USD$100-110 for a single entry and USD$145-160 for multiple entries. Check the official costs with your local embassy, as they change frequently. Tourist visas can also be arranged in the United States by applying in person at the Vietnamese embassy or any one of its consulates, or by sending in the necessary documents and fees by mail. Expedited services are available at a premium. All visa fees rendered outside of Vietnam, whether in the United States or abroad, must be paid in U.S. dollars.

Once in Vietnam, tourists may extend a 30-day visa for up to 60 days by visiting any travel agency that provides visa services. Extensions are also available for 90-day visas, but they are more expensive and generally reserved for emergency situations. Though the extension stamp officially costs about USD$10, the going rate at local travel agencies is around USD$40 for the 30-day visa extension and can reach as high as USD$80 for a monthlong extension of the 90-day visa. This is an unavoidable expense, as the extension process requires the assistance of a Vietnamese speaker, and attempting to complete the process on your own is all but impossible.

If you're entering the country by air, you can save time and money by applying for e-visa processing. This is the most cost-effective option for visitors coming to Vietnam directly from the United States. You will not find information on e-visa processing through the country's official government websites. Vietnamese immigration does not openly advertise this service, but at each of the country's three international airports you will find an official e-visa kiosk through which plenty of travelers have safely and legitimately entered Vietnam.

E-visas can be obtained by contacting a travel agent within the country, many of which provide visa-on-arrival services. You will be asked to supply an image of the identification page in your passport, and within 2-4 business days a letter of approval will be sent to your email. This letter should be two pages: one declaring that you are approved for a visa and the other bearing your name, nationality, and passport number. Upon arrival in Vietnam, you will be required to provide this letter along with a passport photo and a stamping fee, which costs USD$25-50 for 30- and 90-day visas and USD$135 for the yearlong visa offered to American passport holders. An immigration official will then supply you with a visa sticker and send you to the customs line. Along with the stamping fee, you will have to pay an additional fee (usually USD$15-30) to the company providing your letter of approval. All of these costs must be covered in U.S. dollars, including the stamping fee at the airport.

While there are dozens of websites providing e-visa services, exercise caution when applying. There are many safe and reliable websites that provide travelers with legitimate letters of approval, but it is still wise to research reputable companies.

EMBASSIES AND CONSULATES

Within the United States, Vietnam has consular services in several cities, particularly near large communities of overseas Vietnamese. In addition to the **Vietnamese embassy** (1233 20th St. NW, Ste. 400, 202/861-0737, www.vietnamembassy-usa.org, 9:30am-noon and 2:30pm-5pm Mon.-Fri.) in Washington, D.C., there are also consulates in **San Francisco** (1700 California St., Ste. 580, 415/922-1707, www.vietnamconsulate-sf.org, 8:30am-noon and 2pm-4pm Mon.-Fri.), **Houston** (5251 Westheimer Rd., Ste. 1100, 713/850-1233, www.vietnamconsulateinhouston.org, 9am-noon Mon.-Fri., afternoons by appointment only), and **New York City** (866 UN Plaza, Ste. 428, 212/644-0594, www.vnconsul-ny.org, 9am-5:30pm Mon.-Fri.). Each of these offices provides visa services. The hours listed here are only for telephone inquiries; any in-person applications must take place in the morning, 9:30am-noon.

The United States has an **embassy in Hanoi** (170 Ngoc Khanh, 2nd fl., D Ba Dinh, tel. 04/2850-5000, www.vietnam.usembassy.gov) and a **consulate in Ho Chi Minh City** (4 Le Duan, D1, tel. 08/3520-4200, www.hochiminh. usconsulate.gov), which are able to help American citizens in the event of an emergency. Any visa problems relating to your stay in Vietnam are better dealt with by a travel agent, as American consular services cannot assist citizens in arranging Vietnamese visas. Both the embassy and the consulate have separate hours for specific services; check their websites before paying either office a visit.

BORDER CROSSINGS

Border crossings in Vietnam are fairly straightforward. The only way to enter or exit overland is by bus, as there are no international trains connecting Vietnam to its neighbors. Frequent buses travel through Vietnam's many border gates, at which time you pass through two sets of border control offices: one for Vietnam and one for the country you are entering or exiting.

POLICE

The police in Vietnam do not have a stellar reputation. A 2013 survey by anti-corruption nonprofit Transparency International found that 37 percent of the Vietnamese population considers local law enforcement the most corrupt institution in the country. A large part of this stems from the fact that most police officers are underpaid and use traffic violations and other infractions as a way to line their pockets. Politicians have vowed to crack down on such behavior, even discussing a possible salary increase in order to deter both law enforcement and government officials from taking bribes; however, the practice remains common. Most cops steer clear of foreign visitors, in large part because of the language barrier. If you need to contact the police, have a Vietnamese speaker on hand, as few officers speak English.

BRIBES

It's rare for foreigners to have to deal with bribery during their trip. The only instance in which a traveler may be required to supply a bribe is at a police checkpoint, where traffic violations are meted out. Since it is illegal for anyone to drive in Vietnam without a local driver's license, if you are pulled over by a police officer, you will have to pay a "fine." In these instances, good manners and a little patience can help to minimize the dent in your wallet, but you will undoubtedly have to part with some cash. Refusing to pay the bribe is a bad idea. Legally, the police are allowed to impound your motorbike if you fail to provide a license. It is unlikely that the traffic authorities will actually do so, but don't call their bluff.

Accommodations

Throughout Vietnam, accommodations run the gamut from dingy budget hostels to luxurious high-end resorts, sometimes even within the same neighborhood. While there are plenty of good beds available at any price, certain rules hold true for most accommodations. Thanks to the size and volume of many of Vietnam's coastal cities, for instance, noise levels should always be considered when booking, as rooms closer to the ground floor tend to be much louder than rooms higher up, and the same goes for street-facing accommodations versus those in the back of the building. Windows are not a given; it's customary for travelers to ask to see a hotel room before committing to stay the night. A few other amenities, such as elevators, are not always included, but hot water and air-conditioning typically come standard with a room.

Furthermore, though public double-occupancy rates are listed in this book, it is often possible to secure a discount from hotels or guesthouses depending on the season, the length of your stay, and the number of rooms available. Many hotels and guesthouses in larger cities use online reservation sites like Agoda or Booking.com, which can sometimes work to the traveler's advantage by providing cheaper rates, though there are a handful of accommodations that cost more when booking online. For the best price, consult both the hotel directly and their online booking site when available.

When you check in to a hotel in Vietnam you will often be asked to hand over your passport. This is often a source of worry among travelers, but holding one's passport is common practice in Vietnam. Since hotels are required by law to register their guests with the police, many will hold your passport at the front desk during your stay, partly for the authorities and partly for insurance that you don't walk out on your bill (these things occasionally happen). It is acceptable to request that your passport is returned to you after the receptionist has filled out your registration form, though you may be asked to pay in advance.

MAKING RESERVATIONS

Depending upon your location and the time of year, the need for booking accommodations may vary. Most major cities in Vietnam do not require a reservation. With such an abundance of hotels and guesthouses in places like Ho Chi Minh City's Pham Ngu Lao area and the Old Quarter of Hanoi, travelers will never find themselves out in the cold. If you prefer to stay in nicer accommodations and would rather not do the door-to-door legwork, then booking a room is recommended. Be sure when making a reservation that you ask the price up front, as rates may change, and take care to confirm your reservation at least once before arriving at the hotel. Even online sites like Agoda and Booking.com, while reliable, can sometimes make mistakes or lose reservations.

ESSENTIALS
ACCOMMODATIONS

HOTELS

You'll find all manner of accommodations that refer to themselves as *khach san* (hotels). These tend to be larger buildings with more rooms. There is a star rating issued by the Vietnamese government each year, but the criteria for the rating seems to focus on the size of the building rather than the quality of the accommodations. Two- to four-star accommodations are a mixed bag, with plenty of outstanding rooms as well as deteriorating facilities. Boutique and privately owned hotels are usually more impressive, though these are often more expensive, too. Depending upon the rates and quality of the hotel, amenities vary from as little as a bed, air-conditioning, and a hot shower to safety deposit boxes, in-room computers, and fresh fruit or complimentary breakfast.

GUESTHOUSES

Almost interchangeable with budget hotels, Vietnam's guesthouses *(nha nghi)* are smaller versions of the same lodgings, often providing 5-6 rooms where a budget hotel might have 10-12. In general, amenities at a guesthouse include air-conditioning, hot water, and sometimes a refrigerator or TV. These places tend to be the most bare-bones and often the most affordable.

HOSTELS

Hostels and dormitory accommodations are only popular in Vietnam's major cities. While there are a handful of these lodgings in Saigon, Hanoi, and a couple other coastal cities, only one or two hostels actually stand out. All dormitory lodgings should come with proper bedding and a secure locker for each guest, and many also include en suite bathrooms, which limits the number of people sharing a shower.

HOMESTAYS

While there are still plenty of authentic homestays throughout Vietnam, particularly in the Mekong Delta, this is an interesting term nowadays, as "homestay" is often conflated with "guesthouse." Bar a few exceptions, most homestay accommodations are akin to a remote guesthouse, offering the added benefit of home-cooked meals and a bit of interaction with locals, though not as much as you might expect. A growing number of high-end "homestays" are cropping up in more heavily touristed areas—Hoi An, for example; these take on the feel of a bed-and-breakfast, offering more of a local connection along with fancier accommodations.

CAMPING

Camping in Vietnam can have a few different meanings. You may find yourself in a one-room beachside bungalow, a log cabin in the woods, or a tent on the ground. While the lodgings vary, most of these accommodations are located either in national parks or on beaches across the country.

Pitching a tent just anywhere is not accepted. In more remote areas, travelers may be able to get away with overnighting in their own accommodations, but along the coast you'll be hard-pressed to find a place to set up camp. In designated areas, camping fees tend to be inexpensive.

Food

Some of the freshest, most flavorful, and most varied dishes in Southeast Asia belong to Vietnam. From Hanoi's *bun cha* (grilled pork in fish sauce with noodles) to Hue's *bun bo* (spicy beef noodle soup) or the dozens of southern meals unique to each small village and town, Vietnamese cuisine's complex and irresistible flavors win over many a hungry traveler. Most meals consist of a rice or noodle base, a few fresh greens, and either meat or tofu. Portions tend to be smaller here than in Western countries. With the cost of meals so low, there's usually room for seconds in the budget.

STREET FOOD

You can't make it to the end of any city block in Vietnam without encountering a street food vendor. Meals are everywhere: in the park; on the sidewalk; outside of government buildings and public meeting areas. Men and women push metal carts down the road or hustle along with a bamboo pole slung over one shoulder. At first glance, the setup appears to be nothing special, but take a closer look and you'll be amazed by what someone can do with a portable stove and a pair of chopsticks.

While you can buy anything from hot bowls of soup to quick sandwiches or smaller snacks for the road, there are a handful of dishes more commonly found on the street than in a restaurant. Sticky rice *(xoi),* for

food vendor waiting for customers

example, is a popular street-side snack; the rice is often cooked in different leaves or with certain ingredients that turn the rice green, purple, orange, or black. This snack can be served sweet with sugar, coconut, and mung bean, or savory, often accompanied by chicken. A handful of other sweets, including a hot tofu dessert with ginger and tapioca or fried rice cakes with mung bean, are also found on street carts or in a basket on someone's head.

There is something to be said for cooking your food out in the open: Street food kitchens, while simple, are almost always more transparent. You're able to tell which vendors are clean and which are not.

REGIONAL FOODS

While dishes like pho, Vietnam's national soup, and *banh mi* (Vietnamese sandwiches) come standard almost everywhere, local fare is divided into three main regions: the north, central, and south. Shaped in large part by its weather and surroundings, each region's cuisine relies upon both rice and fish sauce as main staples but also has its own distinguishing characteristics. Furthermore, nearly every hamlet and every village across the country has its own unique recipes.

Northern fare is more meat-heavy, shying away from seafood in favor of chicken and beef, though fish sometimes makes an appearance. Hot dishes like *chao* (rice porridge) and what is officially considered the country's best pho are native to the north, as is *bun cha,* a simple but mouthwatering combination of cold rice noodles, fish sauce, pickled vegetables, and grilled meat.

Things heat up in the central region, where spicier dishes like *bun bo Hue* (spicy beef noodle soup) are all the rage, not to mention the dozens of tiny, bite-sized foods found in the Nguyen dynasty's former capital, including *banh beo* (steamed rice cake with shrimp paste), *banh duc* (sticky steamed rice cake), *banh loc* (steamed shrimp and pork fat dumplings), and *banh hoi* (bundles of rice vermicelli).

By the time you reach Saigon and the rest of the south, foods are sweeter, with more sugar found in local dishes. Whether it be the massive river fish of the Delta or the tasty grilled octopus of the southern coast, seafood features heavily in southern cuisine and many dishes are fried, including all varieties of *banh xeo* (savory pancakes), as well as a handful of local specialties like *banh khot* (Vung Tau's delicious, bite-sized rice cakes).

BEER AND RICE WINE

Along with local favorites like southern Saigon Red or Huda, a brew from the central region, freshly made beers are a popular fixture during local happy hours. *Bia tuoi* (fresh beer) is a locally produced lager sold in 100-liter barrels to small shops across town (also called *bia hoi*), particularly in Hanoi. Often going for as little as VND4,000 a glass on the street, this

The Stranger Side of Vietnamese Cuisine

In a nation as food-focused as Vietnam, it is all but impossible to come up with dozens of savory masterpieces without having created a few strange dishes along the way. While pho and *banh mi* (Vietnamese sandwiches) have gained worldwide acclaim as delicious, accessible facets of local cuisine, there are several specialties that manage to make some travelers wrinkle their noses.

Century eggs: A traditional Chinese delicacy that has carried over to Vietnam, century eggs are regular chicken or duck eggs that have been preserved in a combination of clay, ash, salt, lime, and rice for several weeks, during which time the pH of the egg elevates, changing the yolk to a dark green, creamy ball at the center of a gelatinous brown egg. The resulting dish is slightly off-putting in appearance. It's often included in local meals and is something of an acquired taste.

Dog: While foreign perceptions tend to suggest that Asia is far more into dog meat than it actually is, the majority of Vietnam's canine consumption occurs in the north, where dog is still considered something of a delicacy. Down south, you're less likely to find locals indulging in dog, but there are still people who enjoy it every now and again, and Saigon does have a small street dedicated to the sale of canine meat. Most meals are prepared in much the same way as chicken, beef, or other meats—roasted, steamed, boiled, or barbecued—and served with rice or added into a soup.

With a government ban on the sale of dog meat and growing concerns over its safety, this delicacy may be harder to come by over the next few years. The harsh reality of this dish is that most of the animals slaughtered and prepared are actually pets or strays that have been kidnapped. Given the persistence of rabies in Vietnam, contaminated meat is a risk. Many people also believe that canine meat is at its best when the animal has suffered, so the dogs are often killed in a brutal way. As demand increases throughout Southeast Asia, more and more dogs are being smuggled into Vietnam and killed, and the quality, safety, and humane treatment of these animals is fast decreasing.

Embryonic duck egg: Known locally as *hot vit lon* and more widely as *balut,* embryonic duck eggs are regularly consumed in Vietnam and several Southeast Asian countries, namely the Philippines. Larger and more dense than your average chicken egg, *hot vit lon* is consumed when the fetus is 19-21 days old—still too small to hatch but old enough that its wings, feet, beak, and eyes are visible. Like any egg, the yolk is thick and a little dry, while the tiny bird makes up the majority of the shell. *Hot vit lon* is commonly enjoyed on the street with salt, pepper, or lime and an ice-cold beer.

Pigeon: In the mountainous north where protein is scarce, small birds are often a part of local fare. Creatures like pigeons and other forest-dwelling birds are grilled and eaten with rice and rice wine or beer.

Rice paddy rat: In the Mekong Delta and parts of Cambodia, rice paddy rats are a delicacy. Much cleaner than their city-dwelling counterparts, these countryside rodents are sold at the market on a seasonal basis and usually grilled, barbecued, or boiled. Dishes are best enjoyed with beer or rice wine.

Snake: Particularly in the north, snake meat is a delicacy. While some creatures are simply slaughtered and prepared like any other meal, eating snake is more often than not an almost ritualistic experience. First, the live animal is slit from neck to tail, slicing open the skin to reveal its flesh, before its blood and bile are drained into separate shot glasses and combined with rice wine. After the blood has been consumed, the snake's still-beating heart is removed and swallowed by the guest of honor.

Drinking in Vietnam

Though it is largely reserved for men, drinking is a large part of Vietnamese culture. As one of the world's top beer-drinking nations, this country takes its alcohol consumption seriously, as evidenced by the dozens of drinking slogans that can be heard during a weekend drinking session or at happy hour. Phrases like *mot tram phan tram* (100 percent, or bottoms up) and *khong say khong ve* (you can't go home until you're drunk) spell out the Vietnamese attitude towards imbibing. Drinking is a social event and is often accompanied by *do nhau* (drinking food), such as snails, grilled meat, or other savory snacks. Beer is enjoyed with ice and shared among the group. If you go out drinking with a local crowd, be prepared to clink glasses a lot: *Mot, hai, ba, DZO!* (One, two, three, CHEERS!) is a phrase commonly repeated throughout the night.

Drinking in Vietnam can be an enjoyable experience but it can also be a dangerous one. Drinking and driving is a common practice in a country where road safety is already dismal at best. Exercise the same good judgment you would when going out at home: Never get on the back of a motorbike with someone who has been drinking or appears to be drunk, and always opt for an alternative means of transportation in the event that someone in your party is not able to drive.

While it is not a widespread problem, methanol poisoning can occur as a result of poorly produced homemade alcohol or counterfeit spirits. This is a very serious condition that can result in permanent disability or life-threatening complications.

watered-down beverage is incredibly popular up north and must be drunk the day it is made, as its shelf life is very short. Men regularly gather at *bia hoi* after close of business to enjoy a few drinks and catch up. While fresh beer would not under most circumstances be considered a fine beer, the cultural experience of hanging out at a *bia hoi* in the city is well worth the dirt-cheap price tag.

Much stronger than fresh beer, rice wine is a high-octane spirit that is often enjoyed in the countryside and becomes a major fixture during Tet, the Vietnamese lunar new year. Across Vietnam, locals make their own alcohol, storing it in massive plastic jugs for the coming festivities. Glutinous rice is steamed and left to sit for several days, adding yeast to the mixture, to produce a spirit that can carry a concentration of up to 22 percent alcohol. While you won't often find rice wine in local shops, it is everywhere in the countryside. In many cases, making local friends off the beaten path is likely to earn you at least a shot or two.

Conduct and Customs

GENERAL ETIQUETTE

Vietnam is a very polite country. Though Western-style customer service is not always observed in restaurants or hotels, you'll be hard-pressed to find people who are intentionally rude. Locals rarely raise their voices out of anger or show intense emotions in public. Daily interactions are handled calmly and politely. When problems arise, the typical Vietnamese reaction is often awkward laughter. This can be a frustrating and seemingly inappropriate response. In Vietnamese culture, showing anger is considered a lack of self-control and will likely cause the person you're dealing with to shut down, leaving you no better off than when you started.

As much as the average person is polite and respectful, the rules of etiquette, like most rules in Vietnam, are sometimes overlooked. Lining up, it seems, is the worst: people push, shove, and openly cut in front while waiting for a bus or at the supermarket checkout counter. If this happens, politely ask the person to move and you'll usually get a feigned surprise or even an apology, and most of the time that individual will get out of line. Acts like these are rarely meant to be rude; it's just that they were hoping you wouldn't say anything.

APPROPRIATE DRESS

Though you wouldn't know it in larger cities, Vietnam's sense of style tends to be rather conservative, with most people opting for long pants and shirts that cover their shoulders. Women in particular are usually more reserved, though sheer shirts are in fashion. In professional or religious settings, outfits that hit below the knee are appropriate for women and long pants are a must for men. At night all rules go out the window, as you'll see young Vietnamese women flying by on the back of a motorbike

Offering objects with two hands is considered a sign of respect.

in sky-high stilettos and a mini skirt. For the most part, the same rules apply in Vietnam as in the United States: you wouldn't show up to work or to church in your party dress or shorts and flip-flops; if you visit a pagoda or an office building, the same holds true.

BODY LANGUAGE

Unlike Cambodia or Thailand, bowing in Vietnam, while still respectful, does not carry the same significance. Instead, when handing something to an elder or a stranger, for instance, it is polite to give the item with both hands as a sign of respect, or to offer the item with the right hand while placing the left hand on the right elbow. Certain gestures are inappropriate here where they would not be at home. Crossing your forefinger and middle finger over one another, for instance, is a rude gesture in Vietnam. When beckoning someone, it's better to use an underhand motion.

Vietnamese culture dictates that the top of a person's head is the most sacred part of his or her body (because it is closest to God), while the soles of one's feet are the lowest. Touching the top of a person's head is considered impolite, particularly with children, as is showing a person the soles of your feet. In pagodas especially, directing the soles of your feet at the Buddha is considered an offensive gesture.

TABLE MANNERS

There are several Vietnamese dining habits that break with Western ideas of what is polite. Slurping your soup, talking with a full mouth, and shouting for the waiter are all acceptable practices at a local restaurant. You can shout *em oi!* to beckon a waiter over to your table. While it may seem odd at first, you'll want to get the hang of it, as servers don't check up on quiet tables and only bring the bill when you've asked for it. If you're visiting a street food stall or a more local restaurant, throwing rubbish like napkins and used toothpicks on the floor is also acceptable. This may seem unsanitary, but a restaurant employee will come by and sweep up any garbage that gets left on the floor. Occasionally, wastebaskets are positioned at the end of each table. If you're in doubt, take a look around: if you can see squeezed limes, napkins, and other rubbish strewn across the floor, then you're allowed to do the same.

When eating with a local family, Vietnamese hospitality dictates that no guest go hungry: in a Vietnamese house, you will eat until you're full and then some. Be warned that any time you empty your bowl it will be filled again before you have the chance to decline. Dining family-style means that anyone can pick at the assortment of meats and veggies on offer and drop some into your bowl, and people often do when guests are around. In situations like these, rice is served in a small *chen* (bowl) for each person, while the main dishes are set out in the middle. When eating, it is acceptable to pick up your *chen* and bring it closer to your mouth; as you reach the bottom of the bowl, you may lift it to your mouth and use your chopsticks to shovel the rice in. Take what is closest to you, as any piece you touch is yours, and always put the food in your *chen* first before bringing it to your mouth.

There are a long list of dos and don'ts regarding chopstick etiquette. For most transgressions, foreigners will likely be forgiven. Always lay your chopsticks parallel to one another, never crossed, and do not point them at other people, as these gestures are considered rude. It is also inappropriate to leave your utensils in the shape of a "V," and chopsticks should never be stuck upright into a bowl of rice, as this resembles incense sticks and is viewed as an omen of death.

Travel Tips

LANGUAGE AND COMMUNICATION

As a nation still getting the hang of the tourism industry, Vietnam lacks an adequate number of fluent English speakers. In part due to the complexities of their own language, the Vietnamese have a great deal of trouble with English (and, it's safe to say, English-speakers face the same challenges with Vietnamese). Staying patient and simplifying your requests will go a long way to helping make yourself understood. In English, we often make requests more polite by adding extra words. For instance, at home you might say, "I was wondering if you could tell me where the restroom is?" For a weaker English speaker these extra words add confusion. Instead, "Excuse me, where is the toilet?" will make you more easily understood and locals will not take offense to the shorter sentences.

Whenever you arrange a service—whether it be a motorbike rental, a *xe om* ride, a day tour, or a cooking course—always be clear on the cost and the expectations of both parties before setting out, as this will help to prevent disagreements. Patience goes a long way. Expressing anger or being short with someone will keep you from gaining that person's respect.

WHAT TO PACK

Thanks to a steady influx of foreign visitors, Vietnam offers plenty of Western amenities, but some items are still hard to come by. Sunscreen, for instance, is almost never used among the local population and so can be difficult to track down in Vietnam. When you do find it, sunblock is overpriced and the locally produced version is not particularly effective. You're better off bringing your own sunscreen from abroad. The same goes for insect repellent. For women, feminine products are available at most pharmacies and drugstores, but tampons are less common, so bring your own.

Given the humidity, lightweight, breathable clothing and sturdy shoes are a wise choice for any traveler. Anyone planning to go pagoda-hopping should opt for at least one long-sleeved shirt and pants or shorts that reach the knee. A hat is a good idea as certain destinations like the Mekong Delta and Nha Trang are notably devoid of shade. While backpacking through Vietnam is a dirty business and your standard shorts-and-T-shirt attire is perfectly acceptable, pack one or two nice outfits if you plan to hit the town in the bigger cities like Hanoi or Saigon. You will likely need a raincoat at one time or another while in Vietnam, but bringing your own is optional, as cheap, plastic cover-ups are widely available.

OPPORTUNITIES FOR STUDY AND EMPLOYMENT

As job opportunities at home dwindle, more and more Western travelers are choosing to make a home in Asia, if only for a year or two. A combination of increasing tourism and growing demand for English-language education in Vietnam have created ample opportunities for foreigners looking to experience another part of the world and earn money at the same time. Short-term employment can be found at hostels and guesthouses around the country, where simple housework or other odd jobs are sometimes traded for room and board. For more permanent employment, most companies require you to make connections once you've already arrived in Vietnam. Websites like **VietnamWorks** (www.vietnamworks.com) provide insight into what's available from abroad.

If you plan to be in Asia for six months or more, ESL teaching is an excellent option. Jobs teaching English in Vietnam are widely available in Saigon and Hanoi, while employment in smaller cities like Danang is growing. Most English-teaching contracts range between six months and one year, and several schools within Vietnam offer ESL teaching certification courses, like the CELTA or TESOL, both of which are recognized internationally. **Apollo English** (www.apollo.edu.vn), **ILA** (www.ilavietnam.com), and **VUS** (www.vus.edu.vn) are reputable English teaching centers that employ foreign instructors. You can work under-the-table gigs with a tax-free hourly wage, but these businesses are far less reliable. In order to get a legitimate job with a reasonable salary, you'll need a Bachelor's degree in any field, a TESOL or CELTA certificate, a police background check from your home country or state, and a medical check to confirm that you are in good health. If you decide to teach in Vietnam, it is infinitely easier to apply for a work permit and a legitimate visa if you have an original copy of your Bachelor's degree notarized at home and your police check completed before you arrive rather than coordinating these documents from Vietnam, as the red tape can be exhausting.

Beyond teaching English, a variety of other opportunities are available but often require you to make connections within Vietnam first, which is why a teaching job is often the way foreigners get started in Vietnam. Once you've met some of your fellow expats and gotten to know the lay of the land, you can find jobs in anything from marketing and sales to graphic design, business, science, and even the food and beverage industry.

Vietnam is not easily accessible for travelers with physical disabilities, particularly anyone who uses a wheelchair. Elevators are seldom available outside of major cities, streets and sidewalks are often crumbled and aging, and many of Vietnam's tourist attractions require some mobility. Major cities are better equipped to accommodate travelers with disabilities, including Ho Chi Minh City, Danang, and Hanoi. Particularly around Danang and Hoi An, a popular area for many older travelers, businesses and accommodations will likely be more equipped to serve tourists with disabilities.

WOMEN TRAVELING ALONE

Vietnam is safe for female tourists. Women are able to travel freely without much harassment. Solo women will receive their fair share of lighthearted marriage proposals and occasional pestering from local men, but this rarely results in any serious issues. Always be polite but firm when encountering unwanted attention and, once you have made your point, ignore the other party. This is more effective than continuing to respond.

GAY AND LESBIAN TRAVELERS

Gay and lesbian travelers will find that Vietnam is an accepting place. The speed with which Vietnam has come to accept its own LGBTQ community is incredibly heartening. In little more than a few years, large swaths of the urban population have come to understand, albeit tentatively, the presence of homosexuality in local society. In 2015, the Vietnamese government legalized same-sex weddings, with one high-ranking official even publicly supporting same-sex marriage. (Note the difference here between a wedding and a marriage.) Since 2012, Hanoi has held an annual **VietPride festival** (www.vietpride.info) and continues to push for greater recognition of LGBTQ Vietnamese throughout the country. For the most part, many locals are happy to live and let live, though public displays of affection from any couple—gay or straight—are usually discouraged. More and more young Vietnamese are empowered to come out and a handful of great organizations in the major cities are improving social perceptions of LGBTQ people in Vietnam. The countryside is still a conservative place where tolerance may be less forthcoming.

Health and Safety

VACCINATIONS

As per **CDC** (Centers for Disease Control and Prevention, www.cdc.gov/travel) guidelines, all travelers to Vietnam should be up-to-date on routine vaccinations before going abroad. It is recommended that travelers receive vaccinations against Hepatitis A and typhoid, both of which can be spread through contaminated food or water. For more adventurous travelers and anyone planning to visit remote areas in Vietnam or to stay for a long time, vaccinations against Hepatitis B and Japanese encephalitis are encouraged, as well as preemptive rabies prophylaxis.

Malaria

Though malaria is less common in Vietnam than other parts of Southeast Asia, this flu-like, potentially fatal illness still exists in the southern half of the country. CDC guidelines recommend that travelers to rural areas in the south take malaria prophylaxis. Check with your doctor to find out which prophylaxis is best for you, as Vietnam's particular strain of malaria is resistant to certain drugs. There are many side effects associated with malaria prophylaxis, including minor annoyances like upset stomach, nausea, and sensitivity to sunlight but also more serious issues such as anxiety, hallucinations, and even seizures. Many travelers forgo using malaria drugs and instead take extra precautions in covering up and preventing mosquito bites. While DEET repellents are not intended for long-term use, a couple days of strong insect repellent should be fine. If you believe that you have contracted malaria, seek medical attention immediately. When caught early, malaria is very treatable.

Rabies

For anyone traveling to remote areas, spending a lot of time outdoors, or planning to travel by bicycle, the rabies vaccination is recommended, as people continue to die from the disease in Vietnam each year. Almost always fatal, rabies can be transmitted to humans through a bite or scratch from monkeys, cats, dogs, and bats. Avoid touching animals in Vietnam, even pets, as they are often left to their own devices and not cared for in the same way as Western pets. If you are bitten or scratched by a wild animal, wash the wound immediately with soap and water before seeking medical attention. Typically, an unvaccinated person requires a series of five shots following rabies exposure; those who have had preemptive prophylaxis need only two shots as soon as possible following the encounter. Due to the number of wild animals in Vietnam, rabies vaccines are widely available in the country and can be administered almost anywhere, including remote areas.

HEALTH
Allergies

Travelers with severe allergies may have trouble in Vietnam, especially those allergic to shellfish and peanuts, as these are frequent ingredients in Vietnamese cuisine. Cross-contamination is difficult to manage at street carts or in local restaurants, and even if you explain your dilemma to a local server there is no guarantee that the message will be understood. Take care to read all packaged foods and bring your own means of treatment, such as an EpiPen, to counter an allergic reaction. In the event of a severe allergic reaction, seek medical attention immediately.

Traveler's Diarrhea

One of the less glamorous facets of traveling, traveler's diarrhea is common among visitors to Vietnam, particularly those who enjoy street food. Some guidelines urge visitors to avoid roadside food carts as well as ice and fresh vegetables, but this may make your stay more expensive, not to mention detract from the overall experience. Avoiding specific street vendors or restaurants whose kitchens appear unclean or have food that has been sitting out for some time will help to decrease your risk of traveler's diarrhea and other food-borne illnesses. Dishes that are served hot and meat and veggies that have been fried, grilled, or otherwise prepared with high heat should be fine. In many cases, a good street food restaurant will prepare their meals in plain sight, giving you the ability to see the kitchen for yourself. When it comes to dishes like pho, *bun bo* (spicy beef noodle soup), and *banh xeo* (savory Vietnamese pancakes), fresh greens are usually served on the side, so you are able to easily avoid them if you so choose.

Regarding beverages, the ice at most restaurants in backpacker areas and higher-end eateries is safe to consume. Tap water is not meant for anything beyond showers and brushing your teeth. Though water can be boiled, nearly everyone in the country drinks bottled water or *tra da*, a light tea served at local restaurants.

In the event that you find yourself with traveler's diarrhea, it's best to stick to bland foods and proper restaurants for a day or two until your symptoms subside. Over-the-counter anti-diarrheal drugs like Imodium are available both in Vietnam and at home. If the issue persists, visit a doctor, who will prescribe something stronger. If you visit a physician in the United States prior to your trip abroad, ask about anti-diarrheal medicines, as procuring medications at home is generally safer than doing so in Vietnam.

Dengue

One of the few more serious illnesses that exists in Vietnam's cities as well as in rural areas is dengue. Passed through mosquito bites, the disease causes fever, headaches, and muscle and joint pain along with flu-like symptoms. There is no vaccination for dengue. Anyone who believes to be suffering from the disease should seek medical attention, as dengue is highly treatable but can become fatal if left unchecked. Should you become ill, avoid mosquitoes, rest, stay hydrated, and, of course, see a doctor. Acetaminophen-based pain killers can be used to relieve muscle and joint aches, but you should avoid any medications with aspirin, ibuprofen, or naproxen. Take extra care to monitor your health as the symptoms recede; in rare cases, dengue can turn into a fatal condition just as the initial symptoms appear to subside. If you experience difficulty breathing, pale or clammy skin, persistent vomiting, bleeding from your nose or gums, or red spots on your skin, go to a hospital immediately, as these may be signs of a more serious condition.

Zika Virus

In April 2016, Vietnam's Ministry of Health confirmed the country's first Zika cases. Since then, the southern half of Vietnam has seen a marked increase in the spread of the illness, with dozens of reported cases in Ho Chi Minh City alone. Popular tourist destinations like Nha Trang and the Mekong Delta region have also been affected. A handful of international travelers have returned home after a trip to Vietnam and begun showing symptoms of the virus. Vietnam has also reported one case of Zika-linked microcephaly in the Central Highlands.

The virus is currently considered endemic in Vietnam, meaning occasional cases may follow. It's unlikely that the rate of Zika infection will be so high as to cause an epidemic. As of the time of writing, Vietnam had recorded Zika cases in Saigon, Binh Duong, Nha Trang, and Phu Yen; it's expected the virus will also spread to northern Vietnam.

While there is no vaccination to prevent Zika infection, travelers can limit their risk by wearing long sleeves and mosquito repellent during the day and opting for air-conditioned accommodations at night. Check the CDC website (www.cdc.gov) for the most up-to-date information.

Methanol Poisoning

Though this is still a rare problem among travelers, a handful of cases in recent years have raised the need for awareness regarding methanol poisoning. More commonly known as wood alcohol, methanol is the cousin of ethanol, the type of alcohol found in spirits like vodka, whiskey, or rum. Where ethanol can leave you with a bad headache, a queasy stomach, and all the other trappings of a regular hangover, methanol is much worse, with even small doses causing serious side effects or even death.

As a means of cutting costs, some local businesses attempt to create their own homemade versions of alcoholic spirits using this substance, which they then sell to local bars, some of whom don't even know they're purchasing counterfeit booze. Regardless, unsafe amounts of methanol, which can be virtually undetectable in a mixed drink, have found their way into the hands of locals and travelers. Symptoms of methanol poisoning may not show up until as late as 72 hours after initial exposure and can often mirror the predictable symptoms of intoxication or a hangover, including confusion, dizziness, headaches, nausea, vomiting, and inability to coordinate muscle movements. In more serious cases, it can cause loss of vision; kidney, heart, and respiratory failure; gastrointestinal bleeding; and seizures, the combination of which can prove fatal.

It is extremely important to exercise caution when going out on the town, particularly in backpacker areas and in certain cities like Saigon and Nha Trang. Cheap drinks are available everywhere, but if a price seems too good to be true then it probably is. Purchasing your own spirits from a supermarket or chain convenience store is safer than opting for the local corner store. At the bar, if you order a drink and something doesn't seem right—the taste is particularly sweet or harsh, or the beverage is discolored—don't bother finishing it. For the most part, higher-end bars and lounges are safer than local watering holes or cheap backpacker spots. If all else fails, stick to beer and wine. Should you or a friend become a victim of methanol poisoning, go to a hospital immediately.

Insects
The local mosquito population continues to pester everyone in Vietnam. When traveling both in the city and throughout the countryside, take care to cover up at dawn and dusk, when insects are out in the greatest numbers, and use insect repellent. While it is possible to find repellent sprays in Vietnam, it's better to purchase them at home or in neighboring countries like Thailand, as these products can be more difficult to come by in-country and are usually more expensive. Avoid leaving your hotel room windows open at night and, if possible, sleep with the air-conditioning on or use a mosquito net around your bed. While rare, bed bugs are also an occasional problem in Vietnam, particularly if you are staying in dormitory-style accommodations. Check thoroughly for the critters before climbing into bed.

Wild Animals
Vietnam's largest animal problems tend to stem from dogs and cats, many of which are technically pets but whose owners let them roam freely outside. In more remote areas, locals keep dogs for protection. Cyclists in particular will want to steer clear of these animals, as they've been known to chase bikes. Avoid touching animals, even if they appear to be pets. If you come into contact with an animal, wash your hands thoroughly.

Medical Services
Medical services in Vietnamese hospitals are dismal at best, with major overcrowding and sanitation problems. In larger cities, international facilities provide a reasonable level of quality and will usually suffice in the event of illness or minor emergencies. More serious cases may require airlifting to Singapore or Bangkok; all of this should be covered by adequate travel insurance.

Insurance
Travel insurance is a must for visitors to Vietnam, as even a healthy tourist can become the victim of an accident, and while local hospitals may be significantly cheaper than their American counterparts, the cost of quality medical care can add up. Check with your current insurance provider to see if you are covered outside of your home country and what exactly falls within your plan. Travel insurance can be purchased through providers such as **Travel Guard** (www.travelguard.com). For most minor illnesses and injuries, healthcare in Vietnam is inexpensive enough that you may be

able to cover the costs on your own, but at the very least be sure that your insurance plan covers major accidents and injuries. Confirm your plan's payment policy, as some hospitals in Vietnam require cash up front in order to perform medical services, and emergency evacuations can run in the hundreds of thousands of dollars. For those keen on hiring a motorbike, most travel insurance does not cover road accidents if the driver is unlicensed.

CRIME

The vast majority of crime in Vietnam involves bending the rules in business. While violent crimes occur, these incidents rarely involve foreigners. The most common trouble you'll encounter is petty theft, which, while frustrating, seldom turns dangerous or violent. The second greatest concern for foreign visitors is drugs, which are illegal in Vietnam: Possession in large amounts can garner the death penalty or a protracted sentence for offenders.

Pickpocketing and Petty Theft

Though it's a minor offense compared to more violent crimes, petty theft is a big problem in Vietnam, especially in urban areas. Foreigners just getting the hang of a new country are often the victims. Particularly at night and around backpacker areas, tourists stand out as easy targets. Bag snatching, pickpocketing, and burglary are frequent occurrences, even in broad daylight.

There are steps you can take to minimize vulnerability. When walking around town, opt for pockets that close and keep your belongings in sight at all times. When paying for purchases, avoid showing large amounts of money, as this makes you a target. Anyone carrying a backpack should wear both straps; shoulder bags are best worn across the body and on the side furthest from the street. Avoid walking near the sidewalk's edge, as thieves on motorbikes have been known to snatch purses, phones, and wallets, sometimes dragging the person along with them. The same rules apply when you're on a motorbike: place your bag or backpack in front of you, hugging it to your chest, and tuck any necklaces into your shirt, as they can be snatched, too. Whether you're on foot or on a motorbike, use caution when taking out your belongings in public; even if you're just answering a text message or finding directions on your cell phone, duck into a local shop and out of view. These tips may sound extreme, but the number of tourists who have been robbed multiple times on a single trip suggests that, while slightly over-the-top, such practices are necessary. At night, common sense should be exercised. Male or female, don't walk alone around town, avoid alleyways, and always take taxis rather than *xe om* after dark.

If you are robbed, especially at night, it's best to let the situation go. The majority of these criminals are after your monetary goods, not your life. Your first priority should always be your own safety; remember that goods are replaceable, your life is not.

Not everyone is out to steal your money. Locals are incredibly kind, and if you follow precautions, you are less likely to encounter trouble.

Drugs

Recreational drugs like marijuana, heroin, and synthetic tablets are both widely available and illegal in Vietnam. There is a harsh, zero-tolerance policy for drug trafficking and possession.

Information and Services

MONEY

Currency

The official currency of Vietnam is known as the dong. Bills come in denominations of VND500, VND1,000, VND2,000, VND5,000, VND10,000, VND20,000, VND50,000, VND100,000, VND200,000, and VND500,000. Refuse ripped or torn bills, particularly those with denominations of VND10,000 or higher, as they are often rejected by shops and local businesses and you may find yourself stuck with money you cannot spend.

Exchange Rates

At the time of writing, the exchange rate for the Vietnam dong is roughly VND22,000 to one U.S. dollar. Current rates can be found online at **Oanda** (www.oanda.com) and **XE** (www.xe.com). Businesses within Vietnam operate on a rate that fluctuates between VND20,000 and VND23,000.

Changing Money

Most major tourist destinations have proper currency exchange kiosks, in addition to the countless hotels, restaurants, travel agencies, and gold shops that offer exchange services at various rates. While exchange kiosks are usually not affiliated with a bank, they are safe to use, as counterfeit currency is not a major problem in Vietnam. Ripped or torn bills are not accepted by many local businesses. If you receive any bills in this state, or if they are noticeably worn or faded, ask to have them switched out.

ATMs

ATMs are everywhere in Vietnam, with even the most remote destinations having at least one or two machines. Major cities often have ATMs from international banks such as ANZ, HSBC, Citibank, and Commonwealth Bank, as well as domestic institutions like Sacombank, Techcombank, and Vietcombank. Most domestic ATMs charge minimal fees for using their machines. International institutions sometimes charge more, though the cost rarely exceeds VND10,000 per withdrawal.

Bank Hours

For international banks, business hours are 8am-5pm; domestic institutions follow the same schedule but sometimes close earlier, at 4pm or 4:30pm, and almost always break for lunch, closing at 11am or 11:30am and reopening at 1pm or 1:30pm. All banks are open Monday-Friday, with some open on Saturday mornings as well.

Traveler's Checks

While it is possible to cash traveler's checks in certain banks in major cities, these are often far more trouble than they're worth. Not every financial institution will cash them and, when they do, many banks include fees and surcharges that eat away at the actual value of the check. **Vietcombank** (tel. 04/3824-3524, www.vietcombank.com.vn) is one of the few institutions that accepts traveler's checks, though the service is only provided in larger cities and not nationwide. With the availability of ATMs all over the country and the lack of places in which a stolen bank card could be used, you're better off bringing plastic and withdrawing money from a machine.

Costs

Every price, from food and accommodations to shopping, is up for negotiation. In major cities, a good local meal can go for as little as VND15,000-20,000 at a street stall to as much as VND200,000 in a restaurant. In these instances, what you pay for is the atmosphere—more often than not, the food at a small hole-in-the-wall shop or street cart is just as good, if not better, than what you'll find at a high-end restaurant in the trendier part of town. When eating street-side it is a good idea to ask the price beforehand, as vendors occasionally try to rip off tourists by doubling or tripling the bill at the end. You can avoid being had by agreeing upon the cost from the beginning.

Other goods and services are trickier to gauge in terms of cost. Prices fluctuate depending upon location. More tourist-heavy areas like Phu Quoc or Hoi An are often more expensive, while less-visited areas like the Mekong Delta and the Central Highlands tend to be a fraction of the cost. With prices changing all the time, it's difficult to say what an appropriate amount is for any given good or service.

Bargaining

In markets and shops across the country, bargaining is a common practice. Prices for everything from fresh produce to clothing to motorbike rides are up for negotiation. It is often expected that you'll haggle for goods and services if a price tag is not affixed to them. While it can be difficult to discern what a fair price is, your best bet is to ask around, gauge the average asking price of a few vendors, and then cut that number by 20-40 percent. In some cases this will be too much, in other cases too little. Take care not to enter into negotiations with a vendor unless you actually want the product. It's perfectly acceptable to ask the price of an item out of curiosity, but once you begin haggling it's assumed that you actually intend to buy the item.

Tipping

Outside of high-end restaurants, tipping is not required, nor is it a common practice. Some businesses take on a service charge for their employees, but you are not obligated to include something extra unless you feel inclined to do so. The only exception is in spas and massage parlors where tips are usually expected and you may even be asked to fill out a gratuity form after your massage. In this case, VND40,000 and up is usually acceptable. If you decide to leave a gratuity elsewhere, the amount really is up to you: In a country where one U.S. dollar can buy a meal, a motorbike ride, or even a pair of shoes, any extra cash you leave will be appreciated.

MAPS AND TOURIST INFORMATION

Vietnam is not great at providing accurate or detailed plans of the national road system. Cheap walking maps can be found in many towns. For anyone on a serious navigational mission, the only decent Vietnamese atlas is called *Tap Ban Do Giao Thong Duong Bo Viet Nam* and runs about VND300,000 in local bookshops.

The efficacy of local tourism offices varies depending upon the location. Places like Hanoi and Hoi An are packed with tour companies and travel agents who are willing to help, while a place like Con Dao, one of Vietnam's most remote islands, has maybe one or two English-speaking businesses.

COMMUNICATIONS AND MEDIA

Postal Services

Postage in Vietnam is cheap, with postcards traveling halfway around the world for VND10,000-20,000. The same goes for mail, but once you ship larger packages abroad the costs skyrocket, and in many cases there is no guarantee that the item will arrive at all. Most mail arrives at its destination within 2-3 weeks.

Area Codes

The country code for Vietnam is +84. Each city or province has its own area code, which is included in all phone numbers listed in this book. When calling locally, phone numbers can be dialed as they are listed here. International calls require 1, followed by the country code, but without the zero that appears at the beginning of each number in this book.

Cell Phones

Cell phones in Vietnam run on a pay-as-you-go basis and can be purchased new or used in most cities. For travelers, dirt-cheap brands like Nokia are useful and cost-effective; SIM cards are usually sold with the cell phone.

Internet Access

With the exception of the most remote corners of the country, Internet access in Vietnam is widespread. You can easily find Wi-Fi in local cafés and restaurants, while a smaller number of Internet and gaming cafés with computers are also available. Most hotels in major cities keep a desktop computer in the lobby for guests to use.

Local Newspapers and Magazines

A handful of national publications come out daily, weekly, or monthly in English, namely *Tuoi Tre* (www.tuoitrenews.vn), the online English-language version of the Vietnamese paper of the same name, and *VnExpress* (www.e.vnexpress.net), an online newswire. **Saigoneer** (www.saigoneer.com) is a good source of news as well as information on local history, social issues, arts and culture, and food. **Hanoi Grapevine** (www.hanoigrapevine.com) provides up-to-date event listings for Hanoi, while Saigoneer does the same for HCMC.

Monthly magazines geared toward expats are available for free in the country's two main hubs, Hanoi and Saigon, namely *AsiaLIFE* (www.asialifemagazine.com), *The Word* (www.wordhanoi.com or www.wordhcmc.com), and *Oi* (www.oivietnam.com).

Local Television

Local television leaves much to be desired, especially because only a few channels play programs in English. Popular foreign channels like National Geographic and Animal Planet broadcast English-language programming, while Star World and AXN are filled with dated prime time American sitcoms and reruns of *CSI*. All of these channels can be found on basic cable, along with at least one English-language news station. Hotels and restaurants with specific television packages carry European sports channels, the international version of ESPN, sometimes HBO, Star Movies, a regional channel featuring Western films, and Cinemax.

WEIGHTS AND MEASURES

Vietnam uses the metric system. Temperatures are recorded in Celsius, distances in kilometers, and weight in kilograms.

Resources

Glossary

ao dai: traditional Vietnamese garment

banh bao: steamed pork dumpling

banh beo: steamed rice flour cake

banh mi: Vietnamese bread, or a sandwich made out of this bread

banh trung thu: moon cake, a round, dense pastry whose reputation is not unlike fruitcake at Christmas—pretty, ornamental, and not nearly as delicious as it looks

banh xeo: savory Vietnamese pancakes

bia hoi: locally brewed beer (a variant is called *bia tuoi*); also the name for the shops that sell this beer

bun bo Hue: soup with beef and rice noodles, a specialty of Hue

bun cha: grilled meat and rice noodles in fish sauce, a Hanoian specialty

bun nem vit: soup with rice noodles, fresh greens, and duck spring rolls

bun thit nuong: rice noodles and grilled pork

cai luong: a popular form of traditional Vietnamese music

ca phe sua da: iced coffee with milk

ca phe trung: egg coffee

ca tru: ancient chamber music

cha ca: pan-fried fish

chao: rice porridge

com chay: vegetarian food

com cháy: a Ninh Binh specialty made from rice that is sun-dried, then fried

com ga: Hoi An-style chicken and rice

dan nhi: a musical instrument, resembling a two-stringed violin

doi moi: series of economic reforms instituted in the mid-1980s that transitioned Vietnam to a market economy

do nhau: drinking food

giay: paper

hu tieu: a southern-style rice noodle soup

khach san: hotel

linga-yoni **statue:** a statue representing male and female energies

mam tom: fermented shrimp paste

mua roi: water puppet

nem cua be: square-shaped seafood spring rolls

nha hang: restaurant

nha nghi: guesthouse

nha thuoc tay: pharmacies

nha tro: very basic hotel, a step down from a guesthouse, *nha nghi*

nuoc cham: a diluted fish sauce

phap lam: handicraft of enamel on metal, native to Hue

quat: paper fan

roi nuoc: water puppet theater

tap hoa: convenience store

xe om: motorbike taxi

xoi: sticky rice; popular street food

yen sao: edible bird's nests sold as souvenirs in Nha Trang

Vietnamese Phrasebook

The Vietnamese language consists of six tones. The rising, falling, flat, low, broken, and question tones can morph a single group of letters into any number of different words. Take *ma,* for instance, which can mean ghost (*ma*), horse (*mā*), grave (*mả*), mother (*má*), rice seedling (*mạ*), or which (*mà*), depending upon the tone. It is for this reason that most newcomers to the language have difficulty. Even the slightest change in tone can render a word contextually incomprehensible.

To make matters more challenging, most consonant sounds in Vietnamese are enunciated farther back in the speaker's mouth. When you make the "d" sound in English, for example, your tongue strikes the top of your mouth behind the teeth. In Vietnamese, the same letter is pronounced by striking near the center of the roof of your mouth, producing a duller version of the "d" sound, as in *đi* (to go) or *đỏ* (red). Add to that extra vowel sounds like *ơ* (pronounced "uh") and *ư* (pronounced like the "ou" in could) and you've got your work cut out for you.

On paper, Vietnamese is an easier language. Verbs require no conjugation and can be used without the past or future tense. Pronouns are not always necessary. In informal conversation, sentences can be shortened to nothing more than a few words and still retain their meaning. Vietnamese is also one of the only languages in the region to use a Roman alphabet, which makes navigating most cities and towns infinitely simpler, even for someone who doesn't speak the language.

PRONUNCIATION

A handful of letters are pronounced differently in Vietnamese than in English.

Vowels

a   like ah, as in "ant"

ă   like uh, as in "cut"

â   like uh, as in "an"

e   like eh, as in "echo"

ê   like ay, as in "say"

i	like ee, as in "see"
o	like aw, as in "cot"
ô	like oh, as in "broke"
ơ	like uh, as in "fun"
u	like oo, as in "food"
ư	like ouh, as in "could"
y	like ee, as in "bee"

Consonants

c	a muted "c" sound, like a half-step between "c" and "g"
d	like y, as in "you"
đ	like d, as in "dog"
gi	like y, as in "you"
nh	like ny, as in "canyon"
ph	like f, as in "phone"
qu	like kw, as in "question" (northern) or like w, as in "wood"
x	like s, as in "sink"

BASIC EXPRESSIONS

Hello./Goodbye. *Xin chào.*

How are you? *(Bạn) có khỏe không?*

I'm fine, thanks. And you? *Tôi khỏe. Còn bạn?*

Thank you. *Cảm ơn.*

You're welcome./No problem. *Không có gì./Không sao.*

yes *có*

no *không*

I don't know. *Tôi không biết.*

Please wait a minute. *Xin (bạn) chờ một phút.*

Excuse me./I'm sorry. *Xin lỗi.*

Pleased to meet you. *Rất vui gặp bạn.*

What is your name? *(Bạn) tên gì?*

Do you speak English? *(Bạn) biết tiếng Anh không?* or *(Bạn) nói tiếng Anh được không?*

I don't speak Vietnamese. *Tôi không biết tiếng Việt.* or *Tôi không nói tiếng Việt được.*

I don't understand. *Tôi không hiểu.*

How do you say . . . in Vietnamese? *. . . tiếng Việt là gì?*

My name is . . . *Tôi tên là . . .*

Would you like . . . ? *(Bạn) có muốn . . . không?*

Let's go to . . . *Chúng ta hãy đi . . .*

TERMS OF ADDRESS

Vietnamese terms of address vary depending upon the relationship between the speaker and the person to whom he or she is speaking. There are dozens of pronouns to signify the gender and age of a person as well as the level of intimacy between two people. A mother and her child, for instance, would always refer to one another as *mẹ* (mother) and *con* (child), while a teacher and a young student would use *cô* (female teacher) or *thầy* (male teacher) and *con* (in this context, student).

For most travelers, these terms won't be necessary. On the road, most of your interactions will only require you to use pronouns of age and gender. It's simplest to use the neutral pronoun *tôi* when referring to yourself.

When visiting a restaurant or shop, a waiter or shop assistant will likely refer to you as *anh* (slightly older male) or *chị* (slightly older female) and themselves as *em* (a younger person), not necessarily because you are older, but because it shows respect.

If you happen to choose the incorrect pronoun, the other party will politely set you straight before continuing the conversation. In most cases, locals will be appreciative of your efforts and willing to let an error or two slide. Note that appreciation in Vietnamese culture is not always communicated in a way you might expect. Upon hearing a foreigner speak Vietnamese, locals are often quick to laugh. This is borne more out of surprise than anything and is not meant to offend.

In the chart below, the English pronouns "he" and "she" are not listed. With the exception of *tôi* and *bạn*, each of the pronouns below can be modified into "he" or "she" by tacking on the word *ấy* at the end. This means that *anh* (you, male) becomes *anh ấy* (he) or *cô* (you, female) turns into *cô ấy* (she).

I (neutral) *tôi*
person of equivalent age *bạn*
slightly older male *anh*
slightly older female *chị*
younger person, male or female *em*
female old enough to be your mother *cô*
male old enough to be your father *chú*
male slightly older than your father *bắc*
female old enough to be your grandmother *bà*
male old enough to be your grandfather *ông*
niece/nephew (self-referential; used when speaking to someone old enough to be your parent) *cháu*
child (self-referential; used when speaking to someone old enough to be your grandparent) *con*
we (listener not included) *chúng tôi*
we (listener included) *chúng ta*
you (plural) *các anh/chị/em/bạn*
they *họ*

TRANSPORTATION

Where is...? *...ở đâu?*
How far is it to...? *...cách đây mấy cây số?*
How far is it from...to...? *Từ...đến...cách mấy cây số?*
Do you know the way to...? *(Bạn) có biết đường đi...không?*

bus station *bến xe*
bus stop *trạm xe búyt*
Where is this bus going? *Xe búyt này đi đâu?*
taxi cab *xe taxi*
train station *ga xe lửa* (south), *ga tàu* (north)
boat *chiếc tàu*
airport *sân bay*
I'd like a ticket to . . . *Tôi muốn mua vé đi . . .*
one way *một chiều*
round-trip *khứ hồi*
reservation *đặt vé*
Stop here, please. *Xin (bạn) dừng lại ở đây.*
entrance *lối vào*
exit *lối ra*
ticket office *phòng vé*
near *gần*
far *xa*
Turn left. *queo trái* (south), *rẽ trái* (north)
Turn right. *queo phải* (south), *rẽ phải* (north)
right side *bên phải*
left side *bên trái*
Go straight. *đi thẳng*
in front of *trước*
beside *bên cạnh*
behind *sau*
corner *góc*
stoplight *đèn đỏ*
here *ở đây*
street *đường phố*
bridge *cây cầu*
address *địa chỉ*
north *bác*
south *nam*
east *đổng*
west *tây*

ACCOMMODATIONS

hotel *khách sạn*
guesthouse *nhà nghỉ*
Is there a room available? *Ở đây có phòng không?*
May I see it? *Tôi có thể coi phòng được không?*
What is the rate? *Giá phòng là bao nhiêu?*
Is there something cheaper? *(Bạn) có phòng rẻ hơn không?*
single room *phòng đơn*
double room *phòng đôi*
double bed *giường đôi*

dormitory *phòng tập thể*
key *chìa khóa*
reception *tiếp tân*
hot water *nước nóng*
shower *phòng tắm*
towel *khăn*
soap *sa bông*
toilet paper *giấy vệ sinh*
blanket *mền*
air-conditioning *máy lạnh* (south), *máy điều hòa* (north)
fan *quạt máy*
mosquito Net *màng*
laundry *giặt ủi*

FOOD

I'm hungry. *(Tôi) đói bụng.*
I'm thirsty. *(Tôi) khát nước.*
menu *thức đơn*
to order *gọi*
glass *ly*
fork *nĩa*
knife *dao*
spoon *muỗng*
chopsticks *đôi đũa*
napkin *khăn giấy*
soft drink *nước ngọt*
coffee/hot coffee/iced coffee *cà phê /cà phê sữa nóng / cà phê sữa đá*
coffee with milk *cà phê sữa*
tea/hot tea/iced tea *trà / trà nóng / trà đá*
bottled water *chai nước suối*
beer *bia*
juice *nước ép*
smoothie *sinh tố*
sugar *đường*
breakfast *ăn sáng*
lunch *ăn trưa*
dinner *ăn tối*
check, please *tính tiền*
eggs *trứng*
fruit *trái cây*
pineapple *trái thơm*
mango *trái xoài*
watermelon *dừa hấu*
papaya *đu đủ*
coconut *trái dừa*
lime *chánh*

durian *sầu riêng*
jackfruit *trái mít*
fish *cá*
shrimp *tôm*
chicken *thịt gà*
beef *thịt bò*
pork *thịt heo* (south), *thịt lợn* (north)
tofu *đậu hủ*
fried *chiên* (south), *rán* (north)
grilled *nướng*
boiled *luộc*
spicy *cay*

SHOPPING

money *tiền*
bank *ngân hàng*
Do you accept credit cards? *Ở đây có nhận thẻ tín dụng không?*
How much does it cost? *Cái này là bao nhiêu tiền?*
expensive *mắc tiền* (south), *đắt tiền* (north)
too expensive *mắc quá* (south), *đắt quá* (north)
cheap *rẻ*
more *nhiều hơn*
less *ít hơn*
a little *một ít*
too much *quá nhiều*

HEALTH

Help me, please. *Xin (bạn) giúp tôi đi.*
I am sick. *(Tôi) bị bệnh.*
Call a doctor. *Gọi cho bác sĩ đi.*
Please take me to … *Xin (bạn) đưa tôi đến …*
hospital *bệnh viện*
drugstore/pharmacy *nhà thuốc tây*
I'm allergic to … *Tôi bị dị ứng với …*
bees *con ong*
peanuts *đậu phọng*
seafood *hải sản*
I'm asthmatic. *Tôi bị suyễn.*
I'm diabetic. *Tôi bị bệnh đái đường.*
I'm epileptic. *Tôi bị động kinh.*
pain *đau*
fever *bệnh sốt*
headache *đau đầu*
stomachache *đau bụng*
burn *vết bỏng*
nausea *buồn nôn*

vomiting *bị mửa*
diarrhea *tiêu chảy*
antibiotics *thuốc kháng sinh*
aspirin *thuốc giảm đau*
penicillin *thuốc pênicilin*
pill, tablet *viên thuốc*
cream *kem*
contraceptive *cách ngừa thai*
condoms *bao cao su*
insect repellent *thuốc chống muỗi*
sunscreen *kem chống nắng*
sanitary pads *băng vệ sinh*
tampons *ống băng vệ sinh*
toothbrush *bàn chải đánh răng*
toothpaste *kem đánh răng*
dentist *nha sĩ*
toothache *nhức răng*

COMMON SIGNS
entrance *lối vào*
exit *lối ra*
men *đàn ông*
women *phụ nữ*
toilet *nhà vệ sinh / WC*
information *hướng dẫn / thông tin*
open *mở cửa*
closed *đóng cửa*
prohibited *cấm*

POST OFFICE AND COMMUNICATIONS
I would like to call… *(Tôi) muốn gọi cho…*
collect/collect call *thu thập gọi*
credit card *thẻ tín dụng*
post office *bưu điện*
airmail *thư gửi bằng máy bay*
letter *thư*
stamp *tem*
postcard *bưu thiếp*
registered/certified *thư bảo đảm*
box, package *hộp, gói*

AT THE BORDER
border *biên giới*
customs *hải quan*
immigration *nhập cư*
inspection *sự thanh tra*

passport *hộ chiếu*
profession *nghề nghiệp*
insurance *bảo hiểm*
driver's license *giấy phép lái xe, bằng lái*

AT THE GAS STATION

gas station *trạm xăng*
gasoline *xăng*
full *hết bình*
tire *bánh*
air *bớm xe*
water *nước*
oil change *thay dầu*
my ... doesn't work *... của tôi bị hư*
battery *pin*
repair shop *tiệm sửa xe*

VERBS

to buy *mua*
to eat *ăn*
to climb *leo*
to make *làm*
to go, to leave *đi*
to walk *đi bộ*
to like *thích*
to love *yêu*
to work *làm việc*
to want *muốn*
to need *cần*
to read *đọc*
to write *viết*
to repair *sửa*
to stop *dừng lại*
to get off (the bus) *xuống xe*
to arrive, to come *đến*
to stay *ở lại*
to sleep *ngủ*
to look at *xem*
to look for *tìm*
to give *đưa*
to carry *mang*
to have *có*

NUMBERS

one *một*
two *hai*

three *ba*
four *bốn*
five *năm*
six *sáu*
seven *bảy*
eight *tám*
nine *chính*
10 *mười*
11 *mười một*
12 *mười hai*
13 *mười ba*
14 *mười bốn*
15 *mười lăm*
16 *mười sáu*
17 *mười bảy*
18 *mười tám*
19 *mười chính*
20 *hai mười*
30 *ba mười*
100 *một trăm*
101 *một trăm lẻ một*
200 *hai trăm*
1,000 *một ngàn* (south), *một nghìn* (north)
10,000 *mười ngàn* (south), *mười nghìn* (north)
100,000 *một trăm ngàn* (south), *một trăm nghìn* (north)
1,000,000 *một triệu*
one-half *nửa phần*

TIME

What time is it? *Bây giờ là mấy giờ rồi?*
It's one o'clock. *Bây giờ là một giờ.*
It's four in the afternoon. *Bây giờ là bốn giờ chiều.*
It's noon. *Bây giờ là mười hai giờ trưa.*
It's midnight. *Bây giờ là mười hai giờ khuya.*
morning *sáng*
afternoon *chiều*
evening *tối*
one minute *một phút*
one hour *một giờ, một tiếng*

DAYS AND MONTHS

Monday *thứ hai*
Tuesday *thứ ba*
Wednesday *thứ tư*
Thursday *thứ năm*
Friday *thứ sáu*

Saturday   *thứ bảy*
Sunday   *chủ nhật*
January   *tháng giêng*
February   *tháng hai*
March   *tháng ba*
April   *tháng tư*
May   *tháng năm*
June   *tháng sáu*
July   *tháng bảy*
August   *tháng tám*
September   *tháng chính*
October   *tháng mười*
November   *tháng mười một*
December   *tháng mười hai*
today   *hôm nay*
yesterday   *hôm qua*
tomorrow   *ngày mai*
a day   *một ngày*
a week   *một tuần*
a month   *một tháng*
after   *sau đây*
before   *trước đây*
rainy season   *mùa mưa*
dry season   *mùa khô*
spring   *mùa xuân*
summer   *mùa hè*
winter   *mùa đông*
fall   *mùa thu*

Suggested Reading

HISTORY

Bartimus, Tad, Ed. *War Torn: Stories of War from the Women Reporters Who Covered Vietnam*. New York: Random House, 2002. Written by a group of women ranging from veteran journalists to twenty-something novices, this collection of memoirs presents a different side of Vietnam through the eyes of some of the first female reporters to cover a conflict from the front lines.

Herr, Michael. *Dispatches*. New York: Vintage Books, 1977. Lauded as one of America's most famous firsthand accounts of the Vietnam War, *Dispatches* is the product of Michael Herr's years as a journalist covering the conflict for *Esquire* magazine. The author went on to co-write *Apocalypse Now* and *Full Metal Jacket*.

Karnow, Stanley. *Vietnam: A History*. New York: Viking Press, 1983. The best-selling masterpiece of Stanley Karnow, a veteran journalist and historian who covered the Vietnam War and its aftermath both at home and abroad.

Mangold, Tom. *The Tunnels of Cu Chi*. New York: Ballantine Books, 1985. The fascinating story of the citizens of Cu Chi and the intricate system of tunnels they dug by hand to protect their homes. This book is a must-read for anyone interested in war history, with firsthand accounts of the harsh and unforgiving conditions of life underground and the struggles of NLF rebel fighters, as well as the stories of the U.S. Army's "tunnel rats" – a group of men who descended into the pitch-black tunnels to combat the enemy.

BIOGRAPHY AND MEMOIR

Duiker, William J. *Ho Chi Minh: A Life*. New York: Hyperion, 2000. A comprehensive biography of Vietnam's greatest leader and one of the 20th century's most influential politicians.

Pham, Andrew X. *Catfish and Mandala*. New York: Picador, 1999. In his early 30s, uncertain of his future and curious about his past, Andrew Pham set out from Saigon on a bicycle, heading up the coast of a Vietnam newly opened to the outside world, encountering the country's people, its problems, and its unbreakable spirit.

Sachs, Dana. *The House on Dream Street: Memoir of an American Woman in Vietnam*. Chapel Hill, NC: Algonquin Books, 2000. The memoir of a woman in her late 20s bound for Vietnam just as the country is beginning to open up after years of war and poverty.

FICTION

O'Brien, Tim. *The Things They Carried*. New York: Mariner Books, 1990. A semi-autobiographical collection of short stories, Tim O'Brien's fictional masterpiece follows a platoon of American soldiers in the jungles of Vietnam as they fight their way through the war.

Greene, Graham. *The Quiet American*. London: Vintage Books, 1955. An ominous and controversial novel twice adapted to film, Graham Greene's opus is set in early 1950s Saigon, a time and place rife with political tension and deception. This is perhaps one of the most famous English-language novels to be set in Vietnam.

Butler, Robert Olen. *A Good Scent from a Strange Mountain*. New York: Grove Press, 2001. A Pulitzer Prize-winning collection of short stories that peers into the lives of Vietnamese immigrants living in the United States as they navigate the cultural differences and war wounds of a turbulent history between the two nations.

Internet Resources

TRAVEL INFORMATION

Rusty Compass

www.rustycompass.com

This outstanding, well-researched independent travel guide covers a wide range of Vietnamese destinations, providing travelers with helpful tips and recommendations as well as dozens of photos and videos. Run by Aussie expat Mark Bowyer, who has been based in Vietnam since the early 1990s, Rusty Compass is a great resource when planning your trip.

Travelfish

www.travelfish.org

A handy resource for anyone traveling in Southeast Asia, Travelfish offers independent reviews, practical information, and sound advice on countries throughout the region. The site's Vietnam section covers both major tourist destinations and several less-visited towns.

Vietnam Tourism

http://vietnamtourism.vn

A joint effort between the Vietnamese government and a tourism advisory board made up of local businesses, this site features suggestions on what to see and where to go throughout Vietnam.

PRACTICALITIES

U.S. State Department

www.travel.state.gov

Providing up-to-date information on all things Vietnam, the State Department's website stays abreast of current situations within the country and also offers useful information on practicalities such as border crossings, visas, and health and safety tips.

Centers for Disease Control

www.cdc.gov

Before traveling to Vietnam, check the CDC website for more country-specific information on vaccinations, malaria prophylaxis and other preventive measures.

The Comical Hat

www.thecomicalhat.wordpress.com

The odd and unorthodox musings of a local expat.

From Swerve of Shore

www.aaronjoelsantos.wordpress.com

A beautiful and vivid collection of photographs by Aaron Joel Santos, a Hanoi-based fashion photographer and photojournalist.

Sticky Rice

www.stickyrice.typepad.com

A street food blog devoted to discovering hidden gems along the winding, narrow streets of Hanoi.

List of Maps

Photo Credits

Also Available

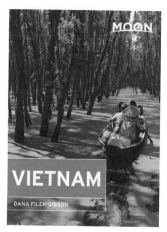

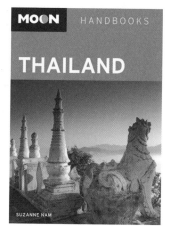

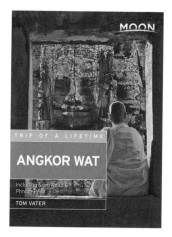

MAP SYMBOLS

▦▦▦ Expressway	○ City/Town	✗ Airport	♪ Golf Course
─── Primary Road	◉ State Capital	✗ Airfield	▯ Parking Area
─── Secondary Road	◎ National Capital	▲ Mountain	≜ Archaeological Site
⋯⋯ Unpaved Road	★ Point of Interest	✚ Unique Natural Feature	♦ Church
┄┄ Trail	● Accommodation	⤵ Waterfall	▯ Gas Station
⋯⋯ Ferry	▼ Restaurant/Bar	♠ Park	◌ Glacier
┅┅ Railroad	■ Other Location	▯ Trailhead	▨ Mangrove
▦▦ Pedestrian Walkway	Δ Campground	⛷ Skiing Area	◻ Reef
▨▨ Stairs			◻ Swamp

CONVERSION TABLES

°C = (°F – 32) / 1.8
°F = (°C x 1.8) + 32
1 inch = 2.54 centimeters (cm)
1 foot = 0.304 meters (m)
1 yard = 0.914 meters
1 mile = 1.6093 kilometers (km)
1 km = 0.6214 miles
1 fathom = 1.8288 m
1 chain = 20.1168 m
1 furlong = 201.168 m
1 acre = 0.4047 hectares
1 sq km = 100 hectares
1 sq mile = 2.59 square km
1 ounce = 28.35 grams
1 pound = 0.4536 kilograms
1 short ton = 0.90718 metric ton
1 short ton = 2,000 pounds
1 long ton = 1.016 metric tons
1 long ton = 2,240 pounds
1 metric ton = 1,000 kilograms
1 quart = 0.94635 liters
1 US gallon = 3.7854 liters
1 Imperial gallon = 4.5459 liters
1 nautical mile = 1.852 km

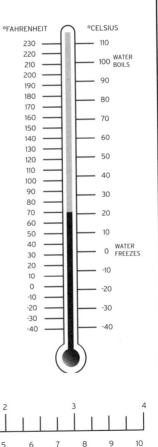

MOON HO CHI MINH CITY (SAIGON)
Avalon Travel
Hachette Book Group
1700 Fourth Street
Berkeley, CA 94710, USA
www.moon.com

Editor: Leah Gordon
Series Manager: Kathryn Ettinger
Copy Editor: Naomi Adler Dancis
Graphics Coordinators: Elizabeth Jang
Production Coordinators: Elizabeth Jang
Cover Design: Faceout Studios, Charles Brock
Interior Design: Domini Dragoone
Moon Logo: Tim McGrath
Map Editor: Albert Angulo
Cartographers: Brian Shotwell, Stephanie Poulain, and Albert Angulo
Indexer: Rachel Kuhn

ISBN-13: 9781631217135

Printing History
1st Edition — October 2017
5 4 3 2 1

Text © 2017 by Dana Filek-Gibson.
Maps © 2017 by Avalon Travel.

31901060969203